the
CHANGE
MONSTER

the CHANGE MONSTER

THE HUMAN FORCES THAT FUEL OR FOIL CORPORATE TRANSFORMATION AND CHANGE

JEANIE DANIEL DUCK

THREE RIVERS PRESS • NEW YORK

Published by Three Rivers Press, New York, New York. Member of the Crown
Publishing Group, a division of Random House, Inc.

www.randomhouse.com

Three Rivers Press and the Tugboat design are registered trademarks of
Random House, Inc.

Originally published in hardcover by Crown Business, a division of
Random House, Inc., in 2001.

Printed in the United States of America.

Illustrations by Gene Mackles

Library of Congress Cataloging-in-Publication Data

Duck, Jeanie Daniel.
    The change monster : the human forces that fuel or foil corporate
transformation and change / by Jeanie Daniel Duck.
    Includes index.
    1. Organizational change. I. Title.

    HD58.8.D833 2001
    658.4′06—dc21

                                                         00-047549

ISBN 0-609-80881-8

10 9 8 7 6 5 4 3

First Paperback Edition

I have enjoyed many blessings in my life, but none greater than my daughter, Jennifer McKee Duck, and my husband, Charles Patrick Carroll. It is with deep gratitude and boundless love that I dedicate this book to them.

CONTENTS

PREFACE

"THE CHANGE MONSTER" is my catch-all phrase for the com-plex, sometimes scary, human emotions and social dynamics that emerge like a dragon surfacing from the ocean depths during any major change effort. Mergers, reorganizations, and transforma-tions all involve people, and that means emotions worn on the sleeve (or hidden, which is even worse) and egos on the loose. Ironically—and in some cases, tragically—many leaders involved in change would much prefer to ignore the people issues altogether. That's why I wrote *The Change Monster*—to talk about the emotional and behav-ioral aspects of the people and organizations involved in change, a subject that has been too long unaddressed. Those leaders who do think about people issues tend to simplify them, brand them as "per-sonnel" issues, and quickly hand them over to the folks in Human Resources. A few wise souls recognize that the human issues are both deep and important, but make the assumption that there is little or nothing to be done about them.

When people—executives, in particular—start a change initiative, they believe they understand what will be involved. But, once they get into the process, they are always astonished at how muddled, painful, protracted, tiresome, complicated, and energy-consuming creating change can be. They wish they had known more going in, had been better prepared, so they could have anticipated messy situ-ations and recognized problems before they arose, or, at least, before they escalated into serious trouble. Some might have chosen not to start the journey at all.

I can't claim to make the process smooth or easy; to change an organization in a significant way is not, never has been, and never will be, quick or easy. That's why the majority of change efforts fail or achieve only partial results, and why the successful ones take so long. What I do in this book is prepare you for the realities of living through major change, so once you're into it you'll be less likely to lose heart, go crazy, give up, bail out, or think you're the only one on the planet ever to have felt so worn out and beaten up by trying to make change happen. I liken the change process to an arduous journey of discovery and exploration, not unlike those of the early voyagers. We can provide better maps and technology than they had, but even the best map won't keep the thunderstorms from striking and the monster from rearing its ugly head.

Those who have completed such a journey will recognize themselves and others and will understand the lessons from hard-won experience. Those who haven't been through a transition yet will be convinced I'm exaggerating or have found only odd people to work with.

My main messages are:

- *For a change initiative to succeed, the emotional and behavioral aspects must be addressed as thoroughly as the operational issues.*

Too many executives focus solely on the operational aspects of change but to implement new ways of working requires people to think and act differently. To be fully effective, changes must address the intellectual and emotional issues—the hearts and minds—as well as the machines and systems.

- *Change unfolds in a reasonably predictable and manageable series of dynamic phases, known as the Change Curve.*

There are five phases of fundamental change, beginning with Stagnation, proceeding through Preparation, Implementation, Determination, and ending—one hopes—with Fruition. Every change initiative I have been involved with or observed proceeds through these phases. And each phase involves a different aspect of "the change monster." Each organization experiences the phases differently. They last longer or shorter and can overlap; different parts of the organization will find themselves in different phases at any given time. In general, the leaders of the change initiative tend to be further along the Curve than are others in the organization, which makes the experience doubly frustrating and difficult for them and their followers.

Change, therefore, is a dynamic process, rather than a series of events. During each phase, downward pressure and negative events will occur, so executives and managers must expect them, and prepare to respond to them. They should also anticipate, create, recognize, and enjoy positive boosts. Dynamics can be subtle, and much more difficult to manage than events. A plant shutdown is an event. The shifting mood of the people within the factory as it faces the shutdown is a dynamic. The dynamics will be influenced and directed by behaviors and attitudes, environments, ideas, and relationships. Failure to see and shape these influences is like wearing a blindfold and then being surprised when you crash into the furniture. Learning how to see and manage these intangibles requires skill, time, and attention.

- *Change can be exhilarating and bring about the best work of a lifetime.*

We needn't be overly gloomy about the change process. Many people find that fundamental change results in the most interesting, involving, and meaningful work of their careers. Executives are seldom so challenged, managers so fully engaged, and individual contributors so intensely connected to the essential work of the organization. For the company itself, a successful transformation brings increased success, heightened recognition, and confidence.

One of my colleagues at The Boston Consulting Group was working with the CEO of a company that was acquiring a competitor. It was a big engagement, involving two global companies, with billions of dollars and thousands of jobs at stake. Not only was Wall Street watching every move, so were government officials in cities, provinces, and countries around the globe. It was not unusual for meetings with the CEO to be interrupted by a telephone call from some concerned senator, minister, or even a head of state. Every shred of rumor, let alone news of every significant move, seemed to land on the front page of the national and international newspapers, triggering reactions from local dignitaries as well as from the stock markets in London, New York, and Tokyo.

My colleague advised his client that the merger would be a hairy one. "You have to expect the unexpected," he warned. "Unforeseen trials and tribulations will occur—protests, strikes, earthquakes, bad news from major customers—anything and everything may come along to stall your progress." Then my colleague looked the CEO in the eye. "But all of that is nothing compared to the extreme emotional ups and downs employees from both companies are going to experience," he said. "People will surprise you in good ways and bad. Executives who have been rock-solid and rooted in self-confidence will be riddled with anxiety and doubt, unable to make even simple decisions. People you've relied on as selfless advisors will become turf-protectors. Some individuals who ought to be worried will act as if they're totally immune from problems. Previously loyal soldiers will abandon the cause, while others you've seen as overly cautious will rise to the challenge and surpass your wildest expectations. And, you, yourself, will be tested to the limit. You cannot imagine the amount of energy and persistence that will be required of you to make this acquisition work for the long haul." The CEO, a seasoned and internationally respected executive, listened patiently to my colleague and then, when he had finished, remarked with more than a hint of condescension, "I think we can handle it."

The first order of business for companies negotiating a merger is to sort out which executives will have what jobs. This process often begins well in advance of the first announcement, and can be so contentious that it has led to the downfall of many an acquisition proposal. But, if the players can be fielded, the regulatory hurdles leaped, and all the financial details agreed on, the deal is consummated. The documents are signed and the new company becomes a reality, at least on paper.

In the above case, one of the executives from the acquiring company had expected to live out his worklife in the position he had attained before the merger. Instead, he lost out in the job-selection shuffle. He was provided with a handsome severance package and bid farewell. No special retirement party, no special attention—after all, he wasn't the only one leaving. The morning after his departure, he dressed in a business suit as usual, left his rural home, and drove his car into a bridge abutment at 90 miles per hour. There was little doubt that it was suicide.

Later that day, my colleague had a meeting with the CEO, who was badly shaken by the event. "You never told me this could happen," the client accused my colleague. "You never said it could get this bad."

This was an extreme case, the only merger-related suicide I know of. But I have been through plenty of other engagements involving fundamental corporate change in which people have exhibited all kinds of extreme, erratic, or unexpected behavior. They have become elated or depressed, gotten divorced or married, turned to prohibited substances for solace or suddenly gone on the wagon, charged around like Superman, found God, lost faith, and behaved in a hundred other weird and/or wonderful ways. And that's just the individuals. The organization itself goes through similar mood swings and accompanying behaviors—an organization as a whole can be depressed or optimistic, lifeless or energized.

Multiply the tumult experienced by a single organization in the grip of change by the total number of such organizations that are involved in massive change efforts—businesses, government agencies, nonprofits, educational institutions—and you begin to think the entire world is populated by anxious people trying to comprehend and manage change. In fact, that's not far from the truth.

Predictions are that the first decade of the new millennium will see even more industry consolidations and therefore, merger activity. We see no abatement in the rate of strategic transformations, privatizations or deregulations, either. Any of these actions can lead to a myriad of other changes within the company, such as reorganization, shifts in power and focus, redesign of core processes, and reallocation of resources. So the ability to understand and negotiate the emotional territory of change will continue to be of urgent interest to the business world and to those who are impacted by those upheavals. We live in an unstable world.

Study after study, however, shows that most of these fundamental change efforts fail to accomplish what they set out to achieve—such as increased market share, higher stock price, faster and more innovative product development, lower costs, and/or entry into new markets.

Why are these change initiatives so difficult to accomplish and so prone to failure? The knee-jerk answer is that people "resist change," as if "resistance to change" were some kind of sorry genetic code that, if it could be reengineered, would magically produce people instantly eager to do things differently whenever anyone asked. The "resistance to change" answer is too simplistic, but it is appealing because it takes the blame off the leaders and puts it on those "no-good followers." There are many reasons change efforts fail, as I explore in this book.

One thing is for sure, organizations do not change until the beliefs and behaviors of the people within it change. (That's why I love the saying, "A good way to go crazy is to expect different results from the same behavior.") Changing behavior—corporate or individual— is inherently an emotional process. But few of us understand emotions and most of us would rather avoid them altogether. Executives, in particular, get antsy when the talk turns to feelings and behaviors. It is territory that most are painfully uncomfortable with, are unprepared for, or simply do not know how to navigate.

In *The Change Monster* we will explore this mysterious territory; we'll learn from others' failures and triumphs. But this is not a how-to book. I assume that you, my readers, know very well how to perform your jobs. You don't need or want me to give you a list of things to do. What I hope I can do is help you understand what is happening and why during each phase of change, so you can calibrate your experiences and realize that you're not alone or crazy. I hope that I can help you see and articulate the issues and dynamics involved, and provide you with a language to use. That will help you think more clearly and communicate more effectively about your situation. And, finally, I hope I can give you the courage you'll need to face the change monster and make your way to a rewarding and successful Fruition.

JEANIE DANIEL DUCK

PART ONE

THE CHANGE MONSTER

THE HUMAN AND EMOTIONAL ELEMENTS OF CHANGE

"I don't know how it started, either. All I know is that it's part of our corporate culture."

1

Battling the Monster

The Need to Think and
Behave Differently

I'M CRAZY FOR chocolate—dark chocolate, that is. Some years ago, a friend of mine sent me, from California, a two-pound box of See's dark chocolate nuts and chews. I was in heaven! As I was oohing and aahing over the box and generally making a fool of myself, my daughter Jennifer, then age three, joined in the excitement. This was a bad sign. If she was excited it was because she expected to share in my newly acquired bounty. Clearly the only way I could get rid of her was to share, so I gave her a piece and sent her to bed. Then I had "just a few" pieces for myself, and went to bed.

Later that night, we had one of those glorious storms so common to Alabama—thunder, lightning, wind, and rain. I got up in the dark and went from room to room, closing the open windows. As I did, I stepped on something crunchy in the hallway. When I turned on the light, I saw that the floor was covered with little round pieces of dark brown paper. I followed the trail of candy wrappers just like the Yellow Brick Road, only instead of the Emerald City being at the end, I found a totally empty box of See's candy! I was stunned. I thought, "She's only three, for goodness sake! How could she possibly polish off two pounds of chocolate?"

I found Jennifer sound asleep in her bed, looking angelic. (Actually, I think she was in a glucose stupor; in any case, she was out for the count.) The next morning, I confronted her.

"Jennifer Duck, you ate all my candy!"

"No I didn't," she immediately replied with a look of earnestness and fear on her face.

"Oh yes you did." I said. "Only two people live here—you and me—and I didn't do it!"

She hung her head. Then, quietly, she mumbled, "I wish I had a baby brother!"

I've never forgotten that incident, much to Jennifer's chagrin—not because of my great chocolate loss, but because Jennifer's response was so to the point. We all have a natural desire to find someone else to blame whenever we're caught doing something wrong or found lacking. I know only too well how she felt. When I realize I have forgotten to fulfill a commitment—whether it's to send a document, to call someone who has asked for some help before a meeting, or to schedule that lunch I've been promising a friend—I feel bad. All too often, I look for someone or some circumstance or event that will excuse or justify my behavior. At least I've learned to do this silently and to stop myself once I realize what I'm doing. I recount this story about my daughter because it exemplifies a central realization of change, a time when we must say to ourselves, "I need to behave differently." We may also need to think differently, to take on a different perspective (or several), to practice new skills, to extend ourselves in new and often demanding ways.

To accomplish change of this kind takes courage. Not the kind of courage we hear about in the news: "Man Saves Child from Sure Death" or "Woman Quells Riot Single-handedly." No, this kind of courage doesn't make headlines. It's a personal struggle that we see as mundane. Without taking away any credit from the heroes behind those headlines, I would suggest that it is an even greater and more difficult act of heroism to change ourselves. When people who have performed bravely in dramatic situations are interviewed, they say something like, "It was pure instinct. I'm no hero." Or, in the case of firefighters, police, and similar professionals, "This is what we're trained for. I was just doing my job." When people who act as change agents in companies are interviewed, they often say, "If I'd known then what I know now, I don't know if I would have signed up for this." Or, "This change initiative was like going on a diet, giving up drinking, and quitting smoking—all at the same time. I'm sure glad it's over." Or, "I've never worked so hard or learned so much." Or, "It was the most exhilarating and memorable time of my entire life."

MY EXPERIENCE WITH THE MONSTER

I have come to know and understand *the change monster*—my term for all the human issues that swirl around change—both personally and professionally. As a senior vice president with The Boston Consulting Group (BCG), I've been involved with many companies going through major change. I've helped senior executives and scores of managers through mergers, reengineering, and strategic transformations. It is fascinating work because the business stakes are high and the human dynamics are as complex and as gripping as any stage play or Hollywood melodrama.

Before I joined BCG, I experienced firsthand what it is like to live through a fundamental change. I was working as a middle manager at a savings and loan institution that, for several nerve-wracking months, teetered on the brink of bankruptcy. The management tried all kinds of tactics and tricks to salvage the business, but to no avail; finally, we went belly-up, were taken over by the Feds, and became part of the Resolution Trust Corporation. The situation wasn't pretty and the process wasn't fun. By the time all was said and done, I—along with about 30 percent of the workforce—got the boot. I will never forget the roller coaster of emotions we all experienced— the slow grinding climbs toward small successes, the sudden plunges toward disaster. Nor will I forget the different ways that my colleagues manifested their emotions. Some screamed bloody murder, some were silent and rode with white knuckles all the way, some jumped ship with no place to land; a few seemed to love the ride and all the drama that accompanied it. It was my first all-out battle with the corporate change monster.

My interest in change, however, predates that experience; in fact, it goes back to my childhood. I have always been intrigued by what people do and why. I'm often amazed at some action and immediately set to wondering, "What was he thinking?" Or, "What drove her to do that?" Figuring out group behavior can be an enthralling puzzle. What made them respond that way? How could that behavior have been predicted or altered? These have been burning questions for me for as long as I can remember.

To try to answer these questions, I followed a rather unusual path of formal and informal study. I started out as an artist, majoring in sculpture and figure drawing. Art is about observation and empathy, about being able to translate what one has observed and sensed into a tangible work that provokes an emotional response in the viewer. At its best, art makes a powerfully intimate connection between artist and viewer—a connection that is both personal and universal. Wouldn't it be wonderful if our work life could be punctuated by moments of connection like those we experience with art? Wouldn't it be wonderful if we all understood that creating such moments is part of our job?

After receiving my degree, I first taught art to students in grades one through twelve, and then went for my master's degree in art education at Pratt Institute in Brooklyn. While there, I also worked in the undergraduate Art Education department, supervising student teachers. I was trying to help them figure out how to teach art in the New York City public school system. Believe me, they weren't interested in art theory; they wanted survival tactics, so I went for anything that was practical and made sense. In our sessions together, we didn't discuss art. We discussed the emotions and the human dynamics that were ricocheting around them and within them. Our discussions were candid searches that focused on trying to understand what was happening and how to bring some positive outcomes to all involved. We found transactional analysis (the study of transactions within and between people) to be particularly useful in explaining the forces that shape individual behavior, how norms are formed for groups, and how ideas for guiding interactions in the classroom can be stimulated. I later became certified as a transactional analyst.

It took me some years to see and validate that the emotional experience of change for individuals is similar to that of organizations—even organizations of very different types. After earning my degree from Pratt, I spent six years in the corporate world, and then—after getting the boot from the S&L—I founded my own consulting firm. Early on, I was working with three very different clients—a consumer goods company, a defense contractor, and the emergency room staff of a large metropolitan hospital—all of whom were confronted with different issues. The emergency room docs bemoaned "the Saturday night knife-and-gun club," which filled the hospital with critically wounded patients every weekend and turned the emergency room into a nightmare. The hospital administrators, meanwhile, were trying to figure out how to improve costs and reduce doctor turnover. The defense contractors were on the opposite end of the spectrum. They were trying to determine the best way to improve their "kill rates" for specific weapons. Neither group, however, could match the stress and earnestness of my clients at the third company—the marketers who were searching for the best way to improve the market share of their fading sugared cereal.

One day, during a meeting with the emergency room staff, I thought to myself, "They sound a lot like the defense guys." This struck me as odd. Later that week, I realized that some of the work I was doing with the defense contractor would also be helpful to my clients at the cereal company. These correlations were intriguing, and I started to look for commonalities, patterns, and dissimilarities. I wanted to know whether companies in different industries, dealing with different issues, always had so much in common. Was the fact that all of them were going through radical change the common denominator? Are human beings so much alike that our "humanness" overrides other factors?

As I watched, analyzed, and probed during the subsequent months, the answer to both questions became more and more clear: Yes. The definition of the word "phenomenon" perfectly describes what I was experiencing: "That which appears real to the senses, regardless of whether its underlying existence is proved or its nature understood." I was convinced that the same phenomenon was at work in all three situations. I then hypothesized that if people—individually and collectively—experience a common pattern when they go through major change, and if that pattern is clearly defined and understood, then it could be managed or, at least, guided.

Over the next several years, I developed a rudimentary framework for what I started to think of as the "Change Curve." I first applied it when I was retained as a consultant by Ray Alvarez, General Manager of Micro Switch, a division of Honeywell. The company—which makes small sensors, controls, and switches for industrial, space, and military applications—had been founded in 1937 and purchased by Honeywell in 1950. For decades, Honeywell left Micro Switch pretty much alone. As thanks for this autonomy, the managers sent fat profits "up the river," as they called it, to corporate headquarters in Minneapolis. Then the market moved toward a new type of electronic switches, but Micro Switch was slow to follow. In addition, Honeywell started diversifying. Companies in growth businesses, such as computer hardware, software, and peripherals, were purchased. The corporation came to rely on Micro Switch's profits to help fund the acquisitions, and the management of Micro Switch felt great pride in being a cash cow for corporate. Over the years, the Micro Switch management slowed their investment in the division and continued to raise prices, cut costs, squeeze service, and starve R&D to keep those profits high. Within a few years, Micro Switch was deep in Stagnation. Key accounts were lost. An overseas company began to snatch market share; the Micro Switch managers, who had considered this competitor as beneath notice, now saw it as invincible. The corporate executives of Honeywell were divided about whether to sell or retain Micro Switch. They decided to bring in an experienced manager—a Honeywell veteran named Ray (Ramon) Alvarez—to turn things around.

When I started working with Ray and his management team, the division was mired in Stagnation. Together, we progressed through the phases that I now see so clearly as typical of every major change: Stagnation, Preparation, Implementation, Determination, and Fruition. For Micro Switch, the process took about three years. But many companies—especially technology and Internet companies—must accomplish their changes much faster, sometimes in a matter of months.

EMOTIONS ARE DATA

Based on all these experiences—as a manager, a consultant, an observer of behavior, a mother, an artist, and a teacher—I have come to believe strongly that the emotional aspects of change are not just important, they are vital. If leaders don't take into consideration the emotional data, all the operational information and numeric data in the world won't be enough to turn around a company. *Changing an organization is inherently and inescapably an emotional human process.* When I say *emotional,* I'm not talking about fleeting moods or surface feelings. I'm talking about the major states of emotional beings: fear, curiosity, exhaustion, loyalty, paranoia, depression, optimism, rage, revelation, delight, and love.

When an organization embarks on a change of any magnitude, its leaders tend to think that they are facing a series of operational tasks that will, if executed successfully, result in a new state of being. They don't realize that they will also have to face an onslaught of emotions and human dynamics. I have come to understand that emotions truly are data and have just as much relevance as data on sales, profits, or any other "tangible" aspect of organizational performance. I also believe that it is possible to address emotional data with rigor and rationality—to identify and define emotions, analyze how they affect performance, and develop strategies and tactics to address them.

Not only is it possible to gather and address the emotional data, it is imperative. Dealing with the change monster is so critical to the success or failure of a change initiative that it is not only the legitimate purview of leaders, it is their major challenge and responsibility. And when I say leaders I am talking not just about the handful of executives at the very top of an organization. I'm referring to the many people who lead divisions and business units, departments and groups, teams and task forces. I know from experience that too many leaders are slow to identify the human issues, fail to recognize their significance, and are very reluctant to confront them directly.

THREE ESSENTIALS OF CHANGE MANAGEMENT

Over the years, I have continuously refined the Change Curve and my understanding of the change monster. When I joined BCG, I was able to validate that the change curve essentially applies universally—thanks to the corroborating data and experience of my colleagues who work with companies of every description, worldwide. We have found that the phases of the Change Curve described in this book are valid in an extremely wide range of companies, industries, and geographies. While the experience of each individual company is always unique, the phases and principles of change are the same. How long those phases last, whether or not they are repeated and what the velocity of movement is within those phases will vary depending on the leadership and the intensity of the changes required.

The Change Curve applies to fundamental change efforts of virtually every kind of entity—nonprofit and charitable organizations; educational and religious institutions; government agencies; community organizations, associations, and clubs; and families. Once you begin to recognize the phases of change and understand the dynamics of each one, the Change Curve becomes visible—and useful—in almost every field of activity.

I do not argue that managing change for any of these entities is *only* about addressing the human dynamics. Rather it is one of three essential elements required for successful change:

1. *Strategy: a passionate belief in where you're going.* The strategy must be sound and the commitment unflinching. The more clearly the strategy can be articulated and the more easily it can be understood and translated into action, the better.
2. *Execution: good, basic management.* A successful transition requires the same good management practices that are fundamental to running an effective organization during times of stability and "normal" operation (if there is such a thing). Good management becomes absolutely indispensable, however, when an organization is undergoing radical change.
3. *Managing the monster requires a heightened sensitivity to the emotional and behavioral issues inherent during change, and a willingness to address them.* I assume that readers have already mastered the first two elements or know where to go for help in doing so. This book focuses almost exclusively on the third element.

THE STRUCTURE OF THE BOOK

I have structured the book around the five phases that make up the Change Curve. To illustrate those phases, I describe how two companies and their leaders go through major change. The first company is Honeywell Micro Switch and its leader is Ray Alvarez. I chose to tell this story because it encompasses so many challenges, and the initiatives taken were tremendously successful. Also, I wanted to highlight a real person, a leader who is not famous or overexposed but who worked hard and figured out how to overcome the monsters he encountered. Ray began the Micro Switch initiative as a seasoned leader who had led two earlier transformations and he had a deep understanding of the emotional aspects of change. Even so, he endured an intense personal odyssey which was a challenging and difficult process for the organization and for Ray.

Because Ray exemplifies a "right" way to go about a change process, his story is undisguised. To introduce many of the things that can go wrong in a change effort, I have created a merger of two pharmaceutical companies—Commando Drug and Venerable BV—both of which find themselves in different types of Stagnation. The story focuses on the process of creating a new, single entity called CoVen. The research and development group is led by Dr. Marco Trask, who, unlike Ray, has little experience in change management and pays scant attention to the human dynamics that accompany any merger. During the course of the year-long initiative, Marco confronts the change monster in many unexpected forms. He undergoes a personal transformation that ultimately helps him achieve success for his organization and himself. This case and the characters are based on my work with several different clients, in several industries, as well as the work of my colleagues at BCG. So while this merger story is fiction, it is true to life.

In addition to these stories, I will include references to other companies involved in a variety of types of change efforts—including e-start-up, deregulation, privatization, and reengineering—and to executives, managers, and consultants who have lived through those changes and done battle with the monster.

IT'S NOT ALL PAIN

Mark Twain once wrote, "When in doubt, tell the truth." I would be fibbing if I told you that if you just follow my guidelines and learn the phases of the Change Curve, you'll slay the change monster instantly and achieve your goals easily and painlessly. However, I do believe that an understanding of the phenomenon of the Change Curve will make the changes you face easier and less confusing, and help you achieve the desired results sooner.

I would also be fibbing if I said that change involves *only* pain and difficulty. It doesn't. The change process may be complicated, time-consuming, and filled with truths you might wish you never had to face, but it can also be the most satisfying, challenging, and spirited work of a career. I approach every new organizational change engagement with both excitement and trepidation. I know that no one involved, regardless of position, will emerge from it without undergoing some personal change. You will have some of your assumptions challenged and will find areas of strength and weakness you did not know existed. Relationships with others will open out or narrow down. You will discover pockets of personal ignorance and wisdom and will learn a thousand new things about yourself and others.

As my mama often said to me when I was obsessing about some teenage crisis, "Well, Jeanie, living through this may be chaotic and trying, but it'll never be boring!" I didn't particularly appreciate that pearl of wisdom at the time, but it gave me a different perspective on the next crisis and made it a little easier to get through. I hope that what I offer here can be equally useful.

2

A Short Tour of the Change Curve

A Map for the Territory of Change

I'M NOT PARTICULARLY good at finding my way to new destinations, which is a bit of a liability for someone who travels 200 days a year, as I do. Too many times, a new client has said something like, "We're just twenty miles west of the airport. Get on the Interstate, go to exit, ah, I think it's 17, or is it 18? Anyway, it's that first one. Take a right at the bottom of the ramp, and then just go straight. You can't miss it." Of course, I always miss it. The most obvious reason is that they forget that there are two Interstates to choose from, there isn't really a ramp at all, and there are three critical turns before you can go straight. But the deeper reason is that the person giving the directions has forgotten how much they've learned—they no longer notice the subtleties that can throw off a newcomer. For them, the route is automatic; they know exactly where they're going. For me, the territory is all new and unfamiliar. Plus, I'm usually driving a rental car, so I'm busy trying to figure out how to adjust the seat, turn on the headlights, and turn off the radio, which has been preset to "gangsta" rap. To make matters worse, I may be in a foreign country—driving on the left or trying to decipher road signs in German.

In such situations, a map is comforting to have but not helpful enough, so I've learned to ask my clients about landmarks. I might then be instructed: "Take a right at the big yellow sign for bingo night, in front of the Methodist church." I also thrive on tips: "Make sure you leave an extra half hour early, because the farmers are demonstrating. The roads will be blocked with tractors." I want general cautions and warnings. "Be careful when you get into our

part of the city. All the streets are one-way, but the map doesn't tell you which way they go." Or, "The cops like to set up a speed trap at mile marker 53."

Traveling into new territory is a pretty good metaphor for the experience of major change. No matter how much you prepare or how experienced a traveler you are, you're going to run into unexpected situations and weird incidents. Some things will go wrong, and fabulous things will come as surprises. Plus, traveling to new destinations intensifies the emotions. Your senses are on alert, your mind is fully engaged, you seem more alive. So, whatever happens seems more amazing, frustrating, painful, exciting, or exhausting than it would under routine circumstances.

The Change Curve below is a kind of map of the territory of change, and a guide to the tricks and habits of the change monster

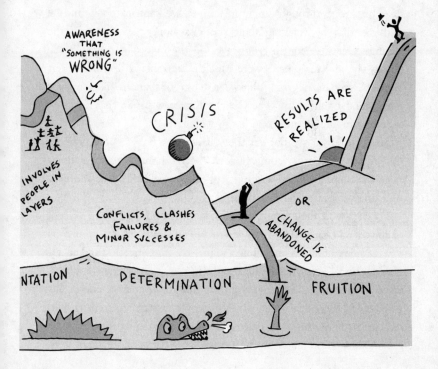

that lurks there. Like children on a long road trip, organizations can constantly be asking, "Are we there yet?" Knowing what to expect—the characteristics of the territory as well as what does and doesn't work along the way—can help leaders and their followers stay the course and calibrate their progress. I've often taught the Change Curve to the leaders of General Electric's businesses at GE's Crotonville Center. After one talk, a vice president of Medical Systems approached me. He showed me his copy of a Change Curve graphic, which he had carefully annotated with dates and events from a series of changes his organization had recently been through. "This clarifies everything for me," he said. "I feel like I've had a series of mysterious symptoms, not knowing whether I was sick, crazy, or normal, and now I've finally gotten a clear diagnosis. Now I understand that what's been happening to me and my organization is normal and predictable. What a relief!" Later, he used the Change Curve to help steer his group through a new initiative. We kept in touch, and he told me that by tracking their progress along the course of the Change Curve—"locating ourselves on the map of change," as he put it—he and his people were much better able to calibrate their progress, stay aware of gaps between subgroups, and manage expectations and momentum. The Change Curve is a map that has been tested innumerable times and has proved useful.

So, before we set out on the journey taken by Micro Switch, CoVen, and the other companies we'll talk about, I want to introduce the map, give you a glimpse of where we're headed, and provide one very important caution.

I'll start with the caution. It's simple, but it's important to voice it explicitly and early. The Change Curve—like any graphic depiction of a complex situation, including a map—is a simplification and an approximation. When an organization is in the midst of change, different departments and subgroups are typically in different phases at any given time. Individuals, too, find themselves experiencing change differently from one another. For example, because the senior executives make the decisions about major changes, it is common for them to be farther along the Curve than are other people in the organization. Understanding one another—which is always difficult during transitions—becomes even more difficult.

It is also the case that organizations, departments, and individuals don't always progress from one phase to the next in an orderly sequence. Some units get stuck in a phase for what seems like forever. Like a sailboat caught in a strong tide, their best efforts only allow them to hold their position and not go under. But in the next phase, they may zip through so fast that they become the pacesetters. Some will slip backward into a previous phase or alternate between two phases. In e-commerce start-ups, each major milestone—going from idea to business plan, securing initial funding, getting a Web site up and running, signing-up the first customer—is so critical and the work to achieve it is so taxing that people often experience the entire Change Curve in the achievement of each major accomplishment.

As different as the territory may look from various perspectives, my experience—and our research at BCG—has shown that the Change Curve applies to organizations in all kinds of change situations. The specifics are never the same, but the commonalities are strong, and the learnings and experiences of one can be applied to others.

STAGNATION:
THE MONSTER IN HIBERNATION

You might think that Stagnation is not a problem if the economy is successful and growing fast. It is. All organizations can stagnate. Technology and Internet companies do stagnate, although the length of their Stagnation phase tends to be much shorter, compared to other industries. In older industries such as manufacturing, periods of Stagnation have been known to last for years. Today, long-term physical and tangible Stagnation is relatively rare. In a booming economy, if public companies stagnate too long, analysts start to scream, shareholders demand action, and insiders start to jump ship.

And no private company will stagnate long before it goes out of business or an acquirer comes knocking.

Stagnation can be caused by any number of factors: poor strategy, lack of leadership, a shift in the market, a product failure, lack of new products or services, too few resources (including, most importantly, human capital), an outdated technology or process, or poor execution.

Stagnation can befall any kind of organization. In the early 1990s, America Online, the Internet portal company, suffered a period of Stagnation caused by a faltering strategy. Hewlett-Packard, a maker of technology hardware, found itself languishing in the late 1990s, primarily because of a confused product line in its nonprinter businesses. IBM suffered badly in the 1980s, when it became culturally rigid and too reliant on legacy technologies. Gillette, the world's largest maker of shaving products, took a dive at the turn of the millennium, because it, too, had become rigid and inflexible and kept trying to achieve success in ways that had worked for the company in the past. Even start-up firms and tiny boutique software shops suffer periods of micro-Stagnation when they find themselves out of sync with the market or unable to come up with new ideas that work.

THE SIGNS OF STAGNATION: EXTERNAL AND INTERNAL

The external signs of Stagnation are quite obvious: outdated products or services, falling sales and share price, customer desertion, and talent drain. In technology companies and start-ups, however, it is entirely possible to be in Stagnation and show none of these signs. Stagnation in such companies can show up as a lack of "buzz" in the press and an inability to attract new capital or sign up the hottest talent.

In some stagnating companies, the change monster is in a kind of hibernation. There is so little change that people feel comfortable and safe; they may or may not be working hard, but they have no sense of threat—which does indeed indicate a delusionary state. Without realizing it, they keep on nursing and pruning the same flowering plants that have been producing for ages; they know what to do and how to do it. This is especially true among companies with legacy products that are still making money. There is an implicit faith that the corporation, and the jobs it provides, will continue to exist forever. If there is a threat, it is regarded as a phantom—not really dangerous, not something to get overly exercised about.

In other stagnating organizations, the management may know very well that change is needed, but can't figure out what to change or how to go about it. Mattel, for example, keeps creating new lives and forms for Barbie, its legacy product, but has had a hard time coming up with a big new strategy, especially one that will embrace e-commerce. Mattel hoped that the acquisition of The Learning Company, a software maker, would inject new life and lead to hot new products and markets. It didn't. The acquisition failed to provide the desired synergies, caused Mattel's stock price to stagnate, and led to the resignation of the CEO.

METHODS FOR ENDING STAGNATION

A period of Stagnation can only end with a forceful demand for change from someone in a position of power and authority—the CEO, the board of directors, a big shareholder, or, possibly, an internal operating committee.

Two categories of actions can be taken to end Stagnation: those externally initiated and those internally initiated. The external category includes takeovers, mergers and acquisitions, leveraged buyouts (LBOs), and restructuring caused by deregulation or privatization. The internal kind includes divestitures, transformations, reorganizations, cost-cutting exercises, reengineering, and initial public offerings (IPOs).

A merger is a powerful way to shake up a really hidebound corporation and force radical change. When a merger takes place, nobody in either company—no matter how delusional he or she may be—can escape the realization that everything is up for grabs. Such mergers have become wildly popular in the past several years, as industries have consolidated and the need for scale has grown. Worldwide, 1.3 million merger deals were completed in 1998; their value was about $2.4 trillion. In 1999, the total rose to $3.4 trillion, according to *The Economist*. Each new merger brings fresh debate about the validity and ultimate benefit of the combination. Study after study has shown that most mergers destroy shareholder value. They fail to accomplish the goals that were intended: higher stock price, faster and more innovative product development, new strategic synergies, sales growth, or entry into new markets.

Mark Sirower, in *The Synergy Trap,* writes: "Whether the premiums paid in M&A represent fair values needs to be challenged. Because acquisitions are complex processes involving different levels of management, different political agendas, investment bankers, law firms, and accounting firms, it is altogether too easy for executives to pay too much. Many acquisition premiums require performance improvements that are virtually impossible to realize, even for the best managers and in the best of industry conditions."

Even so, the incidence and size of the mergers keep growing; at this writing, the AOL-Time-Warner deal is the ultra-super-jumbo—estimated at between $166 and $182 billion. American Airlines is buying TWA and United is buying U.S. Air. Who knows what might be next? "United AmiDelta"? Wal-Mart and Procter & Gamble?

PREPARATION:
THE PHASE LEADERS LIKE TO SKIP

In the case of an internal initiative, the time between the announcement of the plan and its implementation can and should be short. Preparation starts when the decision to change is made. Once made, it is often announced in some dramatic way—at an all-employee meeting or in a special CEO announcement or similar wideranging communiqué. In a merger or acquisition, the Preparation phase begins abruptly with a public notice of the intention to make an acquisition or accept an offer to be bought. Rumors about such an action may have been roiling through the hallways of both companies, but the actual announcement usually comes as a shock because the negotiations have been conducted—as they always must be—in secrecy. The majority of employees will learn from the media that their company is in play.

The Preparation phase can last for months, and sometimes—when approvals are required from government agencies—for a year or more. A huge amount of operational work must be done during the Preparation phase: Design the new organizational structure; define roles and responsibilities; determine which products, services, and capabilities will be critical going forward; and rationalize facilities, to name just a few. The leaders must flesh out the change plan enough so that their managers and employees can add the details that will be necessary during Implementation.

The Monster Wakes

In Preparation, the change monster is rudely awakened from its hibernating slumbers and stretches itself, causing all kinds of emotional tremors throughout the organization. When a change is externally initiated, everyone in the company (and all their friends and relatives outside it) speculates on the initiative and what it means to them. Their emotions heighten. People feel anxious, jittery, hopeful, threatened, excited, betrayed, and distracted. Everybody knows something big is going to happen, but no one yet knows exactly what. The senior executives are not immune to the monster: They worry about their own security, start jockeying for position, and prepare to defend their turf. In internally initiated change efforts, the monster may not awaken immediately. Often, people assume that the announcement of a new initiative is just the latest in a long series of programs or projects. They may feel annoyance, irritation, cynicism, and disbelief, and not take the announcement seriously. In any type of change, when the rush of emotions occurs, it is sure to cause some distraction from the work at hand. Productivity often goes down.

Because it is an in-between stage filled with anxiety and uncertainty—not to mention difficult and often tedious work—Preparation is the stage that action-oriented executives would prefer to skip. They have an overwhelming urge to "get on with it!"—to start doing things. If they give in to that urge, the senior managers generally zoom off in a dozen different directions with only superficial alignment of purpose or agreement about actions or intended outcomes.

LACK OF ALIGNMENT AMONG LEADERS CAN CAUSE FAILURE

The lack of alignment among the leaders is the most common cause of failure for major change efforts. This was the finding of a major study conducted by The Boston Consulting Group (BCG) to identify any common patterns of success or failure in major change initiatives. The sample included companies in every major industry—as well as some government agencies—in North America, continental Europe, the United Kingdom, Scandinavia, and the Asia-Pacific region. BCG examined all kinds of change efforts, including postmerger integrations, new strategies, deregulation, privatization, reengineering, and streamlining for speed. The clearest finding was that the most common cause of failure—across every type of initiative and in every geography—was not the lack of commitment by middle management (as is so often cited), but the lack of alignment of the leaders. I firmly believe that when middle managers are "acting out," they are only slightly exaggerating the behaviors they see at the top.

When the leaders are not aligned, it has a disastrous effect on the rest of the organization. People quickly break into factions and subgroups, aligning themselves behind one leader versus the others. The top executive then is forced to spend too much time playing the roles of police officer, arbiter, and peacemaker within his or her own team and among the various rival groups. The BCG study found that the longer this lack of alignment at the top is allowed to continue, the less likely the change initiative is to succeed.

PREPARATION UNRAVELS WHEN IT GOES ON TOO LONG

Even when the senior executives are in alignment and have done a good job of communicating the need for change, things can start to unravel if the Preparation phase goes on for too long. Consider the case of the merger of two telecommunications firms. Preparation became a new form of Stagnation when the regulatory hurdles took two years between the announcement of the merger and closure of the deal. During those two years, the majority of the workforce did not know what would become of their functions and divisions. Would they have to relocate? What products would they sell? Who would stay and who would go? Who would report to whom?

Both organizations went into free fall. Nothing seemed to matter because no one could be sure which activities would be pursued by the new organization. There was little formal authority because no one knew who would be around in six months or a year. Budgets didn't seem to matter either; no one knew who would be reviewing them or when. Besides, once the deal was finalized and the Implementation phase began, there would be new budgets and new measurements. As a result, people grabbed influence and funding, costs rose, and customers came and went. However, from the outside, the companies looked strong because demand was strong and sales continued to rise. Internally, it felt quite different. Profits were falling precipitously, and the company was actually losing money. People were up one day and down the next. As the uncertainty wore on, many felt a combination of hilarity and weariness.

IMPLEMENTATION:
THE JOURNEY BEGINS

Implementation can be like embarking on a big trip to some faraway exotic place you've only read about—Africa or New Guinea or Myanmar. During Preparation, you spend weeks working on the itinerary, getting your shots, booking hotels and transportation, reading about the political situation at your destination, exchanging money, and writing up contact information for your relatives. Even when you start to fold your undies and put them in your suitcase, the destination and expected adventure can still seem unreal. Not until you get off the plane does it really hit you that your journey has actually begun.

That beginning is called Implementation. The leaders announce the overall plan and assignments, new reporting lines are instituted, and new processes are required. When those things happen, the change monster comes stomping out of its hiding place and there's a virtual free-for-all of reactions. The emotions of threat, fear, exhaustion, and uncertainty, which first appeared in Preparation, are now joined by feelings of confusion, apathy, resentment, inadequacy, and volatility— as well as relief, exhilaration, excitement, and recognition. Employees may feel a sense of unreality. Everything has changed, but nothing has really changed—yet. Most important, no one is 100 percent sure about his or her ability to function or be successful in the new order of things. People are still hedging their bets.

OPERATIONAL CHANGES ARE NOT ENOUGH

During Implementation, it's up to the leaders to help their people understand the overall plan, persuade them that it will work, motivate them to participate in fleshing it out, and then work with them to be sure it is executed properly. Unfortunately, many executives and managers believe that having a clear plan is the final deliverable. They assume that the operational changes will occur and will then beget the full transformation. They take their eye off the ball once the plan is delivered and are surprised, months later, when things aren't working as intended.

I once worked with the leader of a technology company who committed himself to a major change effort and worked like a maniac to develop his Implementation strategy. He applied his considerable energy to every operational issue, and, within weeks, he and his team had ticked off an impressive list of accomplishments. They had designed the new organizational structure, written hundreds of job descriptions, and developed a detailed relocation plan. "The change is complete!" the executive announced to me one day, and thanked us for our help in developing the plan. I argued that the change was far from done; in fact, the hard part was just about to begin—the task of animating the new organization and making it work. He disagreed, but asked us to come back in six months to see how things were going. Six months later, we interviewed key contributors throughout the organization. All of them reported that nothing essential had changed. "The same folks who used to have power still have it, regardless of the new organizational architecture. The same cliques are still in place, and the same bullies are still up to their nasty old tricks." One senior engineer summed up the situation when he said, with pride, "We know what needs to be done, so we just do what we've always done, the way we've always done it. We've survived twelve reorganizations during my tenure."

When he heard our report, the leader turned bright red. "I feel like a guy who worked night and day and spent a boatload of money to renovate his house, and then finds that his kids liked it better the old way." Only after much discussion did he begin to acknowledge that change is not just a blueprint for a new structure; it requires changing people's mindsets and work practices.

DEEP POCKETS AND TIGHTWAD INC.: HOW CLASHING PHILOSOPHIES OBSTRUCT DECISION MAKING

Communication is always critical but never more so than when you're trying to get others to see and do things differently. So often formal communications focus on telling folks what to do—handing out assignments and required actions—rather than on answering why or explaining how the decisions came to be made. People need to understand the thinking that went into the decisions. What principles and goals were used in making trade-offs? What alternatives were considered, and why were they discarded? If leaders want to change the thinking and actions of others, they must be transparent about their own. If people within the organization don't understand the new thinking or don't agree with it, they will not change their beliefs or make decisions that are aligned with what's desired.

In the merger of two large industrial companies, for example, the acquirer, Company Deep Pockets, had plenty of cash and a belief that resources had to be expended to achieve quality. The acquired company, Tightwad Inc., had been starved for resources by its parent for years. The executives of the newly merged company never communicated "decision rules" or clarified any way to make trade-offs; they didn't even make their priorities clear—low cost or high value added.

Each company built and installed massive industrial machines, which required large crews to work together for months at a time, at the customer's site. The crews from Deep Pockets were accustomed to having any resources they might possibly need with them on the job site—back-up equipment, extra tools and components, redundant IT systems. The crews of Tightwad had been so browbeaten that they had learned to pare down, bringing only the bare necessities. They knew from painful experience that getting anything out of their Tightwad management was a hassle. If they spent a dollar that wasn't in the original budget, they would be subjected to a firestorm of outrage and remonstrance from their bosses and the finance guys. If they needed an extra extension cord, they had to go through endless rigmarole; it was easier to just "make do." In a pinch, a worker might even take a ride down to the local hardware store, pick up a tool, and pay for it himself rather than deal with the paperwork and agony of justifying the expense.

On their first joint installation, each crew was horrified by the behavior of the other. Tightwad's crew members were aghast at the quantity of inventory the other crew brought, and they were terrified that the cost of it all would show up as overruns on their budget. The workers from Deep Pockets were similarly incredulous that any professional crew could show up at a site with so little equipment. They had always been measured on excellence and quality, which to them meant the highest possible standards of mechanical aesthetics and the most elegant engineering solution. Deep Pockets workers wanted every piece of equipment and every tool at the ready. They figured if the extras weren't needed on this job, they could always be used for another job later. These conflicting attitudes caused no end of arguments on the site. When a problem arose, the Deep Pockets team wanted to go for the best possible solution, with little regard for implications of cost. The Tightwad team prided itself on its ability to brainstorm innovative solutions that would work without adding cost; the aesthetics and elegance of a job were not high priorities.

The crews got into such endless arguments that they finally appealed to their managers to resolve the conflicts. But the managers couldn't resolve them either because they were just as embedded in their legacy philosophies as were the workers. So, they forwarded the questions to their managers. By the time the dispute reached a manager of sufficient authority to make a decision, he or she had little or no understanding of the problem and regarded it as too trivial to worry about. The typical reaction was: "The people in the field are incompetent." When the problem was tossed back to the direct reports, and they kicked it back to the workers in the field, the reaction was similar, "Our managers are idiots!"

Situations like these often cause companies to get hopelessly lost in the Implementation phase. With so many tasks and so many details to watch, and with little direction or hierarchy of priorities, it's easy to feel overwhelmed. The organization seems to be going a million miles per hour without getting anywhere. People wonder whether they can keep up the pace and whether, in the end, all this activity will really make a difference.

DETERMINATION:
THE MONSTER ROAMS THE HALLWAYS

Now comes the most critical phase of the change process—the phase in which the initiative is in the most danger of failing. If the other phases have been successful, management may think the transformation is over and turn its attention elsewhere—just when reinforcement is most needed. If the organization is still confused, as Deep Pockets and Tightwad were, workers are likely to revert to their old ways, or leave, or, worse, stay in place but not engage. In most companies where Implementation has gone badly, no one wants to discuss it, let alone make a public show of diagnosing the failures and missteps. Rather, the change initiative is allowed to slip quietly into the corporate graveyard of failed programs, and the monster settles down, knowing that it has won.

The Determination phase is critical because the results of all the cumulative efforts should be evident, yet the organization starts to experience change fatigue. People get exhausted from expending the energy needed to rethink their daily work and change their ways of operating. If they feel the signs all point to success, they'll keep up their momentum even when they are exhausted. If it looks like "This too shall pass," they throw in the towel, start to hide, or only go through the motions of change.

One middle manager reflected on his journey, "Trying to figure out what works in this New World that we're trying to create keeps you constantly guessing and experimenting. You have to think deeply about what you're trying to do. It's not like being given orders by your boss, saluting, and then executing the plan. You keep trying to figure out how to make new ideas come to life. Sometimes something works and you feel fulfilled, but most of the time you feel unsatisfied and frustrated."

During Determination, people at last begin to realize that the change is real and they actually have to live their work lives differently. They have to report to a new boss, or work with new colleagues. Pet projects are scrapped in favor of ones with higher potential. Offices have been moved. Headquarters may be relocated from Sexy City to Podunk. Past relationships and processes (even those that hadn't worked very well) now are remembered with "euphoric recall"—they seem, in retrospect, so much more effective than they actually were and so much clearer than the current chaos. People long for an excuse to quit the hard path of transformation.

If the extraordinary focus on change continues and problems are addressed honestly, then progress and commitment can be kept alive even in the most trying of circumstances. But if management does not pay attention and problems are not acknowledged, the overall feeling, even with pockets of success, will be: "There's something seriously wrong here." At that point, the first chords of a funeral dirge can be heard.

The Most Insidious Monster: The Many Guises of Retreat

The most insidious and common monster is retreat. Retreat is very good at disguising itself as something else: apathy, hopelessness, or cynicism. Even worse, it can put on a positive face. The ever-popular ploy of declaring victory and moving on is routinely used. The change leaders will declare a halt in the march toward change, and offer some reasonable-sounding rationalization for the pause. "We need a little breathing space before we start up again." Or, "We just need a little period of normalcy." As innocuous as such explanations sound, they send a clear signal to everyone that the change effort is essentially dead. It's OK to stop pushing. Suddenly, there are no consequences for people who abandon the new processes or violate the agreed-on rules. Leaders make no attempt to stop people who revert to "the way things were." Accountability and follow-through become scarce. But, because the halt is supposedly temporary, the apparent failure doesn't have to be recognized or addressed. The organization refuses to acknowledge the failure of projects that have made it through Implementation but die quietly during Determination. The monster is sitting in the hallway, but no one will talk about it or point it out. In a merger, people give up trying to get the much-ballyhooed strategic synergies to materialize. Old processes exist alongside the new as if in parallel worlds; or, one company's ways are allowed to dominate by default. After a while, the failure of the change becomes a bad corporate memory that is seldom mentioned or is referred to only in corporate code: "I think we tried something like that once before, didn't we?"

To successfully manage change during Determination, the leaders must manage people's expectations, energy, and experience. Negative events will undoubtedly occur, but acknowledging and addressing setbacks can do wonders for credibility and morale.

CANDOR CASHES IN

After the pilot project failed, Fredrick, the executive in charge of streamlining new product introduction at WebMaster Inc., decided it was time for drastic action. He announced an open session and invited all employees to attend. The goal was to figure out how to get the project and the process back on track. Notices of the session went out on the company intranet, and posters were taped to the cafeteria doors. There was standing room only at the session, but folks were mostly curious or skeptical. "I've just come to see the show," said one software engineer who was leaning against the wall.

Fredrick started the session by giving a very candid and forthright review of what didn't work. He then invited members of the project team to add details or other issues he hadn't covered. To everyone's surprise, Janice, a team member, talked heatedly about not being able to get management's attention when extra resources were needed or a dispute had to be resolved. As she talked about these problems, Fredrick went to an easel and wrote on the pad: "Make management responsive and quick." Sniggering rippled through the room. When Janice finished, Fredrick addressed the audience. "Obviously we need help. This pilot project is just that—a pilot. If it doesn't work, neither will the ones that follow it, and that's unacceptable. The team and I are here to hear your ideas. We need all the help we can get, and, in keeping with brainstorming protocol, all suggestions will be considered and judgment suspended."

People were hesitant at first, but when they saw how receptive Fredrick and the team were, they really got going. The session lasted nearly three hours. Some people left and then came back; others wandered in, wondering what the fuss was about, and then stayed to contribute.

Later, I saw the same skeptical software engineer I'd spoken to at the beginning of the meeting. "What did you think of the session?" I asked him.

"That was so cool—I wouldn't have believed it if I hadn't been there. I fully expected some bullshit whitewash, but Fredrick actually laid it all out, and he allowed Janice to criticize his management. No wonder people stayed around to help. When someone is honest and asks for help, it makes you want to help them." Then, after a long pause, he added, "Yeah, I was proud of us today."

At WebMaster, the executive asked for help and he got it. When 3M asked for ideas on how to prevent product tampering as had happened with the Tylenol poisonings, the employees submitted 1,000 suggestions in one day. Avoiding problems is not possible; admitting them and addressing them is. When people band together to confront and conquer the change monster, they are usually victorious and they find their way through to the final phase, Fruition.

FRUITION:
The Monster Is Slain, at Least for Now

Fruition is the phase during which all the hard work and long hours at last pay off. The discrete activities and changes that have occurred in many different areas throughout the organization now combine and fuel each other. The whole enterprise seems new. The place feels different. People who have fought the monster now know it is corraled—at least for the moment— and is nowhere near as scary as it once seemed. The employees feel confident in themselves; they're optimistic and energized, and they're able to get their work done with less hassle, in less time, and with better results. The proof is in the many tangible positive results: The stock price goes up, sales rise, profits improve, costs go down, talented people join the workforce, the company wins more customers by bringing out a great new product or service.

A friend of mine is a natural cook. She can open any refrigerator, pull out what seems like a bunch of random ingredients and—within a few minutes—*voilà!* she's serving up a delicious dish. Her salads are particularly splendid. Their magical combinations transform the individual ingredients into a delightful new and unexpected whole. When I try to do the same thing, I end up with a bowl of torn-up lettuce punctuated by chunks of other stuff—the magical "synergy" of ingredients just doesn't happen. The experience of Fruition is similar. Like salad ingredients, all the individual efforts, projects, and initiatives come together to create a new way that works. There is some magic, and that's what makes it worth the effort and inspires those who have felt it to go for it again and again.

When you reach Fruition, it's important to stop and relish the moment, to acknowledge that the hard work is paying off and that people have successfully transformed the organization. Put the spotlight on the achievements—big and small—and broadly share the rewards. Take time to distill and assimilate the benefits and learnings that have occurred during the journey.

The success of Fruition brings the organization full circle, because the territory on the far side of Fruition is a new period of Stagnation. It won't look the same as the old Stagnation, but it will be just as paralyzing and perilous. The primary danger of Fruition is a lulling sense of satisfaction. The organization feels proud of its accomplishments and wants to bask in the limelight of success for a while. But the limelight fades fast, and the basking can quickly give way to napping. Before you know it, the new thinking—so hard-won—turns into dogma. Meanwhile, the market continues to evolve and the customers increase their demands.

Exceptional change leaders realize that their most important legacy to an organization is not just in creating a single transformation, but in teaching the organization how to perpetually change and adapt, and helping it muster the will to do so. When an organization sees itself as a hearty band of monster slayers, change becomes a challenge they're ready to meet rather than a threat that signals retreat.

PART TWO

STAGNATION

THE MONSTER
IN HIBERNATION

3

Demoralization and Denial

When What You Know Isn't So

I GREW UP in Montgomery, Alabama, where we had our fair share of eccentrics and local personalities around town. When my mother (or, as we say in the Deep South, my mama) and I went out together, she would point out the noteworthy locals, among them Zelda Fitzgerald, widow of F. Scott. The Gordons, another well-known family, had been the richest and the most patrician family in town for many generations. Then, as the result of some bad investments, they lost everything—all their money, power, and position. But you know what? They didn't act that way.

The Gordons paraded around town as if they owned the place, even after granddaddy Gordon had died, grandma had sold the mansion, the daughter had gone to work as a clerk at the dry cleaners, and the son was permanently "away"—that is, in a home for alcoholics. They still expected to get invitations to all the exclusive events in town and to be allowed to dine at the country club long after they'd stopped paying their dues. Once we saw Mrs. Gordon Sr. downtown, wearing gloves and a hat in midsummer, long after that particular fashion had gone out of style. Mama said, "It's so sad to see Mrs. Gordon pretending that nothing has changed. People want to help them but they're too defensive to accept. A friend of mine was recently rebuffed. Mrs. Gordon told her, 'We don't need any help. We aren't broke, we're just temporarily out of funds.'"

Sometimes organizations behave just like Mrs. Gordon—they get very good at ignoring the emotional and financial data. Even when they're bleeding red ink, they deny they have real problems and rebuff offers of help. You often find that kind of denial in the first stage of change, the phase that I call Stagnation. The organization chooses not to see its problems or opportunities. It's not willing to admit what outsiders can tell at a glance—it needs to make a radical change. There are usually plenty of clear, hard, objective indicators: The share price won't budge or is dropping. The market share is declining as competitors gain ground. No new blockbuster products are in the pipeline. Customers are going elsewhere.

An organization in Stagnation also beams out other, more subjective, yet often palpable, indicators: the emotional data. One executive I know says, "If you want to know how healthy an organization is, all you have to do is walk through the factory. You can just *feel* it." I'm sure you've walked through one of those unhealthy places. It doesn't have to be a factory. It can be an office in a fancy downtown tower, or the headquarters building on a corporate campus. It can be a restaurant, a hotel, or a retail store, for that matter. Wherever it is, the energy level is low; people you come in contact with look tired and dispirited. There's no buzz or bustle among colleagues, little laughing, but sometimes a lot of whispering. You get the feeling that everybody is marking time till the day is over. If they have any passion at all, it isn't for their job or their product or their customers.

TWO FORMS OF STAGNATION: DEPRESSIVES AND HYPERACTIVES

Companies in Stagnation fall into one of two categories: "depressives" and "hyperactives." I've seen both, and both are scary. In depressed companies, like those mentioned above, a deadening sense of *ennui* pervades the scene. The organization has no sense of direction; rather it seems to be wandering aimlessly with little sense of purpose. The depressed company exhibits the symptoms seen in an individual in depression: general slowness, inability to make decisions, feelings of inadequacy, no motivation or energy, a feeling of hopelessness. Hyperactive companies, by contrast, engage in frenzied activity. But although the activity consumes enormous amounts of energy, it generates, at best, only minor successes. These companies are like neurotic individuals or children with attention deficit disorder (ADD)—their attention leaps from one thing to the next, but there is precious little follow-through or forward progress. Stagnating companies of both types may or may not recognize what ails them. Some are aware they're unwell; others ignore their symptoms until they collapse and have to be rushed to the hospital.

At one depressed company—we'll call it Ennui International—an executive in charge of an internal transformation said to me, "We're floundering badly. We've lost confidence. Nobody is sure of what to do. Even where we have a good plan, people find it difficult to mobilize the energy and resources to implement it. I'm trying hard to create momentum, but it's tough going."

At a hyperactive company, Worldwide Frenzy, by contrast, a mid-level manager told me:

I was promoted four months ago to my current job. I knew it would be a stretch assignment because it was a new position that combined the responsibilities of two jobs from the old organization. And now I'm a member of two project teams, each of which demands fifty percent of my time. Every day, colleagues on both teams remind me that I have to give their work the highest priority. How am I supposed to do what I need to do for these project teams and still do all the work of my "regular" job? I'm working so hard I've become *persona non grata* at home. My wife is ticked off at me. My kids feel like I've abandoned them. I get home so late so often that the dog growls at me. But the worst part of it is: I'm not sure that all the hard work and long hours will make any difference. I'm really worried that it's just wasted effort in pursuit of nothing.

Life in both kinds of stagnating companies can be unpleasant and difficult. At the depressives, people feel drained and lifeless, hopeless and uncertain. At hyperactives, people feel exhausted, abused, and stressed. They feel they deserve some wins and rewards for their efforts, but, all too often, they get neither. Effort expended does not equal success experienced.

Sisyphus Systems: Depressed and Hyperactive at the Same Time

Sometimes, companies in Stagnation can be a weird combination of both depression and hyperactivity. A defense contractor—I'll call the firm Sisyphus Systems—engaged BCG to help improve its business performance. It wanted its projects to come in on time and on budget—a novel concept for this client and, at that time, for the defense industry in general. We knew we had a lot of work to do. When we started staffing teams to work with us, we found that most people in the company were already severely overcommitted to special projects—they simply couldn't take on any new assignments. It was clear that some of the existing projects had to be dumped, or at least put on hold for a while. But which ones? We decided to begin by taking an inventory of all the internal initiatives so that the executive team could make an informed decision about which ones to keep and which ones to scrap. Compiling the list was an exhausting project in itself. We were astonished to discover that there were more internal initiatives than there were employees—about 3,500 active projects, all with current billing numbers!

During the inventory process, we heard all kinds of cynical remarks. The most common was, "At Sisyphus, old projects never die; they just get underfunded." I began to understand that the company was both hyperactive and depressed. So many projects and initiatives had been created that none of them could reach fruition. Most projects had so little resource and share of mind that a person could work on several initiatives forever, unable to finish or escape any of them. Sisyphus, a character in Greek mythology, was doomed to an afterlife in which he pushed a giant boulder up a hill in Hades. Just as he reached the top, the boulder would roll down again. Then he'd have to do it again, and again, forever. The employees at Sisyphus Systems knew exactly how he felt.

When we discussed the findings of our inventory with the executives at Sisyphus, they were embarrassed but not surprised. "If we needed evidence that we're out of control, too inwardly focused, and have too many people working on the wrong things," one of them said, "we just got it." They were forced to acknowledge that their company was hyperactive, depressed, and in serious need of an overhaul.

The problem with effecting change at Sisyphus was that many of their 3,500 initiatives were change programs, but none of them had produced fundamental change. When a stagnating company attempts one change effort after another, and repeatedly fails to achieve any lasting result, two damaging things occur: (1) management loses credibility and (2) the rest of the workforce becomes change-resistant. When management loses credibility, it becomes almost impossible to push yet another new approach. The workforce, in turn, starts to behave like a prehistoric evolutionary creature (a shark, a roach). It learns to survive and adapt to every event, project, business fad, and administration that comes along, without disturbing its feeding habits. "Why should we change?" employees ask. "We'll just have a new program soon, or a new message. This bunch of idiots will move on to new jobs, and a new bunch of idiots will come in with a whole new plan. Then it's off to the races again."

SOME COMPANIES KNOW THEY'RE IN STAGNATION, BUT DON'T KNOW HOW TO END IT

The leaders at Sisyphus had been only vaguely aware of their Stagnation. In other companies, leaders are all too aware of the situation they're in, but they can't develop a plan for getting themselves out of it. Companies facing deregulation, privatization, or rapid industry consolidation are especially prone to this condition. The executives know that "life as we know it" is about to change drastically, but some can't figure out how they'll compete in the new situation, and others just aren't up for the challenge. One such executive confessed, "I don't have the stomach for this. No one can predict the future. No one knows how this industry will shake out. I don't know if re-making our company is a smart move. Things are working pretty well right now. Maybe we should be 'fast followers' instead. Wait and see how things evolve, then model ourselves after the market leader and catch up fast." The guy was planning to retire in two years. I wondered, "Is he wise or does he just hope he can escape before the pain of changing sets in?" It takes a lot of fire in the belly to lead or even to fully participate in a fundamental change. People with one foot out the door seldom have that fire.

Some management teams don't recognize the seriousness of their situation at all. They refuse to acknowledge the oncoming train of change, and they act as if the strategies that worked in the past will work for the future. In these companies, employees become easily demoralized and may panic. A department manager in a chemical company described himself this way:

> I have a recurring nightmare. I'm working in the engine room of an ocean liner. It's very hot. Suddenly, seawater starts pouring in. I don't know if we've hit a rock or we're sinking, or what. We just keep stoking the engine as fast as we can. It gets hotter and hotter. The water is halfway up

my calves. Finally, I can't stand it any longer. I run up to see the captain to ask him what's going on. I hope that I'll find him at the helm, and that he'll assure me that everything is under control. But when I get to the bridge, there is no captain. There's nobody at the wheel. It's just spinning around. We're out of control.

As the employees become more and more concerned about the fate of their company, they become less and less able to take any action at all. Like "deer frozen in the headlights" they may be eager to make a move but too terrified to decide which direction to go. Of course, lots of them do finally decide: they go out!

AT MICRO SWITCH: FACING A LONG BATTLE

When Ramon Alvarez accepted the job as its general manager, Micro Switch was a business in the depressive form of Stagnation. Its executives were complacent; many of its workers were dispirited. Jim Renier, the recently appointed CEO of Honeywell, gave Ray a simple-sounding charge: "Make Micro Switch competitive for the twenty-first century." Ray moved from El Paso, Texas, where he had been general manager of the Honeywell Keyboards Group, to Freeport, Illinois, where Micro Switch had been located since its inception in 1937.

Ray's quick review of the data revealed the telltale symptoms of a company in Stagnation: slowing sales growth, dwindling profits, and a shrinking customer base. The causes were equally obvious. Investment in Micro Switch had virtually been halted. Meanwhile, competitors were making deep sorties into Micro Switch's traditional core business. Customers were buying from a Japanese competitor whose products offered improved features, better quality, and lower prices. Micro Switch was close to losing its long-held position as number one in the market, and was in grave danger of being shut out, maybe forever, of the emerging market for new technologies. And yet, Micro Switch, despite its decline in profit margin, was still a profitable company and probably could have remained so for some years to come.

Ray needed to get a deeper understanding of the company than the financial data could provide. He set out to gather some of the "soft" data—the emotional data that would allow him to size up the team he'd inherited and get a sense of the morale of the organization. One of his first self-assignments was to visit the three local Micro Switch plants. His first stop was the oldest facility, located just a few blocks from his office. There, he found a factory of the past: poorly-lit, cavernous, loud with the sounds of antiquated cutting and stamping machines. The air was so thick with fine particles of machine oil that Ray could see no more than ten yards in front of his face. When he stopped to chat with a machine operator, he could see that the man's clothing was soaked with oil. Ray was appalled at the nineteenth-century working conditions, and horrified that he was now the General Manager of a company that would allow such conditions to exist. When he asked the operator what he thought about the place, the man shrugged. "I'm really thankful to have a job." Then, trying to be positive, he added, "It's quite a challenge keeping these old machines running." The conditions at the plant strengthened Ray's resolve to change things at Micro Switch. His visit had put a human face on the company's situation.

Ray saw the factory as a manifestation of the many things that were wrong with Micro Switch. The company's outdated equipment and processes were an indication of a lack of reinvestment. The attitude of the workers at the factory suggested a demoralized workforce; they were willing to accept poor working conditions and little say-so as the price of having a job. There was no esprit de corps; no energy was being expended toward keeping the place up-to-date, let alone making it a corporate showplace. The factory was run by a collection of wage earners trying to do their best, but with no understanding of their own potential to do better.

The conditions at the factory were most damning of the Micro Switch executives. When conditions deteriorate and the workforce is demoralized, it reflects directly on management. Ray could only conclude that the current management group was either out of touch with the situation, complacent and unable to muster the will or energy to change things, or just plain deluded. He knew that the transformation had to start with the executives in charge. They would have to change their ways or leave.

Ray spent several more weeks conducting his analysis of Micro Switch, but his findings only served to confirm his first impressions. Micro Switch was running on historic pride and present denial. Ray felt he was being asked to create a silk purse from a sow's ear. He was expected to improve the company's sales and profits, rebuild its technological capability, create a new management team, and revitalize the workforce. Ray knew that he was in for a long battle.

Assessing the Feasibility of Change

When a company is in Stagnation, as Micro Switch was, the leaders need to think hard about their strategic options. Transforming the company is one option; selling the company outright, or divesting or closing some operations are among the other possibilities. Transforming a company is not to be undertaken lightly. What you *don't* want to do is publicly commit to a major initiative, only to discover that it is far more complex and more onerous than anticipated. You would then have to back out for lack of the will or the resources to pull off the change.

A wise leadership team spends time, up front, previewing the factors that will determine the magnitude of the change, as well as those that will influence the timing and likely success.

Many dimensions may need to be altered or completely redesigned in a major change initiative. Some dimensions, such as the number of people and locations, greatly affect the complexity. Other dimensions—incentive compensation, for example—may not be that difficult to change but will have a ripple effect within the organization.

These are some key dimensions that need to be considered when assessing the scope and complexity of any given initiative, as well as the relative level of difficulty:

1. Strategy.
2. Business model.
3. Key processes and IT systems.
4. Organizational structure.
5. Roles and responsibilities.
6. Compensation.
7. Locations of operation and facilities.
8. Size and capability of workforce.

The greater the number of these dimensions that will be affected by the change, the more complicated it will be, and therefore the more critical good project management and overall leadership become. Sometimes a shift in strategy will affect only a small number of people; for example, the company may create a new internal business unit or take on a joint venture partner. But other strategies may require that almost every dimension of the company be altered. At Micro Switch, Ray figured the transformation would require a new strategy, a refined business model, revamped processes, adoption of new technologies, entry into new markets, a new management team, new team-based work in the factories, and the reshaping and retraining of the workforce. And changes in these eight major dimensions would, of course, beget many other smaller changes.

The relative level of difficulty to effect the change in each dimension altered is a subjective measure, but it can be evaluated. For example, if the business model is being changed so drastically that it requires a whole new way of thinking about one's work, that is far more difficult than changing a stand-alone procedure. When the perspective and skill sets required are radically different, intensive training will be needed. One then has to know: Is the training readily available? Will our current employees be able to grasp the new skills? Will we need to recruit a sizable number of new employees? Are they available? How long will all this take? For Micro Switch, for instance, each of the eight dimensions had a fairly high degree of difficulty.

The greater the number of people involved in the change, the tougher it will be to effect and the longer it will take. A team of ten people can adopt a new strategy in a matter of days or weeks. An organization of 500 will require months. When a big company requires new actions from tens of thousands of people, allow a year or more. The number of locations and time zones the employees work in, and the number of languages they speak, also add to the complexity. Think of a company that has only 500 people, all in one location, all speaking the same language. Even if the change involves a number of dimensions, the whole group can be assembled in one auditorium to discuss the issues, provide training, give and get updates—all at the same time and place and in a common language. Compare that to a company with 50,000 people scattered in country headquarters and sales offices all over the world. They speak several different languages, live in different time zones, and use different information systems. Complexity makes everything more difficult, time-consuming, and resource-draining. At Micro Switch, Ray was dealing with a workforce of about 5,000 people located in eleven facilities in the United States and Mexico, and two operations in Europe—plus joint ventures in Japan, South Korea, and India. Not a giant company, but big enough to add complexity to the already multidimensional and difficult change at hand.

President John F. Kennedy's call to "put a man on the moon by the end of the decade" is a classic vision statement—clear, short, compelling, broad enough for all to contribute, and with an emotional hook that motivates. I've known some corporate executives who see no need for a vision and want to keep the strategy a secret. I always wonder how on earth they expect their organization to change! People need and want clear and motivating goals—some reason to come to work; something to get excited about. If the desired state is clearly defined, sharply articulated, and widely understood among the workforce, the employees will be able to absorb it quickly and to begin enacting it effectively. Fuzzy or undefined visions confuse people and erode leaders' credibility.

With Micro Switch, the desired future state was no more clearly defined than Renier's charge—"Make us competitive for the twenty-first century"—although there were also corporate targets for sales and profitability. One of Ray's first tasks, therefore, would be to work with his leadership team to flesh out the vision of Micro Switch's desired state.

The entire change effort is further affected by the amount of time available to make it happen. If there is too little time, people are likely to burn out before the goals are reached. If there is too much time, energy dissipates and people lose focus. Generally speaking, it's better to have a shorter time line in order to keep the organization focused and to generate a sense of accomplishment through results (of course that assumes that demonstrable results are achieved). Because things change quickly in today's marketplace, shorter initiatives are also more likely to be completed in their entirety without being obliterated by another, more urgent, initiative.

The energy, capability, will power, skill, and alignment of the leaders are all-important. No fundamental change takes place without strong leadership. At Micro Switch, Ray had little alignment among his senior management team, so most of the strength in leading the change—at least in the beginning—had to come from Ray himself.

When I work with executives to assess the challenge they're facing, doing the feasibility assessment can have a powerful impact. Sometimes, the realization of the scale will cause them to give up the idea of fundamental change. They recognize that it will take too long, or the resources are not available, or—most difficult to admit—they simply don't have the personal energy or will to undertake change. Better to acknowledge that reality up front than to lead the company—and its employees and shareholders—on a forced march that has no chance of success. That happens. The most obvious example that comes to mind is Roger Smith's quest to transform the General Motors system of conventional manufacturing facilities into an automated "people-less" operation. Didn't work: too many dimensions. Too many people in too many facilities. And Smith didn't have the strength and team support needed to lead it. In a *Fortune* article, he recalled:

> If I had the opportunity to do everything over again, I would make exactly the same decision that I made in 1981 when I became chief executive. I'd begin to rebuild General Motors, inside out and from the bottom up, to turn it into a 21st-century corporation, one that would continue to be a global leader.
>
> But I sure wish I'd done a better job of communicating with GM people. I'd do that differently a second time around and make sure they understood and shared my vision for the company. Then they would have known why I was tearing the place up, taking out whole divisions, changing our whole production structure. If people understand the why, they'll work at it. Like I say, I never got all this across. There we were, charging up the hill right on schedule, and I looked behind me and saw that many people were still at the bottom, trying to decide whether to come along. I'm talking about hourly workers, middle management, even some top managers. It seemed like a lot of them had gotten off the train.

On the other hand, leaders who recognize a challenge, even a multidimensional one, can rise to the occasion. During the debate about whether to go forward, one company president said, "Wait a minute. Before we all start agreeing with each other that this is too complicated, let's consider two things: (1) We control a lot of these factors—clarity of the desired state, resources, timing, and the leadership. We can make sure these parts work. And (2), what do you think will happen to this company if we don't go forward?" His confrontation changed the nature of the debate and escalated the commitment of the executives to make the desired state happen.

AT VENERABLE BV: THE MONSTER ABRUPTLY AWAKENS

Sometimes the realization that a company is in Stagnation comes all too slowly; at Micro Switch, it began as a gnawing awareness. Sometimes it's more like a thunderbolt from Hell, as was the case with

Venerable BV, a respected pharmaceuticals firm based outside Amsterdam, The Netherlands.

In 1995, Venerable was in Stagnation but didn't realize it. Pharmaceuticals companies work with long product development cycles and their products are patent-protected for as long as twenty years. When a company scores a big hit, as Venerable had done with a breakthrough antidepressant, the profits can be harvested for decades. This is a good thing, considering that, for every blockbuster, the company has spent roughly $500 million on the drug's development and will need to spend upwards of $100 million more to market it. The trick for pharmaceuticals, therefore, is to keep the product pipeline filled with potential blockbusters—not "me-too" products or those with small market potential. Because most new drugs will not make it from research to development, management must ensure that enough initial targets are discovered so that when the low-potential drugs are killed off early, there are still enough new products that do make it to market. Coming up with a good drug is only part of the challenge. The company must worry: What are our competitors doing? Is a competitor's product going to beat ours to the market or have greater benefits? Will our drug receive regulatory approval? The path from molecule to market is long and arduous, and most discoveries don't make it to fruition.

Venerable's best-selling antidepressant was going to lose its patent protection in 1999, and the management had focused all their efforts on a replacement—a new drug that was an improvement on the original. It would offer greater effectiveness at lower doses, cause fewer side effects, and could be sold for a lower price. Venerable's leaders expected the new drug to provide needed profits for at least a decade, maybe longer. In late 1997, to their great surprise and distress, the drug did not receive regulatory approval. Panicked, they turned to the new-product cupboard and found that it was bare—no other drug with major commercial potential was anywhere close to being market-ready. They had looked forward to a cozy decade of leisurely harvesting; now they were facing a very uncertain future.

Within a month of the news, the board of directors of Venerable received a purchase offer from Commando International, an aggressive American-based company. The management team, which had just suffered the shock of recognition that their company had somehow slipped into Stagnation, now received a second shock: their world-famous, seemingly untouchable company was "in play." The change monster had not only leaped to life, it had landed in the middle of the boardroom and was causing tremendous turmoil. As one executive put it, "It was like finding yourself being wheeled into the emergency room with the doctors arguing over whether or not they can save you. One minute you're on top of the world and the next you're facing death, wondering what the hell just happened! You always know, theoretically, that this can happen, but you never really expect it will happen to you."

The Venerable Labs research and development facility, which we visited many times, was located in a suburb of Amsterdam, not far from the airport. Built in the 1930s, "The Labs" was a rambling facility. Its central stone building looked like a sprawling university or library. The facility had been expanded many times, but without the benefit of a master plan. By the late 1990s, The Labs was a jumble of wings and towers and covered walkways that nearly engulfed the original building. Here, the researchers of Venerable had developed some of the world's most successful drugs, including three blockbusters that had long since earned back their investment and, for more than a dozen years, had produced rivers of profit for Venerable.

Over the years, The Labs had been home to distinguished scientists who, beyond their roles as Venerable employees, had made significant contributions to the world of medicine and pharmaceutical research. A heritage of contributing to society was part of their proud tradition, whether through basic research, the publishing of scholarly papers, lecturing and teaching, serving in various associations and standard-setting organizations, advising governments, or mentoring young scientists and interns. The Labs, already known as a research center, had become respected as a training ground, an intellectual center for thousands of talented people, and a source of great knowledge and wisdom. Researchers who left Venerable over the years continued to feel loyalty to The Labs, even as they worked for competitors. In short, the people at The Labs—about 2,200 PhDs, MDs, researchers, and support staff—took great pride in the *science* for which their employer was renowned. Their personal identity was linked to the science, not the business.

Before the merger was contemplated, BCG got to know Venerable through an assignment for its clinical development group. It was clear to us, as outsiders, that the company was stagnating, particularly in its research operations—the heart and soul of any pharmaceuticals company. When I visited the Venerable Labs, I realized that they had a lot in common with the outdated factory at Micro Switch. Their work processes had not been examined or updated in years. The result was a workforce that was comfortable doing what it had always done, even if the work did not create shareholder satisfaction. Most important, and most telling, was the devastating lack of urgency about the business. This complacency was as evident among the MDs, PhDs, and support staff at The Labs as it was with the factory workers at Micro Switch.

There were too many drugs in development at Venerable, but not enough that had real potential. Many of them were focused on minor modifications to existing products. A surprisingly large number of development projects involved treatments for rare diseases or conditions that affect very small numbers of people; these drugs might prove helpful to humanity, but they would never be profitable. Other projects involved extremely long-range research that would not yield marketable drugs for decades. When we visited in early 1997, all the projects seemed admirable and interesting, but—when we considered that patent protection for Venerable's best-selling drug was scheduled to end in two years—we got worried. When we asked the scientists about the need for a new blockbuster drug to fund all their research, they agreed and admitted that the company had a problem. But they didn't see it as *their* problem.

Only one group that we interviewed, the oncology team, had a drug in its pipeline with the potential to become a blockbuster reasonably soon—a breakthrough treatment for lung cancer. Dr. Elena Margolis, a relative newcomer to Venerable, headed the unit. She had been recruited from a competitor four years earlier, when the former head of oncology research at The Labs had retired. Margolis, who was in her late thirties, had a sterling reputation and image; she was known for her intellectual power, enormous energy, and persuasive personal style. When she joined Venerable, she was able to attract a team of scientists from a variety of companies. They joined her because they respected her as both a researcher and an administrator—a rare combination of traits. She was also known for her passion, rigid standards, and inflexibility. I remember thinking at the time: This company needs more people like Dr. Margolis. How can Venerable attract more people like her? What keeps her here? And will those same things help retain her? When we heard the news about the merger and were asked to help with the postmerger integration, I wondered how Dr. Margolis and her team would fare.

The intriguing thing about Venerable was the speed with which the situation changed. Like any sudden disruption, it caused immediate disequilibrium and revealed the weaknesses that had been lurking there all along. The board members weren't the only ones in a tailspin. One cynical scientist said, "We just went from Venerable BV to Vulnerable BV." People at Venerable had felt so secure that they were totally unprepared to deal with the possibility of being sold and did not know what to think or how to behave. In the meantime, everything else got shoved aside. In business terms, that can mean that productivity plummets, sales falter, important opportunities get missed, and people just want to get out. When the offer came from Commando, it was a rude wake-up call for everyone at Venerable.

4

Recognizing and Diagnosing the Condition

Helping People See the Truth

THE FIRST TASK for a company seeking to get out of Stagnation is to stop denying that it is, in fact, stagnating. To this end, a crisis can be a very useful tool for leaders who recognize that their company is in Stagnation, but need proof of it in order to convince their workforce or board of directors. As one seasoned supervisor said, "Fear is a motivator. The threat of annihilation will cause people to come together and perform with renewed vigor." When the troops realize that the survival of their company (and their jobs) is threatened, it is relatively easy for the leaders to mobilize them in the cause of change.

Chrysler, under Lee Iacocca, is the classic example. The possibility of bankruptcy was impossible to ignore. It was all over the news; cartoons appeared on editorial pages across the nation. Far less dramatically, in the early 1990s, IBM was in a sufficient state of crisis, if not as dire as Chrysler's, to give Louis Gerstner a mandate to make sweeping changes. And who can forget "Chainsaw Al Dunlap" at Scott Paper and Sunbeam? Such turnaround experts make their marks at companies in crisis. They get called in by desperate boards of directors when dramatic and immediate action is required to avoid collapse. "When the cash cow starts producing red ink, something better start changing fast," a management team member explained during a turnaround. "Unfortunately, even the obvious gets ignored around here. If we want to change something, we have to have a big push, something so big that it cannot be ignored by either the employees or by the corporate executives. So we now call it the 'blessing of red ink' because when you're losing money hand over fist, it gets pretty easy to convince the CEO and the board that the business needs to be radically transformed."

Crisis, however, is a risky instrument for forcing people to recognize the need for change. When a firm's officers make no move until a crisis forces them into it, they lose credibility within their organization. They are seen as the executives who allowed the company to sink so deeply into Stagnation that it reached the crisis stage. Why should they be the ones to turn the company around? What new skills or strategies have they suddenly acquired that they didn't possess before the crisis? What have they learned recently that will make the critical difference now?

GETTING PEOPLE TO SEE STAGNATION

Another problem with relying on crisis to provoke change is that organizations may not recognize Stagnation, even when they're in the middle of it. I worked with a client that had been losing money for several years and was publicly for sale. Even so, many employees confided in me, "Nothing will happen to us." When I asked why they felt that way, they said that the company was too big, too old, too vital—it just couldn't be shut down or sold. They had an unspoken, almost mystical, belief: "A sale would really be awful; therefore, it can't happen." This is not at all unusual. Many employees believe (sometimes desperately) that the company they work for is too important to be shut down. They may cite national security, the local economy, or the importance of the company's products to humankind. When that kind of denial is allowed to continue unchecked and people have not been properly briefed about their probable fate, they have a much harder time coping with extreme measures when they finally come. The company was sold at last, and the assets and jobs were redistributed. Employees were faced with losing their jobs or moving halfway across the country to work for the new owner. Because they were unprepared, they had a harder time making decisions about their future. Many were simply unable to process what had happened to them and to figure out what they wanted to do in the time that had been made available to them.

Getting people to recognize Stagnation becomes more difficult when a workforce that is in denial is coupled with a group of leaders who are loath to declare the bad news. Nobody likes being the bearer of bad news, but some executives hate it so much they simply won't do it. Their excuse is that they don't want to demotivate the workforce. One executive said, "We want to be the good guys, so we never tell people the bad news. We don't deliver negative messages. If there is some message we can't avoid, we sugarcoat it or sandwich it between upbeat messages, hoping that people won't notice or get too upset. I've come to think that we are constitutionally incapable of telling people bad news." This idea that "If I don't tell them, they won't know" just doesn't cut it. In all likelihood, people are already aware of what's up, or they have created their own scenario from rumors. The "old salts" who've been around a long time will recognize the signs. The up-and-comers will smell trouble. If the executives don't address the negative issues, folks start to wonder: Are these guys so incompetent that they don't understand what's happening? Or, if they do understand, are they just refusing to talk about it? And, if so, are they not talking because they don't trust us or because they don't have a plan to fix the problems? None of these questions builds confidence.

As painful as crisis can be, it may be the only way to get a big company to recognize the most common symptom of Stagnation: complacency. In recent years, a number of companies with strong, proud histories and products or services that were market leaders have struggled with Stagnation: AT&T, General Motors, DEC, American Express, and Kodak, to name a few. They all showed signs of being too big, too slow, too complacent, and not innovative enough. An executive at one of those companies told me, just before things got really bad, "We must be doing something right or we wouldn't have gotten this big." But he was also canny enough to remark, "Our past success is the greatest enemy of our future prosperity."

The more successful a company becomes, the more risk-averse its managers are likely to become; they are less and less willing to tamper with the products or services that have built their success. A consumer goods company, for example, offered brands that had become icons of American culture. Although the products remained profitable, the margins had gradually slipped below their peak levels. The brands were managed conservatively; their managers sought, above all else, to cause no harm to the brand's image or popularity. Creating product extensions that achieved predictable returns while minimizing risk became a sure way to get promoted. When we conducted an analysis of the company's major brands, we discovered that most of them had experienced a steady decline in profits for years, even decades. The brand managers had been able to ignore the bad news by blaming profit declines on all kinds of factors beyond their control. My personal favorite was the brand manager for a nation-wide chain of family-fare restaurants that was doing especially poorly in the Midwest. He claimed, "Our problem is that people in Iowa just don't eat steak and potatoes!" Talk about denial!

Powerful and still-successful companies often are the slowest to recognize the signs of Stagnation, especially if they are able to avoid a major crisis. They behave like a train that has built up a lot of speed, but then loses power. It is hard to pinpoint exactly when the locomotive lost steam, because the train can coast at high speeds for miles and miles, especially on downward slopes. The people on board may not be able to feel the loss of momentum. Or, if they do, they may not be willing to talk about it.

Avoiding Stagnation

Many high-performing companies have been unable to avoid Stagnation, but a few have been able to do so for inordinately long periods of time. They do it by developing a culture that emphasizes—and even exaggerates—every threat and perceived danger, and reacts to even the tiniest hints of complacency. Although they have had moments of being at risk, Disney, Intel, Home Depot, Southwest Airlines, First Union, St. Jude Medical, and Dillards are all examples of companies that have enjoyed remarkably long periods of sustained strong performance in spite of recessions, business cycles, and technological discontinuities. They are skilled not only at early identification of potential threats and opportunities, but also at mobilizing the resources needed to establish new competitive advantages and avoid, or even leverage, potential threats. An important by-product of always being on the lookout is that the organization learns to be vigilant, future-oriented, and never satisfied. When Intel's Andrew Grove said, "Only the paranoid survive," he meant that the smart organization behaves as if the competition and the market are out to get it—which, of course, they are.

Companies that avoid Stagnation are constantly changing in a planned, purposeful, and productive way—before they reach a state of crisis. I hate to bring up Jack Welch, Chairman of GE, because he is so widely cited, but I will anyway. When e-commerce was in its infancy, Welch recognized it as a force to be reckoned with, a threat and an opportunity. He saw that it had the potential to destroy well-established big businesses, like the ones that make up GE's portfolio. The GE businesses, however, were hardly in Stagnation. According to GE's 1999 annual report, fourteen of GE's twenty top businesses recorded earnings growth in the double digits. Five of them grew by more than 40 percent, four between 25 and 40 percent, and five between 15 and 25 percent. Hardly what most of us would call Stagnation. And yet, at the annual managers' meeting in January 1998, Welch told his top managers that they had to figure out how an Internet competitor might cannibalize their business and develop a strategy that would preempt such a move. Welch called his initiative "DestroyYourBusiness.com."

The program has produced impressive results. In his 1999 letter to shareholders, Welch wrote:

> While we are already generating billions in Web-based revenues, the contribution of e-Business to GE has been so much more. It is changing this Company to its core . . . this elixir, this tonic, this e-Business came along and changed the DNA of GE forever by energizing and revitalizing every corner of this Company.

Think about that: GE has radically revitalized businesses, some of which were already growing earnings by more than 40 percent annually. Obviously, this is a company that will not accept complacency and looks far into the future to spot looming crises; by doing so, it forces the changes—on its own terms. What many GE observers fail to recognize is that this ability to change is not a recent phenomenon; Welch and his management team have been building change capability into GE's culture for nearly two decades. When GE needs to make a fundamental transformation—as it is doing with the shift from traditional business to e-business—the difficulty and magnitude of the change (as measured by the factors we discussed earlier), while still considerable, are manageable. The executives are already aligned and have the skill and bench strength needed to lead the transformation; the levers are well understood, so designing them appropriately happens quicker; and the infrastructure supporting transformation is in place.

This kind of anti-Stagnation vigilance is a required capability for fast-paced technology companies, especially dot-coms and start-ups. Employees at these companies learn to live with constant shifts in the market, the competition, business models, management, customer base, and investors. The problem with this new breed of company is that it's often difficult to tell the difference between a Stagnation phase (which is more often characterized by hyperactivity than depression) and a phase of Preparation or even Implementation. A dot-com company may be fully implementing a sound strategy without generating any profit. In such a company, the traditional "hard data" are not particularly good indicators of how the company is doing. In biogenetic engineering firms, for example, we have seen that the no-profit condition can be tolerated for years. Yet, nowadays, investors are beginning to ask the hard questions: Is this a company with unrealized potential or unrealizable potential? Is there any way this company can justify its market capitalization? What would this company have to do to earn the profits needed—and how soon will we know whether that will happen? Investors are starting to realize that it is possible to stagnate even in an exciting and exploding market. Is there still money to be made with this stock, or is it time to get out? Amazon.com, one of the Internet sector's most debated companies, is often at the center of such speculation. People are constantly wondering: Is it actually a stagnant company of the hyperactive variety, despite its relative youth and phenomenal growth? Or is it a promising company that makes the right investments but just hasn't quite reached its period of fruition and profitability?

DIAGNOSING STAGNATION

It is not enough to recognize that a company is in Stagnation; the leaders must thoroughly diagnose the condition. They have to determine what is causing the Stagnation and assess just how bad it is. This is not at all easy, because so many factors affect performance and morale. To make matters even more complicated, the diagnosis can be hampered by the leaders' natural assumption that they already know what's ailing their organization. Almost every executive I've worked with has asserted that he or she knows "how things really are around here." I've found, however, that most leaders have less of a feel for their companies than they think they do. Most are insulated from the day-to-day experiences and emotions of the company by all kinds of filters—particularly their well-meaning direct reports, who subtly interpret or modify the company's problems and the facts they bring to the leader's attention. This interpretation may be benign; managers may intend to take care of any problems in their own shop and therefore see no reason to bring an issue to the attention of the boss.

What we hear, over and over again, from even the most hands-on executives who are immersed in their companies' operations, is that the change process reveals how little they actually did know about their own organizations. "I thought I knew how things worked in this company," said one telecommunications company executive. "But when I got involved in running the turnaround, I learned that I really didn't have a clue." In another company undergoing large-scale change, the leader had an even tougher self-assessment. "When I think about what I didn't know about this company when we started down this change road, I just sit and shake my head. Who says, what you don't know can't hurt you? We were lucky. Our lack of knowledge could have killed the whole company."

The best diagnoses involve analysis of three types of information: quantitative data, and external and internal qualitative—or emotional—data.

There is always loads of hard information to be gathered and digested. The numbers reveal a lot about volume, sales, profit from continuing operations, profit from investment, new product development, delivery performance, asset turns, quality, cycle time, ROI, ROE, and so on. The numbers are very important, but they never tell the whole story.

To gather the emotional data, you have to listen to people. Sometimes it's best to start by talking with outsiders—customers, partners, suppliers, professional service providers, distributors, and industry experts who have insight into the company's competitive position—because their input can help you frame the questions and issues that will then need to be followed-up with insiders. People outside the organization often will have a startlingly clear picture of what is going on inside. For example, suppliers who work with many companies in the same industry have a deeper comparative view. A vendor that works with many parts of one organization may have a broader and more complete view of the entire operation, across functions and departments. Because outsiders are less invested in the internal culture, they are better able to see the strengths, weaknesses, assumptions, and values.

There are, however, a number of caveats worth reviewing before starting either external or internal interviews. Listening for understanding is hard to do, especially when the criticism starts. The best way to stop someone from telling you what's wrong is to start defending, justifying, or "enlightening" them about the "reality" of the situation when they bring up a problem. It's hard to keep your mouth shut when you feel that you're under attack.

Early in my career, I worked with Mae, a little old lady who was a troubleshooter for the bank. I watched with amazement one morning as Mae listened to an irate customer who went on and on about problems she'd had with the bank. Mae nodded in agreement, asked a few clarifying questions, and generally commiserated with the customer. When the person finally left, I confronted Mae. "Why didn't you tell her what was going on? You knew she caused some of those problems!"

Mae took me aside and patiently explained, "If I start correcting her, what's she going to say—'oh, of course you're right'? No. She'll either dig in her heels or stop telling me what's going on. Either way, I lose. I want all the information she has to tell me. We may have been right on one thing, but she may point out two others where we need to improve. Now she feels listened to and cared about. Tomorrow I'll call her, tell her I followed up on her concerns, and give her the correct information. She'll know that I went the extra mile for her, and she'll continue to be a loyal customer."

It is also important to keep in mind that all the people you interview have their own position to promote or protect; their own special relationship and history with the organization will affect their view. Some people will exploit any opportunity or invitation to criticize in order to promote their self-interest. They may even exaggerate or make up failings. You have to be skeptical of what they're saying, and ask for counter-examples or specifics even as you encourage candor. That's why it's wise to interview as widely as possible before you draw any conclusions.

If you send out an inexperienced team of eager-beaver would-be revolutionary employees to do the interviews, they will tend to report uncritically, not appreciating every context, and overemphasizing the negative in what they hear in order to "deliver a message" to their stuffy old bosses. When this becomes apparent, it can undermine the credibility of the whole effort. One client researcher warned his team, "You know how our management team loves a juicy quote," he said sternly, "therefore, I want the quantitative data to come first. The quotes come last and are accompanied by an indicator of how representative they are of all of the opinions expressed."

In addition to interviews and conversations, many companies conduct quantitative surveys. These surveys can be very useful but, if poorly designed, can be misleading. We worked with an entertainment company, for example, that thought it understood its customers well, primarily because it conducted quarterly surveys of its customers and paid close attention to the results. Then its newly hired marketing director, Eric Schwartz, decided to personally interview the company's twenty top customers as a way to introduce himself and learn about the business. The interviews revealed some harsh truths not captured in the quarterly customer surveys. The worst example came from Jerry Johnson, the purchasing VP at the firm's second-largest customer. When Jerry met Eric, he launched into a tirade: "You cost me a lot more than just your premium prices. Your ordering requirements and people are so difficult to work with that I have to hire a full-time employee just to interface with your company. And nobody likes that job; it has the highest turnover of any job in my shop." The more Eric listened and learned, the more concerned he became. As he later put it, "You know you're in trouble when the only thing that keeps you in the lead is that your competitors are worse than you are." The problem was that the survey had not been designed to explore the issues of ordering requirements and the cost of doing business with the company; it focused on on-time delivery, quality failures, and the like—areas in which there were few problems.

The lesson here is: To really assess whether your company is in Stagnation, you need a robust analysis—both external and internal. To get this, in addition to the financial and other data, you must talk with people face-to-face, especially those outside. And don't let them be nice to you. Ask the hard questions:

Do you like doing business with us? If so, why? If not, why not?

Do you see our product or service as integral to the health of your business?

Do we provide unique value or are our competitors as attractive as we are?

How has your relationship with us changed over the past X months/years?

What one thing could we improve that would make a difference to you?

How would you describe our company to a colleague or friend?

How would you compare us to your ideal?

From these interviews, general themes emerge. Articulating the themes, supporting them with "actuals" (verbatim comments from one or more of the interviewees), and combining them with the quantitative data can yield a robust picture that is hard to ignore.

Ray Alvarez spent a good deal of time talking with key customers of Micro Switch; what he heard was generally discouraging. "I was getting a lot of phone calls about Micro Switch's performance from irate customers," he said. "Big customers, Fortune 500 companies, were cutting back on their orders or leaving us altogether. We had to stop the hemorrhaging." Again and again, customers delivered a powerful message: "Your product quality is good. You set the industry standard. You have capable people with a high degree of integrity. But, you're not listening to us. Your competitors are outperforming you. They're eating your lunch, and you don't even realize it."

In an earlier assignment at Honeywell, Ray had commissioned a study on customer retention. One of the key findings of that study was that on-time delivery (OTD) was a reliable indicator of customer satisfaction. Customers expected and wanted performance of at least 90 percent, but they would sometimes tolerate slightly lower performance. However, when OTD slipped below 82 percent, the customer would soon take its business elsewhere. Ray gathered the data for Micro Switch's OTD performance for the previous year: exactly 82 percent. No wonder Micro Switch was losing customers.

Such external qualitative findings, in conjunction with internal quantitative data, can provide very powerful knowledge. It becomes difficult for managers to make excuses, explain away the findings, or ignore what they are hearing.

The listening process often reveals a hard truth that leaders seldom face: Getting close to your own organization is tougher than getting close to your customers. For most customers, giving tough, direct, honest feedback and criticism is comfortable. It's in their own self-interest to do so, and it's virtually risk-free. For the people inside your company, however, criticism and tough-minded feedback may be outside the bounds of the company's norms. In many companies, it's the fastest route to being labeled "negative," a "problem," "not a team-player"—the kinds of labels that can rob you of your next promotion.

There are many methods for gathering opinions and insight from employees. We use relatively structured ones, such as employee surveys and focus groups. We also observe meetings, listen to hallway conversations, attend presentations, tour the facilities, chat with workers, eat in the cafeteria, and review employee communication materials to get a sense of the energy level, humor, and mood of the place.

Employee surveys are particularly useful in quantifying and locating issues and providing a general overview of "how things are going." They should, however, be used sparingly or be exceedingly easy and quick to complete. Surveys are like hypodermic needles: People will only allow you to stick them a few times before they get irritated. Moreover, surveys should always be supplemented with other information and interpreted accordingly. Follow-up is very important. The results of the survey should be reported back to the employees, and the leaders should explain what they plan to do with the knowledge gained. Who likes to spill their guts and then be ignored?

Hallway conversations and people-watching also can be effective methods for getting a feel for things. What Harvey Firestone, founder of Firestone Tire, said years ago is still true for astute managers: "I can walk through the front door of any factory and out the back and, in five minutes, tell you if that company is making money or not. I can tell by the way the place is being run and by the spirit of the workers." When Ray Alvarez did this at the Micro Switch factory, it was easy to see whether his people were optimistic or pessimistic, spoke with energy or enthusiasm, or seemed downtrodden and beleaguered.

A marketing vice president who visited the regional sales offices of his company told me:

> It was amazing to me how different each one felt. I hadn't expected to pick that up so clearly. I usually just assume sales folks are high-energy—end of story. I hadn't really thought about the feel of a place or group. I've always thought about the quotas, capacity, output, and quality of

calls—all those tangible and measurable things. But I've been reading *Winnie the Pooh* to my daughter recently. It struck me that the regional offices were like the *Pooh* characters. One place I visited was just like Tigger—bouncy, high energy, lots of movement, exciting. Another was like Eeyore—gray, monotone, depressed, uninspiring. A third one was like Owl—calmly getting on with the work, people congregating in the hallways and the cafeteria for impromptu meetings. There was a quiet energy about the place. The part that really freaked me out happened after I got back. I checked all their numbers and, sure enough, the numbers reflected the feel. Amazing.

Some of the most telling lessons come from personal interactions and observation of human behavior. I once had a confrontation with a group of factory supervisors. In five minutes, they told me why change was necessary and why it would be tough to pull off. We were working with the client to institute new work processes. It required teamwork and very close communications across functions. I had been on the job for a couple of months when I was walking through the factory and heard a shout from across the floor, "Hey you! Duck! We wanna talk to you. We're mad at you." A group of six supervisors came steaming toward me, faces set, muscles tense. My flight reaction kicked in strongly, but I managed to control it and stay rooted to the floor while the gang swaggered over.

The leader of the group fixed his eyes on me, and I suspect he would have grabbed me by the collar if I'd had one. "I've been at this company for twenty-three years," he said, barely able to control his anger. "I'm the bull of the woods. When I bellow, the earth shakes! I've got a management style that works, and I don't need you."

"Yeah!" chimed the chorus of burly guys who backed him up. Meekly, I asked him to describe his wonderfully successful management style. He smiled in a way that sent shivers up my spine. "Kill one; scare the rest!"

That attitude and behavior, in a nutshell, helped me understand why the company was dysfunctional, why it suffered high turnover and grievance rates, low quality, and high scrap. It was in Stagnation and was ruled by powerful "gangs" that protected their own self-interests. (Sometimes, of course, "gang members" wear hand-tailored suits and have manicured nails.) It was one of the many corroborating findings that we carried back to management, to help them realize that things had to change.

The key to learning through talking, of course, is to genuinely listen. Every leader must find their own best way of listening. Some like to drop in on training sessions or work the crowd at sales meetings. Some schedule informal breakfast or lunch meetings with small groups of employees. Some just walk around and talk with people at random. One executive team I know schedules time for informal chats during every site visit. Whatever the method, leaders are always appreciative of the richness of the information and the depth of insight they collect. They learn that their people genuinely care and usually have a solid idea of what's going on. Not surprisingly, executives usually enjoy these sessions. They learn a lot, they feel useful in a direct way, and they strengthen their connections to the organization.

RAY'S QUESTIONNAIRE TO HIS FIFTY MANAGERS

In addition to his walks and talks, Ray circulated a written questionnaire to the fifty top managers and opinion leaders at Micro Switch, to help shape and stimulate conversation among them. He asked only three questions:

1. During the next three to five years, what are the best opportunities for Micro Switch?
2. What could cause us to miss those opportunities?
3. If you were general manager, what are the first three to five actions you would take?

Ray gave the respondents the option to remain anonymous, but he was delighted to see that every one of them signed the questionnaire.

The completeness and thoughtfulness of their responses amazed him. The managers expressed all kinds of pent-up emotions and deeply felt opinions; they offered suggestions and articulated their concerns. It was obvious to Ray that the managers, let alone the employees, of Micro Switch were not used to being asked for their thoughts. He took it as good news that they were eager to talk and share their ideas. The bad news, however, was what they had to say. About leadership, for example, the respondents' complaints were "uncertainty," "indecisiveness," and tendencies to "react instead of strategically managing the business" and to pursue "priorities of the week or month."

Other comments were directed at specific departments and general issues of morale:

On a scale of one to ten, with ten as high, our Marketing is about a two.

There is a widely held perception that our Field Sales force is not fulfilling their role—they don't know the products and they're not selling to the correct users.

Our computer resources don't fully support the needs of the business, our financial systems do not provide accurate cost information, and none of our systems are as flexible and adaptable as needed for our evolving business.

We're hesitant to put our full commitment behind the projects we approve, then wonder why they fail.

Short-term [profit] management has resulted in long-term obsolescence of our manufacturing operations.

Our employees have never been more demoralized; faith in our long-term strategies is low; we do not trust our leadership; we feel overloaded with too many unprioritized, "urgent tasks," and unguided by a consistent sense of direction.

We have "doom and gloom" management. . . . It's almost as if we've lost our collective confidence.

Ray went through all the comments, grouped the common ones, and identified key themes. The important messages from the fifty respondents were depressingly consistent: Micro Switch had lost the will to compete; the division lacked clear strategic direction or focus; people were starved for leadership.

Ray got confirmation of these themes from informal conversations with employees in all parts of the company. A plant superintendent said:

> I know we aren't growing, because we are producing the same number of products every year. But most employees don't realize it because they are regularly moved from one product line to the next. Most line workers have no idea who our competitors are or what they are doing. Everyone just assumes we're safe.

A factory line worker added:

> People think that if the customers are purchasing from us, we're the only ones that they wanted the part from.

Another worker described the environment:

> You come in. You do your job. You don't know how many orders there are 'cause nobody tells you. So the people who do the work know nothing. You don't think about who the customers are. You don't ask how the stuff is getting used. You don't think about competitors. You do your job and you go home.

As happens with most leaders, reading and hearing the comments had a powerful effect on Ray. Survey comments help calibrate the scattered oral comments the leaders may have heard, and they put a human face on the performance data. Since the comments are written, they are easier to quantify and remember than oral remarks. In some cases, they are very hard to forget. In fact, a single comment or theme can so impress a leader that the memory of it will continue to inspire through a long and arduous change program. For example, one respondent in a survey wrote, "This place reminds me of the 1960s." A rather innocuous comment, but one that stuck in the executive's mind. She referred to it over and over again as she led her company through transformation.

STAGNATION AFFECTS INDIVIDUALS AS WELL AS ORGANIZATIONS

When an organization stagnates, the individuals within it tend to stagnate as well. Not everyone in a stagnant organization is personally stagnant; some may be fired up and full of energy about their particular project or job—as was the case with Dr. Margolis at Venerable. It is also possible for people to feel hopeful and positive at some times, and stagnant and depressed at others. But, in general, the stagnancy of the organization has a depressing effect on the people inside. It can even affect partners and suppliers. When working closely with a severely stagnant organization for a long engagement, I have to be careful to keep my own spirits up. Ennui and depression love company.

Dr. Barry Dym, a psychologist and organizational consultant, describes the emotions and behaviors that characterize individuals who are depressed and unmotivated: complacency, indifference, nonchalance, apathy, comfort, boredom, lack of excitement, a sense of isolation or disconnection. The resulting behaviors include listlessness and unconcern, disinvolvement, inattention, passivity, stoicism, low energy, and resignation.

These feelings and behaviors don't necessarily indicate that the people are unproductive; rather, they have little sense of meaning in their work. The organization is failing to provide enough emotional or intellectual stimulation to generate excitement and engagement among its employees. If such conditions persist, the most likely outcome is that people will leave, or, perhaps worse, they will "quit and stay." In other words, they will give up, lose hope, but continue to go through the motions.

People are complex, however; rarely do they feel just one emotion about any issue. Even when they're depressed, they still have the capacity to be curious, ask questions, look for new possibilities, generate useful hypotheses, and engage in wishful thinking. In other words, they can perk up, transform themselves, and make a contribution to a fundamental change effort. The trick for a leader is to determine which people are temporarily depressed but could make a positive contribution if given a different situation, and which people are terminally stuck, drained of energy and ideas, and need to be reassigned or asked to leave.

GAINING INDIVIDUAL RECOGNITION OF STAGNATION: THE SAL THERAPY

There are parallels between organizational diagnosis and individual therapy. A therapist friend of mine once told me about an unexpected breakthrough she had made with a patient we'll call Sal. For the first several months of therapy, Sal generally spent his fifty minutes complaining about his predictable and monotonous life. He was unwilling to take any action to change things, however, and he took this as evidence of his lack of courage. It seemed to my friend that Sal wanted her to confirm his own diagnosis that he was dull and unable to change. Finally, my friend got so exasperated with Sal that she blurted out, "Look, let's agree that you're a wimp. But suppose you weren't a wimp. How would you act?" Sal replied, "Oh, that's easy. If I weren't a wimp I would . . ." and he proceeded to sketch out an innovative plan for change. My friend was pleasantly stunned and suggested that Sal should pretend for one hour each day that he was not a wimp and work on the plan he had laid out. Sal agreed to the one hour per day. Even with his timidity and cautiousness, he began to see his life and work change for the better. Then he picked up speed and increased the number of hours devoted to being bold.

I was able to put Sal's lesson to work for me in my first job as a supervisor. One of my direct reports was not performing satisfactorily, and I had to have a talk with him. The guy scared me, though. He was ornery and uncommunicative; he could be intimidating and unpleasant. So, remembering Sal, I said to myself, "If I weren't scared of the guy, and if I was a real professional who knew what she was doing, what would I do?" I figured out what to do, got through the review, covered all the points I wanted to make, and established an improvement plan which he signed. Boy, was I relieved! Not only had I conducted an effective review, I had also learned a way to manage my own nervousness.

Once I was working with a group of clerks who were upset about their situation but saw themselves as powerless and were unwilling to take any action. We got into a rebellious discussion about how they'd change their work if they could do whatever they wanted. After laughing a lot and coming up with a long list of actions, we reviewed the list to see what they could do on their own, what they needed supervisory permission to pursue, and what required additional resources. They did not feel comfortable just making a request of their manager, so the rest of the meeting was spent in animated discussion of how they could "earn" the resources and the permission. They had already changed their basic assumptions and their interactions without even realizing it. Several weeks later, they had built their confidence in tandem with their accomplishments. As they were ready to submit their ideas and request resources, they were selected to share their success story at the local quarterly meeting. They used that forum to push their expanded agenda. You've never seen such a happy group of people as they were when the visiting regional manager approved all their requests on the spot and told them he wanted a quarterly update.

This approach can be helpful in all kinds of situations because, to be effective, it doesn't require the individuals to change their initial position or sense of self. It merely asks people to consent to an experiment. When dealing with individuals who feel tired and depressed in a stagnating company, that may be the best you can hope for—at first.

I use the "Sal approach" often with people who are facing a major change initiative in an old-line company. Harold, for example, was a thirty-year veteran employee of such an organization. During a kick-off meeting for the change program, he pulled me aside for a quiet chat. I knew Harold to be a thoughtful and conscientious person. He seemed worried and asked, "Jeanie, I have to say that I don't believe everything the executives are saying at this meeting. I don't really believe that the things they're talking about will actually happen. Does that mean that I'm disloyal? Does that make me a change resister?"

I said, "Harold, you've been here thirty years. I'm sure you've seen plenty of programs, initiatives, and leaders come and go. I'd be very surprised if you *weren't* skeptical. It doesn't matter if you believe all this now; I wouldn't expect you to. My question to you is whether you're willing to experiment with the new ideas and to help make them work."

He looked relieved and told me, "That I can do."

STRATEGY LEADS REALITY, CULTURE LAGS REALITY, CULTURE DRAGS STRATEGY

Once a company has recognized that it is, in fact, in a state of Stagnation, and its leaders, after diagnosing the areas and degree of Stagnation, have determined that they want to change the business rather than dump it, the next step is to develop a strategy that will bring them success. Strategy is about anticipating a future competitive reality and determining how to win in that imagined environment. *Strategy, by definition, must lead the current reality.*

Developing a sound strategy is not easy; executing it is even more difficult because the beliefs, habits, and attitudes of an organization—its culture—usually lag behind the current reality. In other words, the culture is defined by one set of circumstances—usually, some earlier reality—but when the reality changes, the culture does not. Like an aging hippie who refuses to acknowledge that the 1960s are over and continues wearing his ponytail, tie-dye, and love beads into the new millennium, a corporate culture can stay frozen in the past. Nathan Myhrvold, VP of Research for Microsoft, said, "If you want to invent the future, the way to get the most positive odds is to get the smartest group of people you possibly can and make sure they are not buried in the past."

So, an important part of executing a winning strategy is to determine the starting point of the current culture. Through observation and conversation with the leaders and with people throughout the organization, you want to know whether the corporate culture is in sync with today's reality. Is it ready for the realities that are emerging? Answers to these questions can flesh out the cultural profile:

Where do we stand competitively?

Where do we think we stand competitively?

How does our culture compare to the current reality?

What beliefs and behaviors drive our organization?

What beliefs and behaviors do we need to change in order to compete effectively?

We find, in organizations of all types, that culture lags reality. In the defense industry, the lagging culture valued technology only, while the Department of Defense had shifted to on-time, on-budget contracting. Pharmaceuticals grew up with a legacy of extravagance, so the culture was accustomed to carte blanche in development projects, but the new reality demanded early pruning of projects and careful allocation of resources. At Micro Switch, the managers continued to think of their company as the leader in the electric switch market for years after customers had come to think of electric switches as dinosaurs. At Gillette, the leaders took a long time to accept that their retail customers, such as Wal-Mart and Target, were controlling the market; the days when Gillette dictated the terms of sale and delivery to mom-and-pop drug stores were long gone. *Culture lags reality.*

When planning a way out of Stagnation, therefore, you must ask: What outdated beliefs and behaviors are prevalent in our organization which will prevent us from conceiving or executing a winning strategy? Consider the case of Merrill Lynch & Co., as it attempted to move into the world of on-line trading. Vice Chairman John "Launny" Steffens was so against on-line trading that his views made headlines in *The Wall Street Journal* in September 1998. The paper reported:

> [Mr. Steffens] who oversees the firm's army of 14,800 stockbrokers, has waged an unusually public campaign over the last few months to dramatize what he calls the dangers of buying and selling stocks unassisted over the Internet. Such trading has exploded over the last two years, but not at Merrill. The always blunt Mr. Steffens first made a public splash with the issue in June when he told an audience at the PC Expo conference in New York: "The do-it-yourself model of investing, centered on Internet trading, should be regarded as a serious threat to Americans' financial lives. This approach to financial decision-making doesn't serve clients well and it's a business model that won't deliver lasting value."

Mr. Steffens admitted that there were "differences of opinion" about the issue within his own company. "But," he was quoted as saying, "I've taken lots of tough positions in my life, and most of them have proven to be correct." Steffens was clearly living in a personal culture that lagged the current reality.

Less than a year later, Merrill Lynch announced its entry into low-cost, on-line stock trading. It seems that the leaders had to be shocked out of their cultural daze by their children. Chairman David Komansky, age sixty, learned that his adult children were buying all kinds of goods on-line. After his 1998 speech, Steffens, age fifty-seven, got a call from his twenty-seven-year-old son, who told him to "get his act together." On June 1, 1999, *The Wall Street Journal* commented on the change of direction at Merrill: "Rarely in history has the leader in an industry felt compelled to do an about-face and, virtually overnight, adopt what is essentially a new business model." Merrill seems to have successfully overcome its cultural lag. In March 2000, Merrill Lynch Direct was awarded four stars in a *Barron's* survey of on-line brokers, one of just three to win the highest rating.

Merrill's story, along with so many others, shows that when the work practices and thinking of a company's leaders—and their followers—are antithetical to the thinking and action that a new strategy requires, the issues must be explicitly addressed. If they are not, the *culture will drag strategy*.

BCG authors George Stalk, Jr., David K. Pecaut, and Benjamin Burnett supported this assertion in their *Harvard Business Review* article, "Breaking Compromises." They wrote:

> Growth strategies built around the idea of breaking compromises are neither new nor limited to a few particular industries. But to visualize such a strategy requires a company's managers to clear their heads of the conventional thinking that pervades their industry.

The most important compromises—and therefore the most potent opportunities—exist because companies have lost touch with their customers. At Micro Switch, the leaders assumed that their customers would be loyal forever because they had come to rely on the company's customized switches and sensors. It also assumed that the customers would understand and accept continuous price increases during tough times—after all, Micro Switch needed to make its numbers and the customers had few alternatives. Over time, such behavior had led to an unarticulated but pervasive attitude: "If the customer is happy, we haven't done our job." Happy customers meant that Micro Switch had left money on the table. The true sign of success was an unhappy customer who was stuck because a better product couldn't be bought anywhere else. Another manifestation of that prevailing attitude applied to delivery dates. If the customer seemed pleased, the date could have been set later. Pushing the customer was considered good business—it was how employees earned their stripes. No surprise that Ray Alvarez got an earful when he went to visit Micro Switch's top customers.

Nothing blasts businesspeople out of their traditional thinking ruts faster than seeing or hearing firsthand what their customers are experiencing or what their competitors are doing. In addition to his son's comments, Mr. Steffen's conversion came about as a result of hearing daily complaints from his top brokers about losing their customers to on-line brokers, as well as from visits with some of the firm's top customers. He and his team were astonished to learn that long-tenured and highly profitable customers had opened on-line accounts with other firms for their more active trading. Adding insult to injury, one of the stocks a favored customer actively traded was Merrill Lynch.

To execute his DestroyYourBusiness.com strategy, Jack Welch realized that he would have to change the way his executives thought about the Internet. They lived in a corporate culture that did not embrace the new reality of the Web. Many of them didn't know how to access the Web. They got their e-mail from the administrative assistants, had never bought a product on-line, and considered the Internet to be the province of geeks. GE was generally an unfriendly environment for Web-savvy people, and the company's rigid hiring policies did not allow many of them to get inside. The few e-people who had made it into GE were much younger than the senior executives and had little visibility or influence. To solve the problem, Welch created a "reverse mentoring" program. He required his top 600 executives to find a Web mentor who could teach them how to use, evaluate, and understand e-business. Some executives found their mentors within the organization, but most had to be hired from outside. The executive-students were put in the position of being ignorant and awkward learners rather than all-knowing bosses. As they learned, the culture began to attune itself to the current (and emerging) reality.

A Personal Aptitude for Change: The Coal Miner's Son and the Southern Lady

No change effort will get very far unless someone at the top of the organization—usually, the most senior operating executive—has a real appetite and aptitude for change. No leader who is in love with stasis and normalcy will be able to take an organization from a state of Stagnation to the glow of Fruition. The same holds true for leaders at every level; to change their division, group, department, or shop, they must have—or develop—an aptitude for change.

Some executives have a natural penchant for leading an organization through transformation and are willing to undergo personal transformation as well. It requires a certain mindset, as well as an interest in and understanding of people. I've known others who seem clueless about people issues. They constantly say the wrong thing and seem to not understand what went wrong. Of the two major characters in this book, Ray Alvarez already had the knack when he began leading the change at Micro Switch, and he helped others develop it. Marco Trask at CoVen did not have an innate awareness about people issues, nor did he think it was of high value when the merger began, but he developed his people skills through transforming personal experience.

Let me tell you a little about Ray Alvarez. He achieved what so many big-name turnaround artists and highly visible leaders have not: He took a stagnating company and led it successfully to Fruition—and did it with no layoffs. Ray's rare ability to deal with change comes, to some extent, from his personal background.

Ray grew up poor in Charles Town, in the mining territory of northeastern West Virginia. Ray's father, Albert, had been sent there from Spain at an early age to live with relatives. Leaving family and the familiarity of home to move to the strangeness and challenge of a whole new world is one of the most comprehensive changes any person can endure. When he was eight years old, Albert was hired to work as a "mule" in the coal mines of West Virginia, and there he stayed until his late thirties, when his black lung disease progressed to the point where he had to quit. He proved himself to be professionally flexible—he learned to train and race horses. He built a business as a trainer and began to invest in horses of his own, which he raced in West Virginia during the summer and in Cuba during the winter. In 1952, Albert was in Cuba when Batista took over. The government confiscated much private property, including Albert's horses and cash. He escaped, but the experience drained his energy and he couldn't muster the will to start over yet again.

Ray had been a good student in high school and was hoping to get an athletic scholarship so he could attend a college out of state. But his father wasn't working, his mother was ill with cancer, and there were two younger brothers to look after. Ray realized that he would have to forget about college. But then Charles F. Printz, a professor at Shepherd, a state college in nearby Shepherdstown, persuaded Ray to attend school while working part-time and living at home. The arrangement worked for the first year, but then Ray's mother died and the family had big medical bills to pay. Again, Ray decided he would have to quit so he could work full-time and help his sister take care of his younger brothers. Again, Professor Printz found a solution. He arranged for Ray to receive his scholarship and work three jobs: full-time as a night watchman, and part-time as a student assistant and as a bookkeeper. Ray made it through Shepherd in the standard four years and graduated in 1962 with an honors degree in business administration.

Before he joined Honeywell's Ordanance Division, in 1968, Ray held a number of jobs. He proved himself to be a talented manager; he was honest and straightforward in his dealings with people, regardless of their rank, and he expected others to act the same way. But he also had a sharp temper and could be surprisingly blunt. He refused to sugarcoat his assessment of a bad situation, and didn't hesitate to name those responsible. But he was a smart team player; he worked hard and contributed to every assignment.

In the early 1980s, Ray got his first taste of major organizational change. He helped Honeywell's Residential Division, a former cash cow that was now losing money, effect a major turnaround. Within three years, the division stopped being a money-loser and became the group that contributed more than a quarter of corporate earnings. Ray was now seen as an executive who could "make things happen"—he could lead and manage change. He was promoted, thanks to the successful transformation of Residential, and, in 1985, took over as vice president and general manager of Honeywell Keyboards, based in Freeport, Illinois. His charge there was to strengthen the product line and the profits and to establish Keyboards as a separate group from its current parent, Micro Switch. Ray moved Keyboards to El Paso, Texas, but some of the workers remained at Micro Switch in Freeport. When he returned as general manager of Micro Switch, Ray was genuinely pleased to see familiar faces there.

The Micro Switch assignment was, without doubt, Ray's biggest and most complex change effort, and he approached it with determination and heartfelt commitment—this would be his crowning achievement and, probably, his final one with Honeywell. As exhilarating as such a change effort can be, it is rare for any leader to go through many of them. The assignments don't come along that often and, when they do, they consume a tremendous amount of time and energy. Executives who complete even the longest careers will remember only two or three initiatives of such intensity in their entire working lives.

What drove Ray? What fueled his aptitude for change? A local businessman who came to know Ray well has said of him: "It's hard to separate the man from where he came from. He grew up in West Virginia in a hardscrabble environment. I think someone growing up that way is going to be disproportionately inclined, for the rest of his life, to be sympathetic and empathetic to people who have never gotten a break. And he has been—to kids, minorities, the disadvantaged, the illiterate, the people who, as the saying goes, 'could use a visit from the good-luck truck.'"

This inclination to improve the lot of the disadvantaged was well matched to the nature and environment of Micro Switch, a manufacturing company with a large population of factory workers. It might not have been so suited to the more professional environment at CoVen, where Marco found himself dealing with highly educated individual contributors who had multiple career options.

Ray's drive was fueled as much by his emotions as by his intellect. "Ray is one of the most complex individuals I have ever met," said the businessman. "He has a brusque, firm, hard visage when, in fact, that's not Ray. I think of him as a steel-covered marshmallow." Sometimes, that's what it takes.

I started my own consulting firm in 1980 and, over the next five years, I worked with the executive team at Residential, helping them with the turnaround. When I first met Ray, who was then VP of Finance and Administration, I found him to be a straightforward and businesslike manager. When I asked him questions, he answered willingly. When I sought advice and suggestions, he contributed both. He was polite, powerful both personally and organizationally, and definitely "a no-nonsense kind of guy."

But Ray had a problem: a difficult relationship with his direct staff. His staff meetings were frustrating, flat, and boring. There was no spontaneous discussion. People seldom volunteered ideas or asked hard questions. No one challenged the boss. Ray asked me if I could help. At the first staff meeting I attended, I understood his concern. Ray talked, the others sat silent. His staff acted like a giant blob of mashed potatoes, absorbing whatever he ladled onto them. I conducted one-on-one confidentiality-guaranteed interviews with every staff member. Each of them said essentially the same thing, "We're afraid of Ray. He has a notoriously bad temper." Most of them had never seen him angry, but they'd heard horror stories. No one wanted to provoke him.

When I gave Ray my feedback, he was stunned. He did not see himself as being powerful, but others did. Nor did he believe that he lost his temper very often—certainly not often enough to be considered a hothead. I told him what I believed: He would have to change his behavior and acknowledge the feedback from the group before they would change. The idea did not thrill Ray. I argued that his behavior and resulting reputation were limiting his effectiveness. What's more, if Ray wouldn't deal with his own shortcomings, it gave everyone else an excuse to avoid dealing with theirs. He accepted my analysis, and we planned how to work together to modify his behavior and his relationship with his staff.

I met with Ray's staff and told them what I had heard from them collectively and what Ray and I had discussed. After a brief discussion, Ray joined the group and talked about his reactions to the feedback. He reviewed specific events, his reactions, and his assessment of himself. He then outlined what he would and would not change, and how he would go about it. You could have heard a pin drop on the carpet during his presentation! This was an unprecedented, gutsy move: a boss discussing his own behavior and committing to change. Ray then asked his staff for help, gave examples of the support he needed, and asked them to hold him accountable. The staff was astonished and engaged by Ray's candor and by the task of finding new ways of working together.

During the next few weeks, I continued to facilitate staff meetings, and we recorded slow but steady progress. At one meeting, Ray and I disagreed over something. I explained my thinking and rationale. Ray disagreed more strongly. As we argued back and forth, the tension in the room became palpable. Ray's staff looked like scared children watching their parents having an argument. Finally, Ray acknowledged that he understood my perspective. I called a break and everyone fled the room. That exchange proved to a be a catalytic event in the life of the group. During the break, it was the major topic of conversation. One guy said, "I've never seen anyone confront Ray and live to tell the tale." Now they had proof that it could be done, and a model for how to do it. Ray had invited me to interrupt him or confront him whenever I thought it was necessary, and that is exactly what I had done—and if I could do it, others could, too. I give him a lot of credit for making himself vulnerable, in front of his subordinates, so we all could grow. Slowly, after that meeting, the group became a team—able to discuss and even to argue about issues, without fearing that a confrontation would lead to anger or reprisal.

Ray's guts and tenacity challenged me, and his staff, to match his courage and his willingness to face the change monster. We were forced to admit to ourselves, "I must change my behavior." I have been fortunate to have clients and partners whose attributes and needs have presented both opportunities for growth and role models. I am convinced that such opportunities abound. Too often, we are looking the other way.

THE END OF STAGNATION

The end of the Stagnation phase is difficult to see, except in hindsight. It most often ends when the leader—or group of leaders—becomes convinced of the need for fundamental change, when someone with power resolves that "things are going to be different." Sometimes the moment is personal and comes from inside; I think Ray felt that way when he stepped inside that oil-soaked factory. Sometimes the moment is shared by a group and is brought on by an outside catalyst—such as when Venerable's drug failed to receive regulatory approval.

When such a moment—or many of them—is combined with analyses, an appetite for change, and the development of a strategy, Stagnation evolves into the next phase of change: Preparation.

PART THREE

PREPARATION

THE MONSTER AWAKES

"And now at this point in the meeting I'd like to shift the blame away from me and onto someone else."

5

Gaining Alignment

Anxiety About the Future

ANXIETY CAN BE HELPFUL OR GET IN THE WAY

ONCE WHEN I was obsessing to my mama about one of my perennial concerns as a teenager—it was either about a would-be beau or an upcoming social event—she calmly observed, "Anxiety touched by hope becomes anticipation." I had to think about that for a while. I concluded that she meant anxiety is neither a good nor a bad thing; it just *is*. But if you add a little hope to it, it becomes positive. Anxiety is what you feel when you care about an outcome but can't be sure how things will turn out. Anticipation means that you've decided to look forward to it, expecting that things will turn out for the best.

Having completed my analysis, I asked, "So how do I go about touching my anxiety with hope?"

"Prepare yourself," Mama said. "Think of things you can do now that will influence the outcome. Obsessing won't get you anything but exhaustion."

Knowing me at that age, I probably translated her advice into calling a friend to talk or going to look at my wardrobe to decide what I should wear.

During Preparation, the organization—leaders and workforce alike—will experience a fair amount of anxiety about what the future holds. This planning-and-getting-ready phase begins when the decision to change is made, and it continues until execution of the plans begins. When people are reasonably hopeful that the change initiative will turn out well, their anxiety can generate commitment, excitement, and even exhilaration. During Preparation, leaders must try to create productive anxiety—an appetite for change. They should work to help people feel hopeful and excited about the future and eager to contribute to it, because these emotions produce the energy that will be necessary when working through the myriad tasks during Implementation.

Not everyone, however, will feel the pull of the dream or wake up every morning eager to help make the vision a reality. Some people will see the new initiative as wrongheaded or not in their best interests. Some just won't want to bother; others will take a dim view of the whole thing. For those people, there must be negative consequences for not supporting the new initiative.

I gave a talk at the Harvard Business School about managing change. When I spoke of negative consequences, one of the students asked, "Why can't you use only positive aspects to inspire the workforce? Why can't you just be upbeat?" My answer was, "I'm not smart enough to figure out the personal motivations of thousands of individual employees in umpteen countries. Plus, I know from experience that some people will only change when their fear of not changing is greater than their comfort with the status quo." That's why I say, "Go for love, but require behavior."

You can't expect people to love the vision, to get excited about the future, if they don't know what the vision is. You can't set requirements for behavior if you don't know what your strategy and objectives are. And you can't generate productive anxiety if you don't create a sense that the status quo isn't working any more. So, during Preparation, the leaders have three major tasks:

1. The management team must be aligned and energized around the vision and strategy.
2. The vision must be articulated and the overall plan sufficiently detailed so it can be understood and executed by others.
3. A healthy dissatisfaction with the status quo and a genuine appetite for change must be generated within the workforce; appropriate expectations of what will happen and what can be accomplished must be set.

HALF-IN AND HALF-OUT

In a merger or acquisition, the Preparation phase begins abruptly when one company announces its decision to pursue another specific company. People instantly begin asking questions and obsessing about what will happen. The speculation doesn't end until long after the deal is closed—a few months or even a year later. During that time, some of the tasks of transformation can be designed, but execution can't legally begin. Only a limited number of new appointments can be offered and accepted before the deal is finalized. In some cases, the people who do receive appointments are forbidden to meet with their new teams. The leaders of the two organizations are prohibited from sharing detailed information about their strategies, new-product portfolio, or other proprietary plans, in case the deal does not go through. There is also the necessity of keeping people focused on their current work, rather than spending too much time on planning and preparation. If people get distracted, the business may suffer. If that happens, the stock price of both companies might plummet before the deal is signed. This half-in and half-out situation can be awkward and frustrating. As one executive put it, "It feels like a long courtship for an arranged marriage. We know who we're going to be with, but we're not allowed to meet the family or get to know each other. There is a mountain of work to do to prepare for the new situation, but we can't really move forward because of all the restrictions."

Preparation is also a tricky phase for start-ups and young companies. It generally comes after the business model has been defined and some initial start-up financing has been secured. The leaders and employees (if there are any!) are working night and day in preparation for the moment when the business finally gets "real."

In any kind of change initiative, the leaders must do most of the work of Preparation, with limited help from others, because the plan and recommendations require senior decision-makers to make the trade-offs and allocate resources. The plan has to be fleshed out before any delegation can begin. The leaders must be intimately involved in forming the vision and strategy and must thoroughly understand the reasoning that underpins the subsequent plans. The leaders have to immerse themselves in the details; if they do, their efforts will pay off handsomely when they begin to inspire the organization and convince the employees of the wisdom of their plans. Their thorough knowledge will also make it easier for them to make well-considered decisions and trade-offs later, when new problems and opportunities arise. The opposite is also true. Leaders who only get short briefings, and who have superficial involvement will have difficulty answering pointed questions from employees. If a leader can't explain (and defend) his vision, he certainly won't inspire others to create it.

AMONG THE LEADERS: LOVING (EVEN LIKING) IS NOT REQUIRED

Early in my career, I was facilitating a meeting of a group of executives, and it was not going well. Some people refused to talk. There were hidden agendas. People were skirting around the edges of the core issues. During a break, the head of marketing approached me. "Jeanie," she said, "just forget about getting us to like each other. I've known most of these guys for years. Two of them I intensely dislike for a lot of reasons we don't need to go into. You're not going to change that by helping us to get to know each other better." She spoke with such finality and vehemence that she startled me. I stood there with my mouth open until I was finally able to say, "OK. You don't have to like each other, but you do have to work together and you do have to help each other succeed." She considered this for several long moments and then said, "That I agree with."

Although the subject of teamwork is outside the scope of this book, I will say that teamwork—particularly among executives—is not synonymous with a love fest. It helps enormously if team members admire and care about each other, but teamwork is essentially about working together for the common good, being committed to the same goals, and helping each other to achieve those goals. Failure to create that kind of teamwork can be fatal to the entire change effort.

The most important aspect of the leadership team is alignment around the vision and strategy; without it, the change effort will not move forward. If each executive goes his or her own way—defending turf, consolidating power, inciting insurrections, and planting doubts among others—the change effort is doomed. Employees are very skillful at assessing each executive's strength of commitment as well as the amount of alignment within a group. If they sense wavering commitment or a lack of solidarity, they take it as an invitation to mischief. Individuals and subgroups will choose sides and align themselves with an executive whom they like and trust, or with the one they believe will win in the end. Others will do just enough to get by, waiting to see which way the wind blows.

I saw this very clearly when I was working with a company I'll call Global Inc. to revitalize their USA Division. Early on, the CEO retired. Within two weeks of our finalizing the restructuring plan, the new CEO forced the resignation of the president of the USA Division, and named a new chief, whom I'll call Joseph. He had been executive vice president of sales and marketing and had had almost nothing to do with the planning for the revitalization.

Joseph inherited a leadership team that included the heads of four different businesses and five functions that supported them; they did not work, think, or act like a team. After our first meeting, Joseph asked me, "Do you think it really matters that we're not a team? After all, we rarely work together. We run very separate units and organizations."

"The problem," I replied, "is not only that your team is dysfunctional, it's also that you don't have alignment around the vision. We all agreed on a single business model for the revitalization, and everyone pledged to use it in their organizations. But two of your business heads are using different business models than the one we agreed on. They're not being subtle about it, and it's obvious they don't think you'll do anything to stop them. Their public lack of alignment is undermining the revitalization effort, not to mention your credibility." Joseph sat quietly for a minute, thinking hard, and then changed the subject.

Two weeks later, Joseph called me into his office. "I'm ready to take on this alignment issue," he declared. "I've called a meeting of my direct reports for this Saturday. I want you to help me design and facilitate it." I was surprised and pleased.

The executives at USA Division were unaccustomed to Saturday meetings, so when the group gathered that morning, everyone was curious and a little antsy. Then Joseph made his entrance. Rather than wearing one of the expensive and elegant suits he usually wore, he appeared in a shirt covered in stars and stripes. He convened the meeting by saying, "I figured that if I wrapped myself in the flag, you might not lynch me when you hear what I have to say." One of his rebellious directors quipped, "No, but we might burn you."

Joseph first surprised and then shocked the group. He reviewed the vision, business model, and values that the management team had defined months before as part of the revitalization plan, and got all those in the room to confirm that they had, in fact, agreed to them. He then went on to cite specific actions of every member of the management team—including himself—that were not consistent with the values, and he talked about how those actions and attitudes had undermined the change effort. When he finished his catalog of executive transgressions, there was stunned silence. The executives had never been confronted so directly before (and never in a group), nor had details of date and time ever been included in such accusations.

After a moment, Joseph continued. "We outlined the values and behaviors that we believed were vital to renewing this organization," he said with great conviction. "We committed ourselves—individually and collectively—to living those values and being role models for the rest of the company. We have not lived up to our promises, and that must change. As of today!" More silence. In the days after the meeting, the two business heads did not change their behavior; they continued to act in ways that were inconsistent with the values. Two weeks later, Joseph fired them both. That was the "shot heard 'round the world." From that moment on, his team came into alignment, and Joseph went on to lead a highly successful revitalization.

MICRO SWITCH:
WHO SHOULD STAY, WHO SHOULD GO?

When Ray Alvarez arrived at Micro Switch, he knew most of his direct reports only as acquaintances or by reputation. He did not know whom to trust: Who should stay? Who should go? How quickly should he move on his decisions? Three members of the group stood out because of the importance of their positions to the change effort: Sam Blair, vice president of sales; Joel Miller, vice president of finance; and Tom Ingman, vice president of human resources.

Honeywell's CEO, Jim Renier, had vowed that Micro Switch could keep and reinvest its profit as its management saw fit, so Ray knew that his VP of sales had a particularly important role in the change effort: Increase sales above budget. But when Ray talked with other managers about Sam Blair, he sensed that they were uncomfortable with him;

Sam was not regarded as a team player. Ray's problem was to try to understand Sam's value to the organization. How strong were his relationships with customers? How deep was his knowledge of the field organization? How willing was he to collaborate with the other members of the management team? And, if he were let go, how would he behave? Would he take customers with him?

Joel Miller, VP of finance, was a calm and deliberate fellow who spoke in carefully crafted sentences. The issue with Joel, Ray quickly realized, was that he represented the "the establishment." He had occupied the center of power in the old order, and was seen as a guy with close links to the corporate power center. Ray needed Joel to endorse dramatic change. Could he loosen his grip on essential information and broaden his role? Could the corporate penny pincher emerge as a financial manager with a long-range view?

In their conversations, Ray began to sense that Joel could change. Reassurance came when he visited Joel to ask about an accounting policy. Joel grinned and said, "In the old days, I would have told you that we do it this way because we've always done it this way. In the new Micro Switch, I can say that it doesn't seem quite right, and we'll come up with a better way." The most encouraging discovery was that Joel's assessment of the division's circumstances was as blunt and clear-eyed as Ray's. "It is obvious that we are in difficulty," Joel stated. "The business has had flat growth for several years. Unit sales are steadily going down. Our profits are declining, and we have taken significant price increases every year to offset the shortfalls. Of course we know there is trouble ahead. You don't have to be a genius to figure out that we can't keep going like this much longer."

The third key player, Tom Ingman, VP of human resources, was a big, blond man who wore his heart on his sleeve. When he got excited or upset, his face became flushed and his bright blue eyes glowed. Ray discovered that Tom had long realized how bad things were. For years, he had worried that the division's leadership was far too focused on short-term results and was giving scant attention to the long-term investments in hard and soft assets that could keep

Micro Switch vital. Tom had repeatedly and unsuccessfully urged Ray's predecessor to "go on the offensive" and provide "inspirational leadership." His pleadings had been ignored.

Ray understood his management group's earlier working conditions and was willing to allow time for them to respond to the new order. But he quickly changed the broad structure of the organization and brought in two new people as VPs. His appointment of one of them to head the largest new division particularly unsettled the existing managers. Ray gave the new division to Alex Fisher, who was younger than most of the incumbent managers and had an undeniable presence and an intriguing résumé. Alex was also a big talker given to spewing ideas, most of which his colleagues considered unworkable. In view of this appointment, some of Ray's managers began to wonder whether Ray really did understand them and if he knew what he was doing.

Ray asked me to work with him and his management team toward developing a vision and strategy for turning around Micro Switch and aligning its various business units. We began our first meeting by agreeing on a number of the serious questions we needed to address:

What do we want Micro Switch to be?

What do we think is possible? Necessary?

Can we make it happen?

How will we work together?

How can this group become an effective team?

What does Ray want and expect from us?

Which members of the group is he going to keep?

How and when will we know if it's working?

In the days following that first meeting, I met one-on-one with each of Ray's direct reports, and I listened as the issues and questions were repeated in greater detail and with more urgency and concern. They were a nervous group, and they were most nervous about Ray. What does he think of me? How can I gain his confidence? Does he plan to dump anybody? One of them said, "We know that not all of us will make this journey. That's OK. Everybody believes that change should happen, but no one wants to admit that he might be one of the casualties." Another added, "We know that no one is 'untouchable'; Ray is going to make up his own mind about who he keeps and who he doesn't. I don't think that Ray will clean house. But he has brought in new people. One of them got the biggest piece of the pie. So, anything could happen."

Most unsettling to the executives was Ray's personal style. Here was a guy unlike any other manager they had worked with. "He has an incredibly high energy level and a low tolerance for nonsense. He has a really short fuse," one of them said. "He's very intense, he's unbelievably focused, and he's willing to put in very long hours. The guy is on a mission!" Some of the managers decided the best thing to do would be to keep clear of Ray. "I just want to stay off his radar screen," one of them confessed.

One executive described how, one evening, the staff had discussed management styles with Ray. "Ray said, 'You will see more management styles from me than you ever thought possible. I will manage with whatever style I think is necessary to get the job done. When the situation changes, I will change.'" Ray's team members found this to be a disturbing comment. "Sounds like an easy excuse for a temper tantrum," they said. And, "How in the world am I going to learn how to manage Ray if he's always changing his behavior?"

About two months later, Ray decided it was time for an off-site session to dig more deeply into the issue of what Micro Switch could and should become in the next ten years; I was to design and facilitate the session. We gathered at a conference facility and spent the morning working through the subjects of vision and mission. Some people thought no radical changes were called for. Others were sure something major needed to be done but couldn't agree on a solution. In the afternoon, we turned to a discussion of values, beliefs, and behaviors.

As is often the case, we made more progress with values than we had achieved with vision. We talked about the need for openness and honesty, congruence, collaboration, and commitment. The group agreed on the values and outlined the desired behaviors. Finally, exhausted, we adjourned for dinner.

The evening demonstrated that talk about values doesn't always translate into behavior. The group looked comfortable and cozy as they took their places around the long dinner table at the hotel restaurant, but events quickly proved otherwise. Sam Blair was dissatisfied with the service, and complained loudly to the waiter, the hostess, and the wine steward. The person next to me whispered that Blair had been blacklisted by one of the major airlines for similarly obnoxious behavior. At the other end of the table, Alex, the new VP, held forth on one topic after another, dominating the discussion, listening to no one. Tom, VP of human resources, who saw the irony of this behavior in light of our afternoon's discussion, flushed red with dismay. Ray sat quietly and watched.

As we struggled through the evening, I realized that this group was a collection of individuals—definitely not a team and definitely not ready to lead a major transformation. They did not know what was going to be asked of them, where they stood in the pecking order, or how to behave with each other or with Ray. We had a lot of work to do.

Misguided Maestro: Warrior or Conductor?

A leader gains alignment with his or her management team through a process that includes data review, one-on-one conversations and group discussions, listening, sharing, and refining. It's important to put data on the table and analyze them together, especially in areas that are likely to be controversial. As one of my clients likes to say when the conversation starts getting airy, "We're opinion-rich and data-free."

Group discussions should be structured around issues that can surface disagreements as well as those that help define areas of convergence. Many times, I have witnessed meetings between a leader and a group that were a series of one-on-one conversations, not a group discussion. This style, which is common, is like a hub and spokes, with the leader as the hub. I'll call one leader I worked with Maestro, because he is a man who enjoys being in control and is supremely confident. Maestro's way of discussing any new course of action is to present his idea to the group and then take on any questions or alternatives from members of the group. He enters these discussions as a warrior to battle and he assumes that once the questions and comments have dried up and the group has fallen silent, his idea has prevailed and he has "won." But by pursuing this series of one-on-one's, Maestro robs himself of the opportunity to hear and understand others' arguments, both pro and con, and to gain insight into their thinking. He misses the chance to allow the group to develop their own thinking. If he were to facilitate the discussion within the group much like an orchestra conductor, and wait until the discussion and arguments had been exhausted, and only then weigh in with his comments, he might very likely discover a greater richness of ideas. By listening to others criticize and defend his ideas, he would learn about the nature and depth of any resistance that might occur in the future, and could foster the development of a repertoire of responses and solutions. What leaders need is enthusiasm, not acquiescence. Having a management team that is resigned to doing the leader's bidding is not adequate in changing an organization. The leader needs a cadre of zealous missionaries. Conversion comes through participation as well as listening and sharing.

GROUP CHANGE REQUIRES INDIVIDUAL CHANGE: THE BEHAVIORAL CONTRACT

When the leadership team reaches alignment on vision, strategy, and values, it also needs to define the behaviors that will support the strategy and those that will be considered unacceptable. Group behavior and organizational change cannot be separated from personal behavior and change. This is one of the hardest parts of any change effort, particularly at the executive level. As Leo Tolstoy wrote,

"Everyone thinks about changing the world but no one thinks of changing himself."

Individuals may accept that their behavior needs to change, but have little or no idea how to go about doing so. Dr. Muriel James, author of *Born to Win* (and a former teacher of mine), uses a "behavioral contract" to help her clients determine some concrete steps they can take to effect a change. I have adapted the contract slightly and used it with clients and for myself. The five questions act as a guide for making fuzzy commitments clear and actionable. I've discovered that when I want to change, this is a very helpful exercise. And, more than once, I've discovered in trying to fill it out that I really don't want to make the commitment I was considering, so I stop pretending that I will.

1. Which of my behaviors will I stop/start or change?

Consider your own behavior and/or activities. (You can't change anyone else!) Sometimes the major hurdle is simply making the decision to change. But, once made, don't leave the decision there. If you plan to stop doing something, you need to start a new behavior to take its place. A simple example would be: I'm going to stop being late to appointments, and I'll start being on time.

2. What, specifically, am I willing to do?

To be effective, actions and behaviors need to be explicit and measurable. Brainstorm multiple possible actions and think through alternative scenarios. To continue our example: I will review my calendar every morning, noon, and evening so that I know where I'm supposed to be and when. If I'm in a meeting or event that is running over time and will cause me to be late to my next appointment, I will excuse myself or call the next appointment to inform them of my tardiness and expected time of arrival.

3. How will others know?

This is a helpful question, for two reasons. First, because it makes cheating just a little harder, and second, because having someone to check in with and talk to is helpful. For example, most folks have learned from experience that sticking to an exercise program is a lot easier if you know a friend is counting on you to join him at the gym (or pool, or wherever) and will be waiting for you. If I'm the only one who knows I've decided to change, then I'm likely to rationalize my lack of follow-through and then act surprised when my commitment has not resulted in demonstrable change. If, on the other hand, I've told my colleagues (or my spouse) that I will be on time, I get a little more motivated to make it happen—and, I will be wary of the harassment I'm sure to get if I show up late. If the change is something that you feel vulnerable about, tell only people you trust—people who want you to succeed. It is important to protect yourself while you are learning new behavior.

4. How might I sabotage myself?

This is my favorite question because I know that when I want to avoid doing something, I can get very sneaky with myself and can develop creative justifications and rationalizations for why I'm not doing it. I once worked with a group of managers on this behavioral contract. In response to this question, one guy wrote, "I'll fade." We took a break, and I intended to ask him what he meant by that when we reconvened, but he didn't come back! Guess he knew himself rather well.

We all have ways of sabotaging our own efforts to change. What are your excuses? How clever can you get? Thinking through as many possibilities as you can now will help you to recognize them for what they are later. For example:

"Everyone's late to meetings so I'll just be wasting my time if I'm there when it's scheduled to start."

"A meeting isn't the opera. It's not like I won't get seated if I'm late."

"I don't like the opening chit-chat part anyway, so it's better to come late."

One of my perpetually late clients had a neat excuse for himself. "If you're early, that means you're insecure. If you're on time, that means you're compulsive. I'm neither. I'm a little late, which means I'm confident," he said, smiling.

"Interesting perspective," I acknowledged, "but when you're late, everybody else thinks it means that you're hostile or arrogant or out of control. Which of these do you want them to think applies to you?"

5. What's the payoff in this for me?

Rarely do people change their behavior just because they know they should. It is easier to change when we know there will be a positive payoff and/or a negative consequence. It may be some rather straightforward reason: "My new boss gets really angry with people who are late." Or it may be that the desired personal change links to a group action. For example: "Our new values statement includes 'Respect for the Individual.' I believe that being late to appointments is disrespectful. This is something I can change immediately to show my tangible commitment to our values. That will make me feel good." Sometimes motivating yourself to change may take some creativity. "If I am on time for every meeting and every appointment for one month, I will reward myself with a golf weekend at Pebble Beach." If you construct a reward for yourself, be sure that the reward is appropriate to the effort, that it motivates you to act, and that it requires you to stretch but is also attainable.

ALIGNING CULTURES, NOT BLENDING THEM

Aligning the cultures of an organization is as important as aligning the members of the management team. I say cultures, rather than culture, because every organization is comprised of many cultures. Some of the cultures are defined by their operating unit, product, brand, or geography. Some are defined by their discipline: sales or engineering or marketing. Some are defined by earlier cultures, from now-assimilated mergers or acquisitions. It is not at all unusual for people to define themselves by the company they originally joined, even years after that company was merged with another. In other companies, cultures are defined around projects or initiatives or teams. At GTE (now Verizon), the traditional telephone company people generally regarded the GTE Internetworking group (now spun off as Genuity) as "the kids." Many companies involved in technology transformations or spin-offs find such generational divides, although they seldom admit it. An even more unspoken cultural aspect involves gender. There are companies in which there exist "guy domains" and other areas where the "girls" are definitely in charge. All of these cultures can be remarkably strong and persistent.

It's important to acknowledge and address these different subcultures because they are still operative and will influence people's acceptance of or resistance to new initiatives. Hopefully, the executives on the management team are the products of many of them so that, as a group, they can understand the various perspectives and think through the most appropriate way to address each one.

One of Ray's early concerns at Micro Switch was that his management group lacked diversity. Their fairly traditional cultures were defined mostly by discipline and level—factory workers, managerial, professional, administrative. CoVen, by contrast, was composed of dozens of different cultures, defined by nationality, professional discipline, therapeutic area, drug, and company affiliation. Ideally, the management team can agree on a set of values that draws on the best offerings from all the constituent cultures. To be powerful, the vision must provide an emotional hook, be broad enough to allow everyone to contribute, and be simple enough to be easily remembered and utilized.

In their discussions of culture, the leaders should think of themselves as corporate anthropologists and ask several key questions:

Where do different allegiances or values either bring people together or keep them apart?

Where do we have the greatest difficulty internally working with each other? What kinds of behaviors create barriers?

What networks are critical to getting work done and/or building knowledge?

How do we best support these networks?

Decoding and mapping these cultural practices will give the leaders invaluable insight into how the company really works and what it will take to change it. I was in a conversation with an executive vice president for human resources who was facing a huge merger. He asked, "When the merger takes effect, we will have about 125,000 employees on two continents. Should we focus now on creating one new, homogeneous culture for the combined organization?" I was happy to reassure him that the objective is not to have one homogeneous culture but to have one corporation with a core set of values that can unite and leverage its many sub-cultures to effectively bring products to the market and to serve its customers.

BUSINESS DIFFERENCES MEAN MORE THAN NATIONAL CULTURAL ONES

In our work with multinational mergers, one of the most surprising lessons we have learned is that specific business philosophies and cultures will make a bigger difference in a merger than will national cultural differences. For example, two U.S.-based telcos with widely different business philosophies and work practices could have more culture clashes during their merger than would a telephone company from France and one from Germany, if their philosophies and work practices were similar. This is not to say the national and societal differences aren't a factor. They are. The point is: Differences of nationality, language, time zones, and customs are obvious and important, but most leaders miss the differences that matter most—the beliefs about the business itself and the resulting behaviors.

The findings of a BCG study of the role of cultural differences in mergers of European Union companies confirmed that business differences produce greater and more destructive clashes than do differences of national culture. We found that clashes of business styles could lead to "massive destruction of value" both in the short term and in the long term. Short-term effects include: loss of identity by the members of the acquired company, a disturbance of their normal business routines, an almost obsessive focus on internal issues (often at the expense of customers and competitive issues), and a plunge in productivity. Long-term effects include a loss of vision—employees no longer understand why they are working and can't make sense of their day-to-day activities; the workforce becomes demoralized by the never-ending conflicts; the culture becomes destructive, with individuals and groups seeking revenge for past wrongs; and people get increasingly frustrated and unwilling to commit to their jobs or projects.

Part of the job of Preparation is understanding those fundamental differences and addressing them directly, albeit at a high level. Are we low-cost or high-value-added? Is product development driven by scientist-stars or by excellent processes and an enhanced infrastructure? Are the major building blocks the countries or the brands? If the philosophical underpinnings of the business are at odds, it will be impossible for managers and employees to resolve their differences after closure and to move forward together. Translation of an

Figure 5.1 Cultural differences can amplify positive or negative working relationhips.

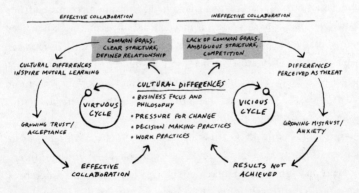

overarching business philosophy to a specific local application will breathe life into the operational changes that will come during Implementation.

Fortunately, we've also learned that when basic good management is in place—that is, the goals are clear and participants understand how decisions are to be made and how success will be measured—cultural differences enhance the creativity and innovation. Cultural differences, whether born from business philosophy or national identity, will have an influence; management's clarity and help will determine whether the influence proceeds in a "vicious" or "virtuous" cycle (Figure 5.1).

You Gotta Believe: Alignment Is Not the Same as Commitment, Which Is Not the Same as Getting Energized

It is possible for a management group to do the hard work of defining mission, strategy, values, and behaviors and reaching general alignment on them, and still not feel commitment or excitement. Alignment alone is not enough to sustain team members through the months and years of fundamental change—they have to believe, they have to get fired up.

Gaining commitment usually requires some kind of "breakthrough moment"—a time when one or more individuals on the team realize that they can't continue with the old ways; they must get on board with the new. Such a moment can come as the result of a crisis (loss of a customer, an analyst's negative report, departure of a key executive), from new information or data (disappointing sales report, disturbing survey results), or from a new understanding of the situation (a metaphor, story, conversation, or personal experience).

I watched an executive group review the results of an internal survey that had been taken to see how prepared their organization was to start a transformation initiative. (It was, in fact, a survey we call Ready, Willing, Able, which I'll discuss in Chapter 6.) The data—which were consistent across geographical areas, divisions, levels, and length of service—showed that the majority of employees did not believe the project would produce any significant change. This made the leaders angry. "This just shows how high the level of resistance is in this organization," one said. "They're not listening to what we're saying. They don't believe us." Then one of the leaders said, "You know, I tried an experiment. I filled out this survey, trying to answer as if I were a member of the workforce. Then, a couple of weeks later, I filled out another copy of the survey, this time as myself. When I compared the two surveys, the answers were the same. That's when I realized that I don't believe this program will make a big difference, and that I don't believe what we're saying either." Everybody in the room fell quiet for a moment, and then the real discussion began, with far more honesty and openness about the survey results. I heard comments like: "If we're not willing to put our time, energy, hearts, and minds into this, why should anyone else?" "The survey shows us that the employees are reading us accurately." There followed an intense discussion centered on the question: What can we do to make this initiative stimulating and exciting to *us*? The eventual outcome of this discussion was a wholly new approach to managing change at the company.

The lesson: Leaders have to be genuinely engaged or the change effort will fail. It is impossible to fake commitment and excitement; the employees will not be fooled. Why should an employee get fired up about a change effort that the management team is ambivalent about?

COVEN:
A MERGER OF EQUALS?

For many reasons, the look of Preparation at CoVen was substantially different than at Micro Switch, and building the management team followed a very different course as well.

Preparation began with the announcement that Venerable would indeed be merged with Commando Drugs to form a large pharmaceutical concern: Commando-Venerable International (CoVen for short). The announcement made front-page news around the world; employees in both companies were dramatically aware of what was happening but desperately short on details. What they knew had been culled from the news and the rumors that flew through the hallways and intranets of both companies.

They knew that Venerable BV and Commando Drugs were multinational pharmaceutical companies that had substantial worldwide operations, many strong products, and revenues in the billions. They knew that the coming together of the two companies was billed as a "merger of equals" but Commando was the dominant player. The deal, worth about $28 billion, would result in what the press called "a global powerhouse" consisting of facilities in 38 countries, a workforce of 45,000 people, and a portfolio of some of the most successful drugs on the market and several exciting new drugs in various stages of development.

Then there were the analyses behind the headlines. One analyst, Piet Jansen, wrote in an international newsweekly:

Many factors drove the acquisition. Commando has been unable to develop new drugs in certain areas of medicine, notably oncology and infectious disease, because the company lacks expertise in these disciplines and has been unable to attract top talent. Venerable, however, employs several world-class scientists in both disciplines. In former times, the European pharmaceutical concern would not have entertained such a merger with the aggressive American competitor, but they now face the imminent expiration of the patent on their best-selling antidepressant, a deadline made all the more urgent thanks to the recent failure of their new drug to gain the necessary regulatory approvals. Suddenly, this industry leader found itself in a slump it couldn't shake, and the stock price reflected the company's uncertain future. According to leadership at both companies, the merger will marry Commando's marketing and distribution muscle with Venerable's drug development brains, creating a competitor that has the right products and the speed and flexibility to get them to market successfully. And, oh yes, the two chief executives stand to walk away with as much as $40 million each in cash, stock options and other incentives. There's a cure for what ails you!

Cynicism about personal motives aside, this was a merger that faced enormous difficulty. According to my change gauge for determining the magnitude and complexity of change, both companies ranked high. Dimensions that would need to be redesigned included: the business model, strategy, organizational structure, key processes, leadership team, factory and facility consolidation, workforce reduction, and IT systems rationalization. Eight dimensions—the same number that Ray Alvarez faced at Micro Switch. The degree of difficulty of each dimension, however, was higher for the drug companies. For example, discovering and developing a drug is far more complex and takes far longer than designing and manufacturing electronic components. Pharmaceutical R&D facilities and factories are far more specialized and are subject to far more regulatory scrutiny than are manufacturing facilities. The number of people involved (45,000 at CoVen versus 5,000 at Micro Switch) further complicated matters. Other daunting aspects of the integration task were: most employees had lots of employment options outside, the number of countries, locations, and cultures involved, and the fact that the companies were headquartered in countries where different languages were spoken.

CLASH OF VALUES: THE PROFIT MONGER AND THE DO GOODER

A gnarly difficulty was that these companies operated with very different and conflicting values and were dramatically different in their business profiles and corporate cultures. Commando, only ten years old, was commercially driven, focused only on drugs that had exceptional market potential, and did sophisticated marketing and advertising. Commando people thought of themselves as being smart, aggressive, and on the fast track; they chose to be at Commando because they wanted to be part of a winning juggernaught. They accepted Venerable as a good acquisition because it strengthened their lead position in the industry and would bring new scale and talent to product development. But apart from that benefit, Commando people saw Venerable as staid and too detached from the competitive race. They felt the takeover was a good thing because Commando could whip Venerable into shape and teach it how to compete on a global basis.

Venerable, by contrast, was a long-established company. Its people strongly believed that their mission was to create and market drugs for the good of humanity. Venerable saw itself as a values-driven company, one which fostered the highest aspirations in its workforce. Many people, even alumni, felt deeply attached to the company and proud of their affiliation, no matter how much they might grumble about current management or the confused state of the marketplace. They felt a strong sense of mission and a righteous indignation at the thought of being taken over by the heathens in Commando. Venerable people felt betrayed by their leaders and could not understand the motivation for the merger. Their only hope was that "right would out" and Venerable's culture and goals would dominate.

The merger was announced with great fanfare and much smiling and handshaking among executives, and the newly formed company immediately entered the Preparation phase. Within a week, a new, combined executive committee was announced. Rick Gurney, the former head of Commando, was anointed CEO and quickly formed the Executive Integration Team (EIT), a group made up of the newly appointed executive committee and business commercialization heads from both Commando and Venerable. The EIT's task was to develop the overall business model and structure of the new organization.

For many weeks, the Executive Integration Team went about their work in virtual secrecy. Neither they nor the CEO communicated with the rest of the organizations about the purpose or specific objectives of the EIT, the process they were following, when their work would be complete, or what would happen once they finished. In fact, they had agreed among themselves that they would not communicate, formally or informally, with their departments, peers, or anyone else about their work.

People in both organizations then began conjecturing. They assumed there would be layoffs and some facilities would be closed. They wondered whether some drug development projects would be axed while others were given more resources. Rumors began to fly, and people grew increasingly desperate for hard information. They searched for meaning in the actions and hallway comments of every member of the EIT. Who was having lunch with whom? Who was traveling where, when, and why? Who was talking with Rick? After an EIT meeting, people interrogated the administrative assistants, trying to find out how long the meeting had lasted and how people looked when they left.

Finally, after about two months of intense work, the EIT made its initial recommendations to the Board of Directors. The next week, CEO Gurney—in conference calls with analysts and the press—announced the overall corporate structure and named the executives who had been chosen for the top two layers. He said that CoVen would reduce the workforce from 45,000 people to about 37,500, a reduction of about 16 percent. The layoffs would affect all locations and all disciplines in both companies. The announcement, although expected, sent shock waves through CoVen. Little work could get done as everyone pondered the same questions: "What will happen to me? Will I still have a job? Will I have to relocate? Who will my manager or direct reports be? Will my compensation change? Will my project survive?"

This anxiety was very different from the kind my mama had talked about. At CoVen, anxiety, fueled by apprehension, fear, and mistrust, became a kind of Preparation cum dread.

NOT ALL MERGERS BRING UPHEAVAL

Mergers and acquisitions do not always result in the momentous change that faced CoVen. When a large company purchases a small company, the "merger" can go one of two ways: (1) the acquired company continues to operate autonomously and experiences change only in a few systems and procedures mandated by the acquirer (usually, accounting, reporting, and information sharing); or (2) the purchaser subsumes the acquired company and immediately integrates the new people into its organization; the small company is swallowed virtually without a trace. It is this first type that typifies Johnson & Johnson, whereas companies like Cisco Systems and GE are models for the second type. All are known for the number and success of their acquisitions. It will be interesting to watch how GE handles its acquisition of Honeywell, given Honeywell's size and complexity.

Even in large mergers and acquisitions, the acquired company may undergo minimal change if there is little overlap of businesses, facilities or personnel. But in mergers of companies that are in the same business and are of nearly equal size, the postmerger integration (PMI) will surely involve substantial change. These companies have no choice but to undergo a thorough process of weeding and choosing. They have to rationalize their facilities and workforce—which means eliminating redundancies and overlaps and often involves closing facilities, laying off people, or choosing one business element (such as an IT infrastructure) over another. They must also integrate systems and processes and cultures, which means finding ways to work together. This complex work is made all the more difficult because of high internal anxiety and constant external scrutiny. Analysts, shareholders, governments, competitors, and customers all watch as the internal reconfiguration and integration are being designed and implemented. To make things even more stress-producing, the company can't ignore its day-to-day business activities—creating and selling products, servicing customers, and maintaining relationships with partners and suppliers with whatever energy is not consumed by the process of effecting internal change.

Although the companies' leaders liked to portray the merger of Commando and Venerable as a tidy interlocking of two puzzle pieces, it actually involved a tremendous amount of overlap. BCG was asked to help the new company with the rationalization and integration that we all knew were essential and would be significant. When we came on board, the EIT had already formed subteams for each major function. Their task was to start addressing the fundamental questions that must be answered in Preparation:

What will be the structure of each function in the new organization?

Which areas of medicine should we pursue, and which ones should we ignore or dump?

Where will manufacturing and service capabilities need to be located?

How will the company go to market?

How will the support functions be organized?

What new processes will we need? And which ones will need to be redesigned?

How should the workforce be deployed?

Because the CEO had significant experience in leading large organizations through change, the EIT made swift progress in gaining alignment. The members of the EIT were highly enthusiastic about the Commando-Venerable merger, and assumed that everyone else felt the same way. They saw it as a bold and aggressive move that would result in a great worldwide company. They honestly believed that both companies suffered limitations that might seriously have weakened their performance in the years to come, and that neither company could have continued to operate successfully as it had been. They also knew that they personally would take their places in the new organization with increased power, influence, wealth and even worldwide prominence; they felt they had control over their own destinies. Win or lose, in or out, the executives stood to benefit. To them, the merger represented the big payoff—both corporately and personally.

COVEN:
CONFUSION WITHIN THE R&D ORGANIZATION

The leaders of the research and development (R&D) organizations, however, did not share the EIT's alignment, clarity of purpose, or commitment to the merger. My role, as part of the BCG team supporting CoVen, was to work with the R&D subteam in analyzing the organization's concerns and areas of excitement. We wanted to have a good start on gaining buy-in and building momentum before Implementation began. My direct contact was Dr. Marco Trask, the newly appointed executive vice president for R&D and a member of the EIT. Naturally, he was also the leader of the R&D subteam.

Marco Trask had been executive vice president for research and development at Commando Drugs. He began his career as a research scientist at one of Commando's competitors. After seven years, he left and worked as president for a biotech start-up. He did well with the company, which went public successfully; he left as soon as he could cash in his options. Working as an independent consultant for several years, he took a number of positions in small and medium-size companies that needed a skilled scientist/manager as an interim leader or to spearhead an important initiative. When he was offered the opportunity to start a new therapeutic area in R&D at Commando, he grabbed it. Over the next five years, he quickly moved through a number of R&D management positions in Commando facilities around the world and became the executive vice president of R&D.

Marco was well respected by his peers, had a good sense of both the commercial and scientific forces that drive drug development, and was an extremely skilled operational manager—one of those polished senior executives who seem to be citizens of the international business community. He was not, however, strong on people skills. He was smart and knew it; he had deeper and more varied experience than most of his colleagues; and he was wealthy enough that he could leave the company whenever it suited him. To his credit, he understood all this about himself and knew that he could not achieve his goals without the support and collaboration of others. He wanted to build the most dynamic and successful pharmaceutical company on the planet, and then he wanted to run it.

In my first meeting with Marco, we talked about what I should focus on during this anxious phase of Preparation. (Others from BCG were analyzing a variety of other important aspects of the proposed change.) For legal reasons, we could not yet start the job selection process or implement any changes. We decided that the most important task for me was to provide guidance to Marco and his team about how to lead change and avoid costly missteps. To do so, I would first have to get a feel for the R&D operations by touring the facilities and talking with the key players.

Commando and Venerable had multiple research centers and locales for development, and both had groups in the United States and Europe and Asia. We decided to focus on seven major sites, leaving Asia and other smaller sites until later. Commando was just finishing construction of a new $200 million R&D facility outside Newark, New Jersey; this facility would become the center for R&D for all the CoVen groups. The major hub of Venerable was the Venerable Labs, outside Amsterdam. Marco wanted me to start there, because he knew none of the Venerable staff and needed a quick read on their reactions to the merger and to his appointment. If it was possible for me to get an idea of who was likely to stay and who would go, and what their particular expertise was, so much the better. Although they couldn't share with me any proprietary information, they could talk generally about their response to the merger and their hopes for its future. As mentioned earlier, BCG had already worked with Venerable on an earlier assignment, so I had some relationships there, and I knew the person

I wanted to talk with first: Dr. Elena Margolis, the head of the on-cology unit.

"I have spent four years building the oncology unit here," Dr. Margolis told me. "I've invested my heart and soul in it and I want to see it through. But I must tell you that I have my doubts about the merger. I can't see any great benefit to me or to my colleagues. I've had dealings with Commando in the past. They are, in my opinion, a short-sighted company. They will always make the decision that benefits Wall Street, or appears to, in the short term. I like to think in broader and longer terms. I'm not concerned about tomorrow or the end of the quarter. I'm concerned about the next generation of human beings that we can help avoid the horrors of lung cancer. If the new management agrees, great, but if not—well, we'll see. Meanwhile, I've heard mixed reviews on Marco Trask and nothing about the plans of the R&D integration team. Why should they keep us in the dark? We are not children and we do have other options. But so far, no one has said a word to me. You're the first person with any connection to the merger that has shown their face here. That alone says something. Aren't we important in this new company?"

I thought: Ignoring Dr. Margolis would be a big mistake. She's al-ready irritated and talking about having options. With her worldwide reputation, she could find a new job tomorrow or start a new com-pany. Marco needs to convince her to stay and explain the constraints he is dealing with. During a merger, the stakes are higher, the inten-sity is far greater, and the period of uncertainty is out of manage-ment's control. Marco had better make the right moves, I thought, or he's going to lose some of the very people who made this merger at-tractive to Commando in the first place.

After meeting with about twenty of the senior people at The Labs and the other Venerable R&D facilities, I reported back to Marco about my conversations. I told him we needed to compare the reac-tions and concerns at Venerable with those at Commando before we finalized any action plans. I couldn't make very good judgments without talking to the folks at the Commando locations. "Don't worry about that now," he said. "I know those people very well. I know they're with me, and I know the skills and preferences they have. Just tell me about the Venerable people. I have to know if we should be looking for talent from the outside, or whether we have the people we need. That's job one. You can talk with the Commando folks later."

I argued that he could not be sure that his Commando colleagues were fully on board. "Weird things happen to people in anxious times like these," I said. "You don't know for sure that they'll stay, and you don't know if they'll support you, until you ask them."

Marco considered my comment. "You could be right," he shrugged. "Go ahead and talk with the Commando people now. But first, give me your initial impressions of Venerable."

"I think you've got some problems," I said. "Naturally, people are concerned about their futures, but I'm also hearing concerns about the culture of Commando. They don't know you or their counterparts. They don't know your style—what you value or what you'll emphasize. They worry that science will take a backseat to commercialization, which they think would be awful. They feel resentful that the sale was made at all. They're angry that their company is seen as failing because they think it's the best place to be if you're a scientist/physician. They are very entrenched at The Labs, so they're worried that they'll have to move from Amsterdam to Newark. If they're asked to move, they'll probably leave the company instead. A couple of the stars there are very uncertain that their projects will continue to be funded or go unmolested by the new company."

Marco listened carefully. "I can't do anything about the fact that they let their company stagnate. I can help them succeed in the new one. Sounds like we have some work to do to help them understand economic realities. Do you have any idea who might leave?"

"Well, I'd pay close attention to Dr. Elena Margolis," I told him. "She has strong convictions and a loyal following. If you lose her, I

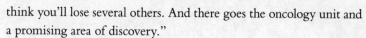

think you'll lose several others. And there goes the oncology unit and a promising area of discovery."

"I'll talk to her when I can," Marco said.

As it happened, he did talk briefly with her before the deal was signed, and got her tentative agreement to stay. Whether he got her deep commitment and real support, I wasn't so sure.

6

Is Everybody Ready?

When Emotions Become a Roller Coaster

AT SOME POINT during Preparation—when the task of gaining alignment and commitment within the leadership team is fairly well in hand—the leaders need to turn their attention to the rest of the organization and assess their readiness for change. They need not wait until all the issues and conflicts within the executive team have been resolved. In truth, gaining alignment and commitment of the leaders is a process that continues throughout the change; it is rare for all of the leaders to be united, fully committed, and energized all at the same time—and to stay that way. Some will "catch fire" without warning; others will cool as the process unfolds. Like the phases of the Change Curve itself—which are dynamic, overlap, and seesaw back and forth—individuals will be upbeat one minute and down the next. They will experience change differently and inconsistently. They are likely to feel multiple, often conflicting, emotions at any given time. As I said to Marco: Strange and unexpected things happen during every phase, and you have to remain vigilant in assessing and inspiring your team.

Leader unity is critically important, but you cannot wait for complete harmony and agreement before you turn to the organization at large to see where people stand and how they're feeling.

THE READY-WILLING-AND-ABLE ASSESSMENT TOOL

We have developed an instrument for assessing the change bias of an organization. We call it Ready Willing and Able (RWA). It is a survey that can be done via e-mail, in focus groups, or one-on-one, depending on the sample size and purpose. Generally, we use it as a quick and broad "radar scan" of the organization. It tells us whether there are particular issues or parts of the organization that need more attention. It addresses three key aspects of change preparedness:

1. Readiness to change. Does the organization understand and believe change is needed? Are people aware of the external pressures their company faces? Do they have an understanding of the performance gaps the organization is now experiencing?

2. Willingness to change. Are they sufficiently dissatisfied with the status quo, and/or worried about the future, that they are willing to change? Do they know what they need to change and what capabilities they need to develop? Do they have confidence that the plans being articulated are the correct ones?

3. Ability to change. Do they believe that the organization possesses the skills and tools needed to affect change? Are they

personally equipped? Do they believe that management has the will and the skills needed to see it through?

RWA is customized to each company and includes some core questions that provide comparison to other companies. By customizing the survey, respondents see that it is specific and relevant to them. RWA also demonstrates that the leaders have put some effort into the activity—rather than buying an off-the-shelf survey—and really care about the results. We don't want the leaders to appear cynical, as if they want people to believe they are interested in listening when they really aren't. Feedback on the results and the follow-up actions that will be taken is critical to building credibility and buy-in.

RWA produces both quantitative and qualitative data. Quantitative data are important in calibrating pervasiveness, locale, and extensiveness of a perception; qualitative responses can illuminate interpretations and intensity of feeling. Both are necessary. There are usually between thirty and fifty quantitative statements that require responses on a scale of one to five, from strongly disagree to strongly agree. The qualitative questions ask for written responses, which often produce great volumes of "verbatims." Demographic questions are limited, to ensure confidentiality.

Here are some representative statements from a typical RWA questionnaire, prepared for Worldwide Frenzy Inc. (WWF Inc), the hyperactive company I described in Chapters 3 and 4.

Illustrative of READY

We face significant competitive challenges in the next five years.

I believe radical change is needed if WWF Inc. is going to meet its strategic goals over the next five years.

Our competitors are making significant advances in their products/services.

I understand the business strategy for my division.

Changes within WWF Inc. are driven by business needs and not by hidden agendas.

I agree that the changes to my job are necessary.

The viability of WWF Inc. requires that we make major changes in our operations.

WWF Inc. is ready to undertake a major change initiative.

Illustrative of WILLING

I understand WWF Inc.'s vision.

This vision is the right one for WWF Inc.

This vision is highly motivating to me.

I understand what I can do in my job to support WWF Inc.'s vision.

If this were my company, I would be pursuing the change initiative as outlined by WWF executives.

I understand how this vision will impact what I do and how I make decisions on my job.

My division's business objectives are clearly prioritized, so I know what I must accomplish.

I am willing to radically change my current role and/or responsibilities to help WWF Inc. compete effectively.

The person I report to translates the WWF Inc. business model into action for our group.

This business model is the right one for WWF Inc.

Illustrative of ABLE

WWF Inc. employees have the skills required to meet the challenges facing WWF Inc.

I can count on my division's leaders to follow through and do what they say they will do.

I feel confident that WWF Inc. senior executives will make the tough decisions that are in the best interests of the company.

WWF Inc. senior executives have the skills required to meet the challenges facing WWF Inc.

When a major project is initiated, WWF Inc. follows it through to completion.

Departments within WWF Inc. are not territorial; communications and cooperation across departments are open, honest, and easy.

WWF Inc. will allocate appropriate resources to my division so we can meet our goals and objectives.

WWF Inc. meets its short-term commitments without compromising its long-term performance.

We have a good track record in completing change initiatives.

I am confident that WWF will be successful.

The trick in analyzing and understanding survey results is to consider both types of responses together. The qualitative data provide headlines and a snapshot of major issues. The verbatims provide lots of color, emotion, anecdote, and grit. They can also be difficult reading for organizations in trouble; sometimes specific groups or even individuals come under fire. The leaders should be prepared for this.

The results of the assessment can be displayed in a number of ways. The spider chart in Figure 6.1 gives a clear visual impression of the three aspects. Each "rib" of the spider relates to a specific statement.

The closer to the outer ring of the circle, the more positive the response; the closer to the center, the more negative. Figure 6.1 shows that WWF feels quite ready to take on change. The most positive spike in the Ready segment shows that most people agree that WWF Inc. faces significant challenges in the next five years. The next most positive spike in Ready shows that people are personally willing to "radically change" their roles and responsibilities. The bad news: The two deepest dips indicate that people do *not* feel that the company as a whole is ready to undergo change, and, even worse, they believe the change initiative is based on hidden agendas. This

Figure 6.1   RWA highlights significant issues for change agenda.

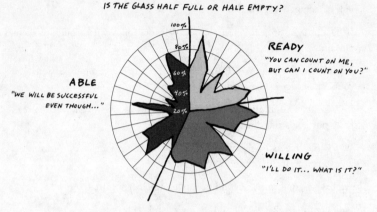

demonstration of a lack of confidence in management's integrity led to our summary statement, "You can count on me, but can I count on you?"

The Willing segment shows that the organization has strong agreement with the vision and willingness to make, and live through, change. The big sticking point is the lack of belief that the new business model is the right one for Worldwide Frenzy. The written comments reinforce employees' belief that this business model would not create future success and, in fact, is out of sync with the new vision. The overall attitude of the organization was a willingness to change but a strong desire for the business model to be revisited.

The responses in the Able segment show that most people are very skeptical about the company's ability to meet its short-term business commitments without scuttling the long-term change effort. They're worried that the company will not allocate the necessary resources to effect the change, and they do not believe that the executives will see the changes through to completion. They make it clear that WWF has a poor track record when it comes to implementing fundamental change. But, in spite of all the negatives, the two strong points are their beliefs (1) that WWF will be successful and (2) that they, the employees, have what it takes to make the changes work.

The data can be sliced and diced in a variety of ways. It is often useful to look at the results in each functional area, discipline, or region, in order to identify any major differences by subgroup. In other words, if the sales organization has one set of perceptions and engineering has a different set, that's important to know so that actions appropriate to each group can be created. In the case of WWF, the data showed that the responses were quite similar across all the functions of the organization, and the biggest differences were between layers of management—specifically, between the vice presidential level and the directors. This conflict, which was a surprise to the leaders, revealed an alarming area of dissonance and mistrust. The leaders realized immediately that they had to pay more attention to the vertical lines of communication and be far more proactive in personally communicating with the directors and gaining their buy-in.

Let's look at the RWA for Ennui International, the depressed company I talked about in Chapter 3. Figures 6.2 and 6.3 show the responses from divisions in two countries, Brazil and France. Figure 6.4 shows the response from the corporate functions. The Brazilian organization is quite Ready and Willing to tackle fundamental change, and the comments on the qualitative questions support an eagerness to get on with it. The French organization, on the other hand, does not believe that change is needed and therefore is not willing to engage in any major change initiatives. The only thing these two divisions have in common is that neither believes that it has in place the capabilities needed to implement and sustain fundamental change.

The corporate functions hold a third opinion, which is at odds with the countries' opinions. They see that change is needed (Ready), but they believe that the plan currently being promoted is the wrong way to address change (Willing) so they are not willing to support this plan. In addition, they see themselves as highly capable of implementing change, if and when the correct plan is proposed.

Figure 6.2   RWA survey results from Brazil.

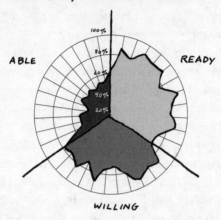

These RWA survey results showed the leaders of Ennui International that their strategy for moving forward had to be tailored to specific groups. Only when they saw these data did the management team for France recognize that its timidity in talking about bad news had a high cost. By not communicating the urgency and gravity of

Figure 6.3   RWA survey results from France.

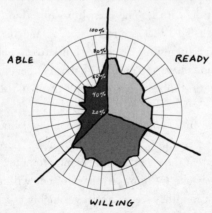

the competitive threat, the team had lulled the organization into believing that there were no serious problems and had, therefore, reinforced the employees' resistance to change. To become ready for the Implementation phase, the leaders in France had to greatly increase their efforts in educating the workforce as to why change was needed and then building an appetite for it.

In Brazil, the leaders wanted to demonstrate responsiveness to the survey results and take advantage of the organization's desire for action. They decided to immediately start some of the changes scheduled for the Implementation phase. They had all-hands meetings at the various locations, reviewed the survey results, and announced two pilot projects that would start immediately. They got high marks for their openness and for the speed of response. Starting early had the added benefit of testing the current change capability. They knew training would be needed but were unsure of what particular skills were lacking in which specific groups. The pilot projects would clarify what training was needed in various locations.

Figure 6.4   RWA survey results from corporate functions.

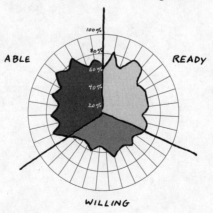

The value of the Ready, Willing, Able assessment (or any other such diagnostic tool) is that it shows the leaders where the hot spots are—or where they are likely to form—and it gives the management team a chance to proactively manage them. With this information, the leaders can target their communications and interventions for the greatest possible return on their efforts.

7

Building an Appetite for Change

Moving to Productive Action

When I was growing up in Alabama, it seemed that my home state was always at the bottom of some national list. I remember that my heart soared when I once heard that Alabama was actually number one in the nation, until I learned that it was for cases of ringworm. My heart sank. We got so tired of hearing negative news that we got in the habit of saying "Thank God for Mississippi," because its residents were usually worse off than we were. (All due apologies to folks from Mississippi!) The lesson is that, when people are eaten up with defensiveness or shame, it is practically impossible for them to experiment with new behaviors. Defensiveness does not generate a spirit of confidence, adventure, or experimentation, all of which are needed in great quantities when embarking on a major transition.

Often, people in an organization know that change is needed, but the need has never been discussed publicly or stated explicitly, let alone forcefully, by their leaders; the leaders need to create a *healthy* dissatisfaction with the current conditions. I use the word *healthy* because, as I said earlier, a little anxiety is healthy and even inspiring; scaring people into a catatonic state is not. The goal is not to make people feel ashamed of their past or panicked about their future, but to move them to productive action. Confidence is success remembered. Reminding employees of what they have been able to accomplish in the past and challenging them to surpass those records in the future is a better motivational strategy than denigrating the past or casting aspersions on past management.

How leaders go about building an appetite for change among their troops will depend on their starting point. If the organization is mired in Stagnation, as was Readers' Digest when Thomas Ryder came in as CEO in 1998, radical and symbolic actions may be needed to shake up the company and to signal that a new day, at last, has dawned. Ryder, whose mission was to turn around the company, made such a dramatic move when he sold the company's $100 million art collection. Its value was not measured only in money: The collection had a rich symbolic value as well. To long-term Readers' Digest employees, the collection—which included works by Picasso and Giacometti—was the proud legacy of the founders and a constant reminder of their successful and cultured way of life. To Ryder, the art collection was a luxury that a company with falling profits and repeated layoffs could no longer afford—a remnant of a bygone era. Selling the collection was a dramatic (and traumatic) event that signaled "the end of life as we knew it."

In mergers, the leaders need to pay very close attention to such symbolic moves; everything from creating a new headquarters for the new company on a neutral site to something far subtler, such as the location and layout of the Board room or the placement of any portraits. Image consultants build their businesses on creating new company names, identities, themes, colors, and all their applications, from forms to uniforms.

MICRO SWITCH:
SHARING INFORMATION AND USING SYMBOLS

When the management team at Micro Switch assessed the current situation, they were quite sure that most of their people did not know the company was in Stagnation. They were equally sure that if they announced their vision and tried to whip up some enthusiasm for it, the workforce would look at them as if they were crazy. They expected that people would react by saying, "Why would we embark on a major transformation of a company that is successful and making money?" The next reaction would be for the workforce to hear the term "turnaround" as code for more layoffs. Micro Switch had a long history of massive layoffs whenever profits shrank.

As bad as these possibilities were, the management team was far more worried about what it saw as a more insidious result of a premature announcement. If the workforce did become engaged and even highly committed to the change, the team worried that the employees would not be able to make or sustain the changes needed for success. They were woefully unprepared for the scope and depth of the changes required to move Micro Switch from where it was to being "competitive for the twenty-first century." As just one example, about 15 percent of the factory workforce could not read or do basic math. How were they going to run the new machines that were operated by computers? How would they be able to adjust their production schedules based on the daily printouts?

Because of these considerations, Ray Alvarez and his team decided not to announce the vision. Instead, they embarked on a program that would have two major thrusts: (1) educating all Micro Switch employees about the competitive realities they were facing, and (2) basic skill building to prepare people for a higher level of success. To do this, they intentionally disregarded one of Micro Switch's longtime unwritten rules: they decided to share sensitive customer and competitive information with employees.

The first communication session was with an extended group of managers. "Historically, we had deliberately withheld the real numbers from the larger management team because many of our competitors would love to have that information. But this time we showed them the real numbers. That was a real break with the past," remembers Joel Miller. "We reminded people of the need for confidentiality, we made no copies or handouts of the presentation, we asked them to honor the confidentiality requirements and trusted that the managers would. They did, and we've been doing it ever since."

The managers were then enlisted to help communicate the need for change to the rest of the workforce. The leaders wanted to emphasize three primary points:

1. The company is in danger and we have to change.
2. It's not your fault; we have great people who can help Micro Switch to win.
3. The company cares about you.

Recognizing the very diverse capabilities of the workforce, which included scientists and inventors, engineers, managers, administrative staff, and factory workers, it was important that the messages be easy to understand but not condescending. Ray and his team settled on two symbols to underscore the necessity for change. The first symbol—"storm clouds on the horizon"—was a familiar and tangible metaphor, given the geography around the Micro Switch locations. Folks in Illinois, Texas, and Mexico were accustomed to watching as storm clouds formed in the west, then moved toward them—sometimes gradually, sometimes with alarming speed—and brought nasty weather that engulfed them. "We didn't want to cause too much anxiety among the workforce," said Ray. "After all, we weren't about to go under. By talking about the storm clouds gathering to the west of us, we let everybody know that there was a real threat coming our way, and that we had to prepare for it by doing things differently." Weather is a universal concern; it affects everyone, regardless of status or wealth, so it worked well as a metaphor for everyone in the company.

The more sobering, and unusual, symbol was the "death spiral," which Ray introduced in a video. He talked about how healthy companies can go out of business very quickly if they don't remain aware of and responsive to the outside forces that are affecting them such as changes in competitors, customers, and technologies. He talked about the threats to Micro Switch, and emphasized that these threats did not come about as a result of uncaring workers. "But if we don't recognize our problems and manage them properly," he said, "we could find Micro Switch in a death spiral, where things get worse and worse very quickly and pretty soon we're out of business." To emphasize the point, Ray was videotaped outside an abandoned manufacturing facility that had once been the main plant for Rawleigh Foods. Most Illinois employees knew Rawleigh Foods well and had fond memories of delightful cooking aromas wafting through the streets of Freeport. Knowing that it had been a successful and stable part of their lives and that it no longer existed added to the impact of the "death spiral" symbol.

Ray and his team used these symbols over and over again in communications throughout the company. One Micro Switch manager, Judy Fox, recalled that the communications made people uneasy at first:

I had worked with another Honeywell division and then left to work with a different company in Los Angeles. When I took the job with Micro Switch, I was excited. I thought, "I have a new lease on life; I'm back in the Midwest and back with Honeywell!" But when I got here, everybody was talking about "storm clouds gathering in the west" and Ray was distributing these videos about death spirals. I thought, "Whoa! This company is not in good shape. I've signed up with a loser!" I was upset that they were recruiting people when the company was in such bad shape. It made me afraid for my career. So I watched very carefully. Gradually, I came to understand that Ray was trying to educate people about the business and get them to understand the competitive pressures facing Micro Switch so they would realize we had to turn the company around. After a while, I stopped worrying, and started looking for opportunities to contribute to the effort.

COMMUNICATING THE MESSAGES: OVER AND OVER AND IN MANY WAYS

Communication is a vital part of the change process during every phase of the Change Curve, and it is imperative that the communication channels be opened during Preparation. It takes time to establish the channels, find the right tone, and get all the leaders involved in the communication process. When you plunge into Implementation, the communication process should be in place so that people are able to talk with each other as easily as possible.

Although all the communication tools (print, video, e-mail, intranet sites, and so on) are useful and necessary, most people prefer to get their information from a human being whom they trust—someone they believe has the inside scoop. For most employees, that person is their immediate manager/supervisor. That's why Ray Alvarez held briefing sessions every month with all the managers and supervisors. A big part of those sessions was to prepare the managers and supervisors to do communications sessions with their own people.

Building an appetite for change takes time—primarily, face time—and repeated application. No single communication (even a stellar video) will suffice. Besides, videos often play to an empty cafeteria or conference room. The most powerful communication is done face-to-face, especially if people have the opportunity to ask questions and engage in dialogue. Although this is time-consuming, and, for many executives, uncomfortable, there is no substitute. The benefits of face-to-face communications are numerous—not the least of which is getting to know your audience, which is critical in any communication or leadership effort.

It is equally important to allow the audience to get to know you. I worked with the new CEO of a large telecommunications equipment manufacturer who faced a daunting challenge. Her predecessor had been enormously popular, in part because he had been lucky enough to enjoy perfect timing—he arrived just after a major layoff, enjoyed the profits generated by it, and left before major shifts in the industry called for additional dramatic changes in response. He had charisma and was at his best in front of a large group. Employees were crazy about him; they saw him as a caring person with an upbeat attitude.

My client, Harriet Grindstone, came into the job with little recognition and a reputation for being capable but remote, severe, and numbers-driven. Harriet knew that public speaking was not her strong suit; moreover, she learned that rumors about her were flying. Dire predictions circulated, from location to location, that she would ruthlessly drive the organization toward making the numbers come out right so that she would look good. Harriet knew that she would have to make big changes not only in operations and how people worked together but also in their basic beliefs about the business and how they—individually and collectively—succeeded. "Not only is my timing lousy, but the organization already has me pegged as the Wicked Witch of the West! How am I ever going to get them to work *with* me instead of *against* me?" she wondered aloud. Harriet decided not to let her predecessor's legacy intimidate her; she recognized that she would have to be bold in her own way. She committed herself to meeting every employee in the company and enlisting his or her support for the upcoming changes. In her first year, she visited every location, made formal presentations with question-and-answer sessions, and held informal meetings with small groups. She listened intently to employees and made sure that she really understood their concerns and aspirations. She took all questions and did her best to answer them.

Harriet also got her management team involved in the communications process. To explain and sell the new strategy, each management team member held multiple two- to four-hour sessions with groups small enough to allow for questions and dialogue (usually thirty to fifty people). The sessions provided a rich opportunity to test the new strategy. Employees asked their questions directly and offered their suggestions. The executives learned what was on the minds of the workforce by meeting with all 10,000 people in the organization. "It was one of the best things we've ever done, because we really got to know the organization," one of the executives reflected. "And we never would have invested that kind of time if Harriet hadn't made us." The time and energy spent in these meetings paid off handsomely when Implementation began. Everyone understood what was expected and why, had had time to think about it, and was committed to meeting the challenges ahead. Implementation went far more smoothly than any deployment the organization had experienced before. Harriet's ratings as a leader went up, not because she had the charisma of her predecessor, but because she made the management team and the employees feel important, capable, and needed.

This is an important lesson. Many executives think that, in order to communicate well, they must become polished public speakers, a cross between John Kennedy and Winston Churchill. "That's just not me!" they'll say. When I suggest that they take some speaker training, they resist. "I don't need a bunch of smooth handlers telling me how to dress for television. I'm not going on *Oprah,* after all." Good communication, however, is not about being slick or camera-ready or knowing how to use a TelePrompTer (although that couldn't hurt). The most critical steps are: genuinely believe that communication is important and care about your audience. Everything after that is details.

THE CHIEF COMMUNICATOR BECOMES THE DE FACTO SHAPER OF CHANGE

Sometimes, an unexpected individual emerges as a strong and influential communicator. In one company, it was the Chief Technology

Officer (CTO). After every executive committee meeting or any other important gathering, the CTO would send to his direct reports a voice mail giving his interpretation of the events, including his views on discussions and decisions. His direct reports loved getting these voice mails. They made them feel that they had a direct link to the inner sanctum. And, to show their privileged status of "being in the know," they quickly passed the voice mails to others—and so on and so on, until 70 percent of the division was listening to these voice mails. Furthermore, because they were unofficial (and because of the mystique that each person only got them because of his or her status), these messages were deemed the most credible communications of any within the company.

When we informed the executive committee members about the voice-mail phenomenon as part of our communications analysis, most of them were stunned. The CTO feigned surprise; I'm convinced, however, that he had worked tirelessly to build his following. The voice mails (and similar e-mails) were never marked "private" or restricted in any way that would prevent their being passed on. He was not only Chief Technology Officer but, by default, Chief Communicator. Too bad he and the CEO didn't see eye-to-eye on many critical issues.

The Chief Communicator, whoever it may be, will often become the de facto shaper of the change. In one merger, for example, the Change Team in the acquired company organized a toll-free telephone number with a new message every morning and afternoon, as well as answers to frequently asked questions. The acquirer, on the other hand, had no such service, and its written communications were infrequent and ineffective. Word of the toll-free number immediately spread, and people from both organizations began bombarding it with calls. It came to be regarded as the best source of merger information. As a result, the acquired company significantly influenced not only the messages but the attitudes and beliefs of both sets of employees and even the course of the merger itself.

RICH CONTENT DOES NOT REQUIRE ENDLESS DETAIL

Many leaders are reluctant to use the available channels of communication broadly during Preparation, because of their belief that they
don't have any "new news." But often, how the leaders or task team
members define news is very different from how the rest of the organization defines it. Instead of focusing only on what has been decided, it might be easier to discuss the process that is being used, who
is involved, what has been learned, or even what ideas have been discarded. It's understandable that leaders and their teams would prefer
to speak when they have lots of content—specific decisions, details,
new information. But if the assessment and decision making happen
over several months, it is not adequate to inform the organization at
the start of the effort and then leave it hanging for months while all
the details and decisions are being worked out. It's like that old joke
about the man who told his wife on their wedding day, "I'm telling
you now that I love you. If that changes, I'll let you know; otherwise, I see no reason to repeat myself."

   In the absence of good (or any) communications from the leaders,
employees find themselves relying on another source for news: the
media. People are never happy to learn about major corporate decisions
or developments from newspapers, television, radio, or the Internet.
They want to hear company news directly from the company—prefer-
ably from their own managers *before* it has become public knowledge.
Why should the press get information before the people it most affects?
Why should my neighbor know something I don't know when I work
here and he doesn't? Of course, corporations do not control the press,
and many stories about large companies are not placed by their own
communications people. Instead, they are the result of speculation,
rumor, and investigative reporting. Telling folks directly—and, whenever possible, *before* the media—is desirable; the second-best approach
is to respond immediately when an important story appears in the
media.

Especially in times of uncertainty, it is important to tell people what they will know and when they will know it. At CoVen, for example, the first concrete news the employees heard was that 7,500 of them would be laid off or nudged into early retirement. At that time, they were told nothing about who would be laid off, when, or how the process of selection would be managed. It is quite helpful to explain what you are doing, describe the process you will employ to make decisions, and estimate when you will be able to tell employees what they most urgently want to know. Transparency of the process is critical to building trust and easing anxiety. Be careful with time lines; you can always be early with promised actions or announcements, but you can never be late. If people don't know how decisions are being made, or if the decisions are late, their distrust of management will grow alongside their anxiety.

Too often, however, leaders are so wrapped up in the issues of running the business that they fail to recognize the importance of communication; they say too little and often say it too late. One thing you should count on: *People will connect the dots in the most pathological way possible.* In the absence of communication from the leaders, the organization will seek information from other sources, whether those sources know what they're talking about or not. Your silence doesn't stop the conversation; it just means you're not participating in it.

COVEN:
MARCO GOES ON A ROAD SHOW

Knowing that the conversation was raging at both Venerable and Commando, we recommended to Marco that he should communicate with the nearly 3,800 members of the combined research and development organizations, even before the deal was signed. His purpose would be to explain the design process currently in place as well as the change process that would be followed once the new company was a reality. He resisted, using the common argument that he didn't have enough information to say anything useful. "We don't yet know how many people will go, or who they will be," he argued. "We don't know which facilities will be closed. We don't really know anything, so what am I going to say? I don't intend to get up there and speak banalities to them." Marco needed to introduce himself to the organization. People were curious about who he was and what he was like. And although he couldn't be specific about people and dates, we argued that there was a lot of information he could and should share. He could explain the objectives and the expected impact of the merger on research and development; the various tasks of the R&D change team, including the success criteria; the process and the time line for the appointment process and for designing the organizational structure. Plus, we could help him educate people about the phases of the Change Curve, so they would have a better understanding of the emotional dynamics of the change they were entering and of what to expect at each phase.

Marco finally agreed and we put together a communications plan for all of the research and development groups. Because Marco was unknown to so many employees, he needed to personally visit all eight facilities. Each visit was coordinated with the local management team and followed up with monthly progress reports. To ensure that the communications were continuous, we set up an interactive intranet site, which gave employees a place to ask questions. A bimonthly electronic newsletter provided answers to common questions, as well as integration-related news. We also produced a video for other departments, in case they had any questions about what was happening in R&D.

Marco's visits to the R&D locales were well received. People were relieved to know how the decisions were to be made and to have a relatively firm date by which their fates would be known. However, interviews and surveys of the R&D staff, taken just after this first wave of communications, showed that people from both companies were harboring mistrust and were feeling an underlying anxiety. The

Venerable people expressed a strong sense of disappointment and betrayal because their board of directors had chosen to sell the company. It seemed to most of them that their company's problems could have been solved without a merger. And, to make matters worse, many felt that Venerable had been purchased by an inferior company. They saw the new CoVen executive team as untrustworthy and cited the appointment of a higher number of Commando executives (versus Venerable executives) to new top-tier positions as evidence that the pledge of a "merger of equals" was a farce. The Commando people, although they understood the proposed R&D reappointment process, were surprised and annoyed that they too would have to go through it; they had assumed, as members of the acquiring company, that *their* jobs were safe. They found it hard to accept that they might lose their jobs to Venerable people. Even more troubling, we found evidence that senior managers within R&D were contributing to the "us versus them" discussions.

These findings showed that many people in the organization harbored strong feelings of concern and doubt about the intent of the merger and the process of change. Marco and his team talked about these issues. "The merger is a fact," Marco said. "People just have to accept it and move on. And if they thought they wouldn't have to compete for their jobs, they were being naïve."

I responded, "That may be, but the fact remains that some senior managers are participating in these gripe sessions, which gives license to everyone else to be negative and difficult. Instead of providing leadership during times of high emotions, they're contributing to the problem."

Marco was uncomfortable with these "soft" issues. "Let's just focus on the operational tasks," he replied. "Once everyone knows where they stand, this will blow over."

I pushed back on Marco: "Each member of this team needs to deal directly with their managers now. We need to talk with all the managers about the process, answer questions that we can answer now, and urge them to reassure people to stay the course during these months of uncertainty. If this isn't done, the morale of the organizations will continue eroding. And eventually, you'll have managers who aren't credible or capable of addressing sensitive issues."

Marco felt we were being alarmists. He pushed away from the table. "We'll deal with that if and when it happens." I was still concerned. I knew that when it came time to "live the change" in Implementation, people would be far less inclined to accept the challenges and hardships involved if their direct managers and supervisors had been voicing disagreement and skepticism. Marco and the other R&D leaders needed to talk with them, understand their concerns, and insist that all of the management team address the issues in a professional and straightforward manner. They needed to explain the context and rationale as well as the motives behind the merger and its positive potential. They needed to be sure they understood the decision-making criteria, the process, and the time lines so they could reassure their employees without adding fuel to the fire.

TALKING TO THE ICONS

The communications campaign had been designed to reach every member of the R&D organization, and it had done so, but we also needed a more detailed and in-depth conversation with an important subgroup: the key knowledge workers. I think of these people—the PhDs, MDs, and specialists who were CoVen's primary assets and were highly regarded by the organization—as important human "icons." Everyone else in the organization watched how they were treated and considered their actions and reactions carefully. We agreed that Marco would conduct a personal communications campaign with the R&D icons. About thirty physicians and scientists met that description and were not on Marco's Functional Integration Team (FIT).

It was a difficult assignment. These were highly educated, highly skilled, and highly paid professionals who had plenty of autonomy and were used to being in control of their destinies. In addition, most of them had greater allegiance to their discipline and projects than to the company itself. Marco's talks with them were intense and sometimes prickly. The topics ranged from practical matters, such as project selection and funding, to strategic and philosophical issues: What was the role of R&D in this new company? Which therapeutic areas would be chosen? What did each scientist want to accomplish?

Marco did well; the scientists agreed to support the integration and to stay if chosen for the new positions in CoVen. I was particularly impressed that Marco had been able to connect with Dr. Margolis and persuade her to make a more explicit commitment to the company. She promised not to talk with any headhunters and to come to Marco first, whenever she had any concerns. I suspected, however, that the fundamental issue of values still had not been resolved. I knew from experience that a clash of values is a tricky situation; peaceful coexistence, rather than a full conversion of the unconvinced, is often the best that can be achieved. I thought it likely that Dr. Margolis had been sufficiently convinced by Marco to "wait and see" how things progressed but still might quit. Marco saw it differently. "She's a professional. She has made her deal and if she has as much integrity as you say she has, she'll stick to it," he said. "Besides, she's going to be a star. Why would she quit?"

On to Implementation

There is generally no clear and definite end to Preparation—as there is no clear and definite end to any phase of change—but milestones can signify a moment when one phase is on the wane and the next one is gathering momentum. In mergers and acquisitions, announcement of the merger begins Preparation in earnest, and closure of the deal is the "official" start of Implementation. These may or may not, in fact, be so clear, given regulatory approval or delays. It is possible for two organizations to linger on in their separate states, waiting and wondering when things are going to get rolling, while the leaders scramble to respond to regulatory requirements. In other types of change, the Implementation phase may start, in a small way, when the first pilot team is chartered and begins its work. Or it may begin in a grand and public way, with a big kickoff event composed of speeches explaining the plans, new assignments, training sessions, and team-building exercises.

However the phase begins, a beginning does not always guarantee a positive ending. More than one change initiative has foundered early in Implementation—usually because two key challenges of the Preparation phase have not been met:

1. The leaders have not achieved alignment. The resulting inconsistencies among missions, business philosophies, and priorities cause tremendous confusion and conflict between teams and groups. People become frustrated and disillusioned, and the organization retreats. The leadership team falls into bickering or isolation, and the better managers may leave the company.

2. People do not sufficiently believe in the need for change, or they don't endorse the plan. In either case, when it comes to chartering teams and asking for help from the entire organization, recruits will be hard to find.

The lesson: Go slow early, to go fast later. Take the time to prepare the organization for change. Resist the urge to "just do it," or doing it will be tougher than it needs to be. Instead, relish your period of hopeful anxiety; it will be a source of energy throughout the change to come.

PART FOUR

IMPLEMENTATION

THE MONSTER STOMPS OUT OF ITS HIDING PLACE

Courtesy of Roger Beale.

8

Plunging In

Time to Start Walking the Talk

TIME FOR ACTION! Implementation is a welcomed phase, especially among those who've been itching to "do something" and those who feared "analysis paralysis" during Preparation would keep the company frozen. Just as the senior executive needed to recruit, align, and engage his or her leadership team to begin the change initiative, now the successive layers of management must involve the rest of the organization in implementing the change.

In Implementation, as in all the phases of the Change Curve, the leaders have to manage the expectations, energy, and experience of the organization. During Stagnation they had to build an appetite for change. During Preparation they wanted to enroll the workforce in the dream of what might be. Now, during Implementation, it's time to put that pent-up anxiety to work animating the new organization. Now, people are expected to do more than listen and ask questions— they have to act and participate. It's time to start walking the talk.

This is no small task. As my mama told me (more than once), "When fantasy and reality compete, fantasy always wins." It's no wonder fantasy wins—there are no limitations, no sweat, no negative consequences. It's just us soaring in our imaginations. When the time comes to implement the plans, folks often find that the reality of what it takes to get there is radically different from their fantasies about the process. Implementation is the hard part. Implementation is reality. And, as twentysomethings like to say, "Reality bites."

When I was a young girl, I sometimes thought about becoming a mother. I pictured myself going to the hospital to deliver the baby. I would arrive fat, slightly awkward, and a little uncomfortable. In the next scene, I was lying in a bed with a beautiful baby, wrapped in either a pink or blue blanket. Sweet. Clean. Very romantic. Then one day I asked my mother if having a baby hurt. She said, "Yes!" I was shocked. I thought, "You weren't supposed to say that. Even if it's true, you're not supposed to tell me." Well, I gotta tell you, creating radical change in an organization hurts and, like childbirth, it's messy and painful, but ultimately rewarding.

Along with the organization, the leaders will experience pain during this phase, especially if a leader wishes to create significant change *and* be universally loved. When one person (the leader) tells another person (an employee) that he or she needs to change, it rarely inspires love; tension, embarrassment, or even resentment are more common. Some folks flare up when they learn the new requirements, but then they cool off; they may agree with the leader's assessment after they've had time to reflect. (That still doesn't mean they like it.) A few will respond like serious athletes to a good coach; they'll be interested, attentive, and willing to follow orders. However, some will exhibit amazing powers of denial and sabotage.

The same patterns show up in an organization as a whole. As a colleague of mine says, "Expect the rule of thirds—one third will see the changes as irrelevant to them, one third will embrace them with varying degrees of enthusiasm, and one third will disagree and resist either openly or in secret." Educate the first group, reinforce the second, and address the third with some hope of converting them. One of the early questions to ask is: "Are there groups that will not be affected by the change?" If so, it's important to tell them. However, those who see an initiative as irrelevant often haven't understood the second- and third-order effects of a change. They need to be educated by someone who understands these dynamics.

Anywhere in the organization—among the executives, middle management, or the individual contributors—some folks won't want to see the implications because they are on their way out, have settled in, don't care, disagree, or are distracted. Some will have a habit of just going along, doing only what is required of them but never getting deeply involved. For these people, the move into action—especially pervasive change—may shake the foundations of their work world with the power of an earthquake. For all the people in the organization who are experiencing a healthy dissatisfaction with the status quo, the move into action should be exciting and welcome. Even so, successful change leaders are respected and admired more often than they are loved.

The crossover moment from Preparation to Implementation differs, depending on the type of change involved. In a merger, it's once the deal has been approved by all the regulatory bodies and signed by the leaders of the respective companies. At that point, the new logo and slogan can be used in advertising. The new signs can go up on the buildings. The new organization can be put in place. The new management team can take charge.

In an internal transformation, Implementation generally begins when the plan has been fleshed out with enough detail to start making assignments. If the leadership has made its case that major change is needed, people within the organization may agree or get excited or antsy, but until they know what they are supposed to do differently, everything is still theory. When vision statements became popular in the mid-1980s, it wasn't uncommon for an executive team to issue what I call a "disembodied vision"—an aggressive statement of aspirations with no plan for how to achieve them. (My favorite example was a client who tried to excite the workforce with: "We're going to be big with the bigs.") Even when the vision statement is intelligible, it may only tell employees what management wants the company to *be,* not what it wants the employees to *do.* One of my colleagues says, "I know we're still in Preparation when the plan has far more holes than cheese. We're not ready for Implementation until we can tell people what to do Monday morning."

The beginning of Implementation may not be clear or consistent across the organization; it can begin in a variety of ways, depending on the particular situation, the style of the leaders, and the nature of the desired change. Having clear lines of demarcation between phases is not, for the most part, necessary or advantageous. Customizing the change process to fit the particulars of the organization is.

OPTIONS FOR STARTING IMPLEMENTATION

There are numerous ways to start Implementation; what's critical is to proactively choose what, when, and where to begin so that you have the greatest chance for success in the required time frame. In some Implementations, all of the methods will be deployed. In others, one may do the trick. Here are some of the options.

Test, then deploy. Stagger the beginning of Implementation by chartering one or more pilots to test the design before instituting it throughout the entire organization. This works best when the transformation involves a new process that can be tested—and perfected—on a small scale, separate from or parallel to the rest of the organization. Examples: A new team-based approach to customer service that can be deployed for a single brand or product line; a new manufacturing process that can be tested on small runs of a new product.

Build behavior first. To demonstrate that the organization can succeed, focus on a single objective that involves people throughout the organization. This is the reverse of a coach who says: "You gotta have a winning attitude!" The "behavior first" method works best when the downtrodden are saying, "You help me win, then you'll be amazed at my attitude." This approach is useful in organizations where change is believed to be impossible. When Ray Alvarez took over Micro Switch, he first focused the attention of his management team on one important goal: on-time product delivery.

Enlist star power or have a public hanging. Assign (or hire) someone impressive (look for high credibility and impact) to head the change effort and/or fire a recalcitrant executive who isn't leading the charge. Either move can demonstrate the seriousness of the commitment to change. Nothing gets people's attention more quickly than a hiring or firing. This move is particularly effective when the "old guard" has been in power for some time and everyone assumes they're immovable.

Convert by attraction. Work through the changes in one division, plant, or business unit, and use their success as a model for others. This is a good approach when the units see themselves as similar and are willing to learn from each other. It's a bit harder if "sibling rivalry," strong cultural differences, or closely guarded autonomy characterizes various parts of the organization.

Planned replication. Start the change process only in a few locations, but seed the efforts with the leaders who will manage the next wave of Implementation. Make this explicit, and provide time for them to share best practices as they go. Knowing they have to implement this process in their organizations will make them eager to develop an experience-tested, greatly improved plan for the next round. Make observation, reflection, and documentation of learning part of their requirements; it will jump-start the building of a change capability. This is a particularly useful approach when the change involves replication (for example, at bank branches) of a system or procedure that is reasonably mechanical and quantifiable, such as utilization of a new software tool.

Implementation is, by definition, an operational phase. It is about defining and managing the implementation of new organizational structures, job definitions, processes, and interfaces. Excellent project management skills will go a long way to reassure the organization. When people are clear about their assignments and expected deliverables, and the processes and performance metrics that will be used, they feel a greater sense of control and are more optimistic about succeeding. Given that many companies have numerous project management professionals, I will assume that readers possess good project management skills or know where to get them.

What distinguishes the change effort from established project management methodology? The scope and timing. Many of the basic good practices are applicable, but managing the creation of a new product is a quantum leap from creating a new organization. This is true not only in mergers, but also in the creation of new companies for e-commerce. In mergers, scale and complexity are the dominant factors; time may or may not be of significant concern. In creating e-commerce companies, speed drives decision making and Implementation in ways not experienced by most businesspeople. In both situations, managing the emotional fallout is critical.

HUMAN DYNAMICS CAN SCUTTLE GOOD EXECUTION

Even great execution can be scuttled by human factors and dynamics that are common to the Implementation phase. It is wishful thinking to believe that plunging into action will solve underlying conflicts and eradicate lingering doubts. For example, don't assume that once a person knows he or she has a job, and what it is, he will be fully engaged and loyal to the new organization. Don't assume that just because he or she got "a good job" he will forgive and forget any disappointments experienced to date.

Other faulty assumptions are: A team that has been chartered will function and achieve the desired results. An organization that has been restructured will snap into place. Oh, that it were true!

I worked with a junior manager who was the leader of a team charged with installing a new computer system—a task always fraught with complications and unexpected twists and turns. As the work got under way, the number of requests coming from users multiplied, even as the team struggled to complete the tasks already assigned. "They want the moon and the stars, but they're not willing to give us even a minute of their oh-so-valuable time," complained one IT employee. Schedules started slipping, and irritation grew. The project manager acknowledged the frustration they all felt, and decided that it was important to get it out in the open. He decided to hold biweekly meetings that would include the IT project team and any users who were having problems.

At the first meeting, he said, "We're going to start every meeting with a fifteen-minute gripe session. Anyone can complain about a problem or a disappointment. We can visit Pity City during these sessions, but we're not going to relocate!" One participant said, "This is the time we all get to say 'Ain't it awful' and 'Poor baby' to each other. Sometimes we get mad, but other times we get tickled or overly dramatic. It relieves the stress." Twice a week, they visited Pity City, but only for the allotted fifteen minutes. The next part of each meeting was a fifteen-minute brag session; people swapped stories about small victories, problems resolved, and appreciative customers. The remaining time was spent on problem solving and determining what to do next. Over the ten months of the project, these meetings helped build camaraderie and confidence among the team members and their users. It was a good way to defuse the stress, build problem-solving skills, and help everyone to realize that they were all working toward the same goals.

MICRO SWITCH:
BUILDING BELIEF

Ray Alvarez chose the "Build behavior first" approach to Implementation. He wanted to increase the sense of urgency within the organization—rev up people and get them to move faster on critical issues. He decided to focus on a single issue of critical importance to the customer—one that would make a difference to them and to Micro Switch. Ray's research had shown that customers cared most about on-time delivery (OTD) and that the OTD rate at Micro Switch now hovered at 82 percent. Customers' dissatisfaction was dangerously high. Fixing OTD would be Ray's rallying point.

From the moment he arrived in Freeport, Ray had been talking with his staff about improving the division's performance of on-time delivery. "Ray wanted to see who the smart people were," recalls one director. "He wanted to see who could understand what needed to be done and go do it." But, despite his pronouncements that improving delivery performance was a high priority, nothing much had happened. On the theory that "people watch what gets watched," Ray decided that on-time delivery would be the behavior-building issue. He would monitor the managers' behavior personally and very intensely, and he would ask his direct reports to do the same. He established a weekly meeting, held every Monday at the crack of noon (no lunch served), to discuss one and only one subject: the improvement of on-time delivery performance. He set a target of 96 percent OTD and told the attendees that the meetings would continue until they reached their target. The meetings were attended by about twenty-five employees, including senior managers and a variety of people who were close to the problem. The group served as a kind of steering committee and de facto project team.

Ray refused to tell the members of the group how to improve OTD; in fact, he probably didn't know himself. Instead, he challenged them to develop their own plans, charter their own small teams, and do whatever it might take to improve delivery performance. Every week, he asked them the same questions: "What are we doing to increase OTD? What did we do last week? What are we planning to do this week? What more can we do to achieve our goal?"

This weekly scrutiny in front of peers was a new and uncomfortable experience for the team members. One participant recalled,

"Ray essentially said to us, 'I'm not going to listen to excuses. I'm going to be in your face on this. I'm going to hold you responsible.'" At one of the earliest meetings, Ray announced that he planned to visit a number of suppliers and ask for their support in the OTD initiative. The head of procurement resisted the idea. "All of our suppliers are under contract," he argued. "We can't make any changes with these guys until the contracts come up for renewal. It's a waste of time to try changing our agreements before then." The debate got heated; the head of procurement would not budge.

Soon after the meeting, Ray decided to use another of the standard Implementation options: the public hanging. Ray advised the reluctant procurement manager that it would be wise for him to look elsewhere for a career. The manager wasted no time finding another assignment in a different division. His departure—which everyone knew had been prompted by Ray—underscored the importance of the OTD issue and demonstrated the lengths to which Ray would go to achieve the goal.

After the departure of the head of procurement, the OTD meetings were anxious and edgy. Said one member, "The majority of us were thinking, 'Am I going to survive this?' We genuinely didn't know what might make a difference to our delivery performance." The tenor of the meetings, however, gradually changed from tense to collaborative and productive. "The intriguing thing about them," the member said, "was that we didn't develop any new tools or take any radical new actions. Because Ray was paying attention to OTD, we started paying attention to OTD. And, gradually, our delivery performance improved. It was primarily a matter of paying attention and keeping a sharp focus. From that initiative, we learned that if we all focused on any problem together, we could find a way to solve it."

One of their actions to improve OTD involved a rather simple and undramatic activity. "For years, we had used a twelve-digit number to identify customers, rather than their name," Ray said. "That number had no meaning to the employees who produced the products. One of the ideas the OTD team came up with was to print the name of the customer on all the order documentation, along with the twelve-digit number. That made a huge difference to the folks on the line. All of a sudden they saw the relationship between their work and the work of another human being, the customer. It increased their awareness of the customer and deepened their commitment to getting jobs out the door on time."

Another simple idea generated by the OTD team was the daily "fall down" report, which showed not only how the company had done on delivery performance for that day, but where it had fallen down on the job. The report compared that day's performance to the figures for the previous day and week, and identified the causes of delays and bottlenecks.

The leaders pointed to a longstanding ban on overtime pay as a factor in poor performance delivery, and decided to lift the ban. Supervisors could now authorize overtime work when it was needed to meet a customer's delivery date.

With these and many other changes in place, Micro Switch felt confident enough to give its customers a guarantee: "If we're late, we'll pay the freight." This simple, tangible signal told the outside world that things were changing at Micro Switch; the company was putting forth its best efforts to serve its customers and would take the consequences if it couldn't deliver.

Micro Switch reached its target of 96 percent OTD within six months. "It was our first success," said Ray. "I wanted to prove to the organization that we could pick something to fix and do it. Everybody rose to the challenge. We had to demonstrate winning behavior before we could believe that we could win. It worked like a charm."

As soon as the OTD initiative began to show signs of success, Ray identified the next action: Clean up the factories. He started to talk about the importance of housekeeping and safety in Micro Switch plants, and he made regular unannounced inspections of the facilities. In response, the plant managers instituted far more stringent requirements for cleanliness and asked for capital to purchase new machine housings, splashguards, and lighting. Ray approved the expenditures, but also challenged the managers of the plants to come up with a plan for improving productivity and profit. They accepted his challenge and worked hard to come up with a turnaround plan of their own. Part of their plan included a long-term program to replace outdated machinery with new, state-of-the-art equipment. When they met their short-term milestones and demonstrated that they were on track to meet the long-term objectives, Ray approved the purchase of the new machines. The arrival of the first new piece of equipment had a dramatic and intense impact and meaning for the plant workers. "We hadn't seen any new equipment in a long, long time," said one worker. "Most of our machines were here before we came to work at Micro Switch—and a lot of us have been here fifteen to twenty years—so it was really special to see those new machines! It was nice to have the feeling that the managers cared about the plant, and about the people who work here. We were really proud and excited."

One of the objectives Ray outlined during Preparation was: "Earn the right to ask employees to make further changes, by demonstrating that the company cares about them." One plant supervisor observed, "I gotta admit I was a skeptic when Ray started hammering away at us about OTD and housekeeping and safety, but he sure 'put his money where his mouth is' and made a believer out of me. Plus, he's a fella with energy to burn and you don't want to come across like a slacker when he's doing so much." These relatively minor actions—meeting regularly, removing a manager, improving on-time delivery, and making the plants cleaner—did not, in themselves, make Micro Switch "competitive for the twenty-first century." They did, however, go a long way in preparing the groundwork for the transformation. Summarizing their effects:

- They showed that Ray was serious about making change happen and was capable of getting his management team to take it seriously, too. The organization saw that he would use his authority and influence to force others to act.

- They involved a wide variety of people from all levels of the organization. This cross-section of involvement proved to be extremely important because it demonstrated that everyone had a part to play in turning around the company, and it gave a larger number of people a taste of the difficulties and rewards of making change happen.

- They showed that Ray was willing to use his spending authority when the expenditures were well thought out, and he would help the organization reach its goals. This respect and reciprocity helped build trust.

- They set a new standard of involvement and energy. Ray showed that he was personally going to work diligently and with focus, and he expected others to do the same. Energy begets energy. People respond to their role models.

- They were measurable and tangible. OTD levels could be expressed as a number. Customer delight was tracked on a monthly basis. New machinery could be seen and touched. Such positive and tangible actions led to intangible reactions: feelings of accomplishment, collaboration, and hope. A new spirit of renewal seemed to be spreading through the organization.

At the time, one of the directors commented, "I sense a titillating hint of new excitement around here. It reminds me of early spring in Minnesota. You have those first warm days when there is still snow on the ground but you know that you've broken the back of winter and warm days are coming."

COVEN:
WELL-PLANNED DEPLOYMENT OR FIRE DRILL?

When the deal papers were finally signed, each member of the CoVen Executive Integration Team (EIT) got the green light to start implementing the full selection process and managing the new organizations. R&D had created subteams responsible for developing all the specifics of the new organizational structure: which capabilities would be required in each area; where the people would be located; what the compensation and new job descriptions would be; how many people might be expected to leave; and what services and severance would be offered to whom. Other teams were chartered to design core processes, review the product pipeline, and identify cost-cutting opportunities.

During Preparation, it had seemed that only a small, exclusive, and secretive group had been involved; now, CoVen became a beehive of activity. People and functions were moving, the appointment process was in full swing, conference rooms were booked nonstop for groups finally getting to work together, people were being interviewed, factories were crawling with touring strangers, and document swapping was straining the capacity of the e-mail system. As one manager put it, "I sure hope all this planning pays off. Right now it feels more like a chaotic fire drill than a well-regimented deployment."

We had started monitoring the morale and confidence of the R&D organization about a month after Marco Trask was appointed, and we continued as the integration proceeded. After every major announcement, we collected data—through face-to-face interviews, short written surveys, and focus groups involving about 20 percent of the population—to help assess and calibrate perceptions, concerns, and expectations throughout the process. These data were critical in guiding communications, addressing any potential hot spots before they erupted, helping to understand how attitudes were or were not changing, identifying events that triggered reactions among particular groups, and measuring their intensity. We knew that we were likely to hit periods of low productivity, confusion, protest, excitement, or anger, and we wanted to be as prepared as possible. Being blindsided was not our idea of a good time.

Our "temperature checks" mostly told us what we had expected to hear; people had an overwhelming appetite for more information. One unexpected finding was that when a particular group was *not* mentioned in a major communication, the anxiety of the people in that group spiked. They read all kinds of messages into the omission, and rumors ran wild. The first time this happened, we were surprised but reacted quickly. We prepared briefing packages for the managers of the "omitted" groups so they could explain why their function or department was not included in the communication and when they might expect information about their group. After that incident, we prepared briefing packages for *all* departments and distributed them to the department heads on the evening before any announcement or communication. As one of our team members quipped, "Planning works better when it happens before the event."

Another key finding during the first weeks of Implementation was that the members of the management ranks felt concern and even alarm, especially after the overall organizational structure was unveiled. Attrition at the top is common in a pyramid structure, but there is more attrition when two pyramids combine. There simply were not enough important management positions to accommodate all those who currently held leadership positions in Venerable and Commando. The Human Resources, Communications, and Change Management teams worked together to figure out how to curtail the talent flight and how to manage the problems that would result from the loss of the "icons" from each organization.

At the beginning of Implementation, only Marco's direct reports had been appointed; now his team began to select people for all management positions in R&D. Marco had decided that everyone would have to apply for a job, on the theory that the process would give people from both companies a fair shot at the new positions and would help generate buy-in for the new management team once they were chosen. Human Resources, under the direction of the R&D Functional Integration Team (FIT), developed a job description and grading for each open position, as well as selection criteria, the schedule for accepting applications and interviewing, an estimate of how long the evaluation process was likely to take, and roughly when the chosen candidates would be announced.

No team was charged, however, with developing a vision or strategy for CoVen R&D. Marco had decided that the vision and strategy, core values, and desired culture could be addressed later, along with the clarification of which therapeutic areas and projects would be emphasized or exited. "We can address that stuff after we take care of the most urgent priority—deciding who has what job. I don't buy the argument that we might choose people differently if we had a defined vision, strategy, or culture," he argued. "We need to focus on scientific credentials; the rest can wait."

Not surprisingly, people responded with remarkable swiftness once the selection process got under way. The executive team began accepting and rejecting applications within days. Some of the selections sent shock waves through the organization. Several physicians and scientists with long-term experience found themselves without a position. What's more, some of the rejected people were from Commando. The Commando employees had been slow to understand that their jobs were up for grabs too, just as were those from Venerable. There was a shift in attitudes toward the R&D FIT team: feelings of distrust and disappointment mingled with the feelings of excitement and pockets of hyperactivity. People grumbled and complained and ran tallies of who got which jobs from which company. Cynical cartoons began to appear on cubicle walls and in public gathering spots. Those who were chosen clustered in their offices and tried to hide their relief and exhilaration. No one was blasé.

9

Broadening the Involvement

Building Bench Strength and Leadership

MICRO SWITCH
BUILDING BENCH STRENGTH AND LEADERSHIP

To INVOLVE PEOPLE at lower levels of the organization, Ray Alvarez launched a process he called "inclusive strategic planning." He asked each department to develop a strategic plan, which the management team would review. The idea was to jumpstart discussions and force people to focus on defining their department's strategy and what they needed to learn and do to achieve their goals. An additional benefit of the process was that it provided a way to assess management talent throughout the division. Ray asked a few of his trusted senior executives to participate in the reviews and rank the presenters into one of three groups: (1) those who were already managing in ways that supported the vision; (2) those who could manage that way with some help; and (3) those who were unlikely to complete the journey successfully. One of the executives involved said, "When the teams presented, I wanted to shout 'Hooray!' and cry at the same time. The hooray was because they had come so far in the weeks they had been working. Cry because I knew how far they had left to go."

Ray took particular notice of a young product manager named Rick Rowe, who worked in the electronics business. Ray's predecessor had characterized Rick as a maverick who could be difficult to work with. Ray saw different qualities. "At the first strategic planning session we had, Rick got up to speak in front of a couple of hundred people wearing a flowered shirt and a pair of cut-off shorts, sunglasses, and a straw hat. He started off by saying that, if we really wanted to go after the Asia-Pacific market, we ought to be headquartered in Hawaii, and he would volunteer to transfer there. This was totally different behavior than this group of people had seen at any management meeting, and it was in front of the senior execs. They couldn't believe he was going to get away with it. But I was thinking, 'This is my kind of guy.' He's smart, he knows what he wants to do, and he has the gumption to do something out of the ordinary. It wasn't long before Rick got his first promotion."

Ray decided to spend much of his time developing a cadre of strong leaders who could help implement the transformation. He identified fifty people—about 10 percent of the managers and supervisors in the company—who, he believed, could contribute the most to the change effort, either because they were already committed or because their current management style and capabilities were what he was looking for. Rick Rowe was one of them.

Ray invited the chosen fifty to a special offsite event at a resort known as Eagle Ridge, in nearby Galena, Illinois. When the invitations were received, the company grapevine went into a buzzing frenzy. Some people who had expected to be invited were not; others—many in positions of less traditional authority—were. In a few cases, the boss was not invited but the subordinate was. Those who were invited felt honored and excited. Those who were not began to wonder what they were doing wrong.

After dinner on the first night of the meeting, Ray unveiled the new Micro Switch vision and mission statements to the group. He said, "Our track record to date shows that we can achieve miraculous results through concentrated bursts of energy. We improved our delivery performance in just six months. But now we seek sustainable performance excellence. I ask each of you to commit yourselves to leading and completing that journey of revitalizing Micro Switch."

Over the next two days, Ray and his team talked with the group about the vision, strategy, actions taken to date, and key success factors going forward. The objective was to share management's thinking as completely as possible. This meant encouraging discussion, testing ideas, adding to them, and, ultimately, creating the buy-in needed to get the commitment and participation of these fifty important players.

In one of the sessions, I introduced the Change Curve and asked the participants which phase they believed Micro Switch was in. Many believed that Micro Switch was still in Preparation. Some argued that the company had moved into Implementation. A few felt there were still pockets of significant Stagnation. It was proof that everyone experiences and views a change effort in his or her own individual way. One executive stated, "It is very difficult to orchestrate the change effort, especially now that we have people spreading out all along the path. We have part of the organization that's way out in front and other parts that still don't have a healthy discontent."

Ray accomplished his objectives with the Eagle Ridge meeting. The participants agreed that they would act as missionaries and translators. Their job, as they saw it, was to help other managers and employees to fully understand and accept the vision and to work diligently toward its realization. They would manage, speak, and act in ways that would demonstrate to the organization that they themselves believed in the vision and were aligned in how to achieve it. In the final session before they left the resort, Ray dubbed the participants as "Eagle Visionaries" and promised that they would gather for similar retreats twice each year. He knew he needed this group and he was aware that they would need to be refueled and refreshed.

The group returned to work all fired up. Rick Rowe recalled, "Some months before, I had been given the task of transforming my part of the organization from its present state into some undefined world-class operation, but I wasn't given any real training or tools to do the job. At Eagle Ridge, for the first time, I felt like there was some method to the madness. The meeting generated camaraderie and trust. Following that meeting, the degree of cooperation between functions at the director level improved substantially. In fact, it was the best it had ever been in my years at Micro Switch."

By sharing his feelings and information with this core group, which made them feel valued and honored, and by asking for their help with the tangible tasks of Implementation, Ray created a powerful force for change. Not only did he now have fifty new allies (albeit with varying degrees of commitment and understanding), he also knew that, through them, he could reach out to the rest of the organization.

MAKING AN OFFER THEY COULD REFUSE—OR NOT

As he basked in the success of Eagle Ridge, it became clear to Ray that it was time to focus on the flip side of the management development task—trimming his management team. When the strategic planning sessions were complete, his team agreed that a number of individuals needed a lot of help, and some would be unlikely to make the cut, even with help. But Ray was reluctant to simply move or remove these directors and managers; they had, after all, met the division's performance expectations in the past and he felt that Honeywell owed them the opportunity to succeed. He called a meeting of all managers and supervisors and explained how he wanted the business to be run, and how that vision would alter their roles and responsibilities. "For example," he said, "I expect you all to be directly responsible for communications within your work groups. I want you to ensure that your people understand critical information, such as customer needs and competitive threats." Ray concluded the meeting by inviting people who felt that they could not, or did not want to, do the job as it was now being constructed to meet with him privately. "If you come to me now, I will see that you get another job within Micro Switch or another division of Honeywell," he promised them. Then he added, "But if you don't meet with me and I find that you're not doing the job as outlined, there are no such guarantees."

It was a dramatic moment, and a fair offer. Within the next few days, several managers, including some at the highest level, met with Ray and asked for new assignments. "We had a few people who clearly couldn't articulate their ideas. They didn't have the strategic focus or the capability to develop a strategy. We couldn't have them leading our teams. Their careers got changed. Many of them are still with us, doing their jobs well but not at a director or vice president level."

About a year later, Ray spoke to the group again and repeated his offer. "We've been working hard for a year to implement the changes needed to transform Micro Switch. Now that you know firsthand what is expected of you, I'd like to reissue my offer. If you're having difficulty fulfilling the demands we're placing on you, for whatever reason, come see me." This time, a larger number of managers and supervisors took Ray up on his offer and were reassigned. As a result, Ray thinned his management ranks by about 35 percent over a two-year period without having a layoff. This thinning had several benefits; for example:

1. It removed the people who might slow or obstruct the change process—and did so with grace and affirmation.
2. It was a highly visible activity. The rest of the organization could not help but notice that people were being moved or

removed. Those who had been opposed to the changes found themselves required to rethink their positions.

3. It made the 65 percent who remained feel more exposed and more valued. They realized that they would be expected to perform and probably shoulder more leadership responsibility than ever before. And they felt that they were among the "chosen."

GO FOR LOVE BUT REQUIRE BEHAVIOR

During Implementation, you sometimes have to use action to gain understanding and commitment, rather than starting with a base of understanding and expecting that it will lead to a willingness to act.

This was demonstrated to us when we worked with an industrial equipment company, HeavyDuty Industries. We were engaged to help them dramatically improve their order fulfillment process and reduce the time from order to delivery. In particular, they wished to speed up their production and delivery of special orders, because they wanted to be able to charge a healthy premium for fast delivery on customized orders. Considering that HeavyDuty made high-ticket components—averaging hundreds of thousands of dollars each—the premiums could have a significant positive impact on the bottom line.

The change did not involve a complete transformation of the company, but employees in the marketing and sales groups had to understand the new procedures and premium charge rates, and those in procurement, manufacturing, logistics, and IT needed to conduct their work in fundamentally new ways. We had worked with client teams not only to develop the new special-order process, but also to complete the work necessary to support the process in the factories, warehouses, and IT systems. We were well into Implementation but were not getting the results we wanted and expected. To find out why, we decided to talk with the order entry clerks.

We met with them and immediately discovered that they were not committed to the change. In fact, they had attitudes and beliefs that had not been addressed and could soon completely scuttle the

Implementation efforts. In particular, we learned that the clerks suspected that the real purpose of the rapid-response process was to eliminate their jobs. That surprised us because a layoff had never been part of the plan. We asked the clerks why they were so suspicious. One of them summed it up boldly: "The more order backlog there is, the more work we have in scheduling, tracking, and keeping the factory and the customers informed. If orders are delivered on time, we'll have nothing to do." This got us into an animated discussion of job security. I said, "Your jobs are only secure if you meet your customers' needs. The faster you do it, the more secure you are. And the proof that you're meeting your customers' needs quickly is to have no backlog." They weren't buying it. It was obvious that they thought of us, the consultants, as the enemies. Why hadn't they heard about all this from their own supervisors? Why hadn't we heard about their concerns? Obviously, communication about the plan had not been very effective.

We moved on to a discussion of the volume of special orders, which hadn't increased even though the process to fulfill them was in place. Why? The unofficial spokeswoman of the group nailed it again, "The factory has been telling us for years that we shouldn't take special orders. It messes up their scheduling. And we don't want the factory on our case." We explained again that changes had been made in the factory to solve the scheduling problem. The factory could now handle the special orders easily. In fact, they needed more special orders to run at optimum capacity and maximum productivity. The clerks still weren't buying it. Who were we to tell them that the factory had changed? They had no proof.

Our next topic was the price increase for handling special orders. At this, the clerks just scoffed and rolled their eyes. They knew their customers well; they knew the moaning and hassling they got from customers about the current price schedule! We explained that we believed the customers would be willing to pay extra if they received their orders faster, because the sooner they got their equipment the more valuable it was to them. Again, the clerks did not accept our arguments. While the organization around them was moving nicely through Implementation, this small band of resisters was in its own Determination phase and had the potential to sink the whole effort. Could we break the log jam somehow, or would they dig in their heels and refuse to use the new guidelines?

Finally, one of my colleagues took a new tack. "Let me ask you a question," he said. "When you order pizza, do you prefer to have it delivered right away, or would you rather wait for a while?" Everyone stared at him, as if the question were irrelevant and the answer blindingly obvious. He went on, "Have you ever ordered a pizza and been told they'd deliver in thirty minutes or less?" A couple of clerks nodded in agreement. "So, what happens if it doesn't arrive in thirty minutes?" One clerk answered, "I get mad." Another added, "I eat a snack and ruin my appetite." My colleague nodded. "So, the pizza finally shows up an hour later. You're mad. You're not hungry anymore. The pizza's cold." Everybody was imagining the situation now, and feeling a little angry at the imaginary pizza delivery guy. "OK. What if you called the pizza place and they gave you some delivery options: (1) They'd get it to you in an hour at a discount price. (2) You could get delivery in 45 minutes at the regular price. Or (3), you could choose their new Pizza Pronto Express Delivery service—delivery is guaranteed in twenty minutes, and the pizza is packed in a new ultra-insulated container that keeps it piping hot. For that, you pay an extra dollar. If it's late, you get the pizza free." Everybody started nodded and wishing the service were available in their area. "Well, if you'd pay another dollar for a ten-dollar pizza to get it when it is of most value to you, don't you think your customers would pay more if you could deliver their four-hundred-thousand-dollar piece of equipment when they really need it? Every day it's late is costing them money!"

The clerks began to acknowledge the possibility that this could be true. But we couldn't hope to change in an hour the beliefs and attitudes that had been developed over a period of years. We asked the clerks if they would be willing to try an experiment for a short period of time, to see whether the new special-order process could work. If it did, we knew it would change their beliefs. They finally agreed. They would implement the new approach for special orders for a trial period of three months. We checked in with them six weeks later. "The customers love our special-order service," the spokeswoman told us. "What's more, they don't mind the premium at all. They say it's about time we cared more about their problems than worrying about our factory!" Management was also pleased. At the end of the quarter, profits had risen 26 percent on the same volume. To reward and reinforce their efforts, the clerks were given a percentage bonus for new Special Delivery service orders. Everybody won.

In this case, the clerks went through the Change Curve on their own schedule, apart from the rest of the organization. When we first met them, they were stuck. They had understood the need to change as it was explained during Stagnation, and they knew that changes were being implemented. But no one had translated the overall change message into what it meant to their specific tasks. They had made only a few modest changes during Implementation; they hadn't wholeheartedly embraced it. At the time of our meeting (and the pizza story), they were in Determination. After they experimented with the new procedures and experienced success both internally and with the customers, they moved rapidly into Fruition.

The most important point of the HeavyDuty story is that many people in the organization will not become part of the change until they really understand what is being asked of them, why it's required, and how they will win under the new rules. Their resistance may stem from lack of understanding or conflicting beliefs. (The clerks thought they were protecting their jobs and supporting the factory by not adopting the new procedures.) All too often, no one works with specific subgroups—walking them through the desired actions, taking questions, and helping them to deal directly with their concerns. Often, when this is done, the resistance melts or useful adaptations are made. At other times, people are coaxed or prodded into action first; their beliefs and attitudes change after success is experienced. We want people's excitement and enthusiasm, and the sooner the better. But sometimes, only after doing what's required—and seeing that it works—will attitudes change and enthusiasm build.

WHEN THE NEW WORLD REALLY IS NEW: EMBRACING E-COMMERCE AT A CLICK AND MORTAR

When transformation involves embracing a fundamentally new business, such as initiating e-commerce activities in a traditional company, the change may require profound adjustments—new ways of thinking and the speed of decision making and acting are two typical modifications.

The speed at which e-commerce ventures must move is overwhelming, and the sheer energy and stamina required are staggering. Instead of having months for analysis and strategy creation, both must be done in weeks. Formation of the organization must be completed in months. When consortia are formed, the new entity is brokered, staffed, funded, and operating in less than a year. One executive who is in charge of the e-commerce start-up for his Old Economy company said, "Mere urgency is not enough; we need to think emergency. If we don't transform ourselves, and do it fast, we will not survive. Meanwhile, the world we want to create will be inhabited by others!" This means that all the phases of the Change Curve become condensed and may overlap more than in other types of transformations.

Two of my BCG colleagues, Grant Freeland and Scott Stirton, have closely studied the culture and management profile needed to succeed in e-commerce. In analyzing one failed attempt at creating a click and mortar, they concluded that the company "lacked the bias to action and willingness to take risks that are essential in the e-commerce environment. What's more, the culture and processes of the new business mirrored those of the traditional organizations—minimal stock options, traditional management processes, and, in the words of one participating manager, 'a culture that is too similar to that of the mother ship.' As a result, the business has not achieved traction."

As more and more traditional companies get involved in e-commerce, the ability to leverage the assets of the existing organization through the new channels becomes increasingly important. In such cases, it will be as difficult to get the members of the click organization to adjust their behavior to the ways of the mortar company as it was in reverse. There will be a nexus of the two enterprises, and it must be staffed by people who can embrace both cultures. My colleagues, in their paper "Organizing for E-Commerce" call them "guerilla networkers"—people who know how the traditional business works, have a network to make things happen, and understand the needs and methods of the e-commerce venture as well. They describe the situation at a large Canadian bookseller:

> A critical component of the leveraging strategy is getting salespeople to direct customers to in-store kiosks where they can search for out-of-stock books on-line. The company made a veteran salesperson head of sales in the on-line venture. Her knowledge of the traditional business and her personal relationships with key [mortar] players allowed her to communicate the potential value of the new on-line offering to the in-store staff and build active support for the on-line strategy.

Although the speed and the novelty of this change were greater, the method is similar to how Ray Alvarez used his fifty top influencers. The key is to identify the people who have the potential to understand and embody the desired change, and to have them demonstrate to others how it can work.

HARRY WINSTON: CONVERTING A KEY OBSTRUCTIONIST

Sometimes a single individual can play an important role in championing or obstructing the change process. Every champion should be treasured, recognized, and supported. The obstructionists, however, often require far more effort to contain or convert. They often are important—but negative—influencers. If they can be brought around, they can become extremely powerful allies for the cause. A cynic who becomes a proselytizer has a tremendous impact on the rest of the organization. People see that this great doubter has been convinced, so who are they to argue? A converted rebel is often the best ally a leader could ever hope for.

One of my clients, an equipment components manufacturer, decided to reinvent itself. The company had always competed on cost; now it wanted to take the leadership position in value-added, custom-designed work. For the Reinvention Initiative, the staff members had to rethink all of their assumptions and ways of operating. This was particularly critical in manufacturing, where they wanted to get ideas from the line workers as well as the engineers. This was going to be a challenge for the factory supervisors who believed that their success could only be achieved by being tough taskmasters. The environment in the plant had always been "Don't speak unless spoken to," so to solicit ideas for product and process improvements would not be an easy transition.

The vice president of manufacturing, Harry Winston, epitomized the "old way," and he was a key—if unwitting—obstructionist. He was a lean man, tall, with gray hair, wild black eyebrows, and piercing green eyes. When he stood near me, I felt like a vulture was looking down on me, waiting for me to die. His boss had suggested that we meet to talk about the culture in the plants and how to design the necessary changes. When I came into his office for our first meeting, Mr. Winston did not get up. In fact, he didn't even bother to look up. He mumbled, "Sit down" and kept doing whatever he was doing. Fifteen minutes later, during which time I assumed I was supposed to be repenting for my sin of intruding on his busy day, he finally looked up and gave me a visual appraisal. His inspection seemed to confirm his expectation; I was a waste of time.

"I have a daughter about your age."

Immediately I felt sorry for her.

"Most people in your line of work are psycho-babblers and charlatans," he went on. "I think this culture stuff is a lot of baloney."

Thus started a relationship that was strained and startling.

Two months later, I walked into Mr. Winston's office to update him on some work I was doing with the plant supervisors on the Reinvention Initiative. Considering our history to date, I wasn't looking forward to our session. However, for some reason, he seemed amused that day and eager to share whatever it was that tickled him. I was eager for any possible diversion, so I inquired if something funny had just happened.

"Yeah, I always enjoy seeing how my managers react when they bring me a problem." Seeing my confusion he continued, "You see, it's like this. Whenever someone brings me a problem, I give them a hard time—to see what they'll do. The lead supervisor just came in here to tell me that one of the lines in the factory is having a recurring quality problem, and they may have to shut the line down if they can't figure out how to fix it before the next shift starts. I got mad, grilled him on what he'd done so far, and then told him to stop wasting my time when he should be out on the line fixing the problem. He turned bright red, got quiet, and left."

"What's funny about that?" I asked with unmasked incredulity. "Did he deserve to be grilled and insulted, or is it just part of your routine?"

"I always do that; it's how I prioritize," he answered.

I thought, this makes no sense to me whatsoever. So I said, "I'm sorry but you'll have to explain this to me because I'm not following you at all."

He gave me a condescending look but went on to explain. "It's really very simple. When someone brings me a problem, I give them the third degree. If they go away and I don't hear any more about it, then it's one less monkey on my back. But if they come back again and ask for my help, then I know it's serious and I'll help them. It's a quick way to prioritize problems."

"But don't you worry that, because you always give them a hard time, people will stop coming to you and you won't know about a problem until it gets too big to hide?"

"No, because one of the cardinal rules around here is 'No surprises.' They know if they *don't* tell me they'll be worse off. Besides, those who have come back a second time have learned that I will help them."

"So, basically," I ventured, "your managers either get yelled at a little or a whole lot, and only the brave survive."

"Right," he smiled. "Only the strong survive and you need to be strong to run a plant. It's good development for them and it helps me rank their performance."

No wonder the plants were having such a hard time adjusting! Harry Winston's personal style of management was the opposite of what we wanted, yet he was the man in charge. His chief lieutenants often complained, "Harry just doesn't get it." Harry had agreed with the analysis and the action plan of the Reinvention Initiative. He had committed himself wholeheartedly to it, but had not recognized that he himself would have to change. He had preached convincingly about the need to change, endorsed the plan, and participated in all the activities required. His organization was, in fact, making the required changes. When Harry walked through the plant, he noticed that his managers had started acting differently. They seemed enthusiastic. They were having more conversations with each other, and with the workers, than ever before. Workers from one line were often visiting with those on another. He even saw some folks from different shifts coming in for meetings or staying late. He saw engineers clustered at machines with the operators. He noticed, but never joined in himself or inquired what all the talk was about.

While his organization was heavily involved in the Implementation phase, Harry Winston was in a state of personal Stagnation. He had been stagnating for years and hadn't realized it. He had not seen himself as others saw him nor had he realized the effect he had on others. He needed a personal wake-up call.

About three months into the project, Harry surprised me by asking me to come see him. When I did, he got up from his desk, thanked me for coming, and closed the door. I was now on full alert.

"You've been working with some of my guys in the plant," he said. "I don't know what you did, but I like the results. I figure if you can help them, you can help me." He sighed heavily and then went on to explain that during his annual review he had gotten severely criticized for his leadership. His boss had said, "What we need in this company is teamwork, trust, creativity, and a high degree of collaboration. Your style doesn't promote that kind of environment. Most of your people are so busy covering their tracks that they never volunteer ideas or take risks. Harry, do whatever you need to do to fix this, and we'll review your progress in three months."

We sat quietly for a few moments. It seemed there was still more to the story. In a very subdued voice he went on to say, "And my wife told me the other night that we either go to therapy or she's going to leave me." He looked up momentarily with a brief, sad smile. "Of course I told her I'd be glad to help her out by going to therapy with her," he joked. Then looking down again he said, "But, of course, I know it's about me. I never meant to hurt my wife or to instill fear in my employees. I just didn't realize. . . . "

Harry and I spent a long time that afternoon going over his past history, his perceptions, and what he wanted going forward. One of the things we talked about was the fact that intention does not equal effect. A person may intend one thing and yet cause a totally different response in someone else. I had come to believe this was the case with Harry. I illustrated my point by describing an interaction I had witnessed between Harry and his general supervisor a week before. I had been sitting in Harry's office while he was finishing some work. The general supervisor walked in to tell him about a problem they were experiencing and what he was doing about it. Harry didn't look up. He grunted a few times as the supervisor went through the details. When the supervisor had finished, Harry looked at him and said, "That's why we pay you the big bucks." And then he looked down at his paperwork again. The supervisor looked at me, rolled his eyes, and left the room.

I followed him out of the room, intending to ask him how he felt about that interaction. Before I could say anything, he immediately started in, "You see, Jeanie, you see what I mean? The guy doesn't even look at me! He gives me no feedback and no help. He either grunts or gives me some smart-ass remark! He knows a ton about the business and this plant, but working for him is a royal pain!" I went back to Harry's office and asked him what he thought happened between him and the supervisor. He said, "I showed him that I trusted him."

Harry's intentions were positive: to demonstrate trust in the supervisor's judgments and affirm his actions. But the effect was all negative. The supervisor didn't feel affirmed at all. He felt alienated, discounted, and dismissed. Harry was totally unaware of the enormous disconnects between his intentions and others' reactions. He never stopped to concentrate on the other person, to see their reactions, to be sure that what he intended was having the desired effect. And he certainly never asked. He had always assumed that what he intended was what resulted—some superhuman version of cause and effect. He thought that the principles of engineering, which he loved, applied to people too. If things didn't seem to work out, it was because someone wasn't acting rationally or was stupid.

"Let's use your analogy to think about this," I said to Harry. "Haven't I heard you talk, any number of times, about different machines in the factory and how quirky they become over time and how it takes a really good operator to make those machines produce at optimal levels?"

"Sure. Most machines wear in different ways or develop their own patterns, but a good operator can compensate for that."

"How does an operator learn to do that?" I asked.

"Well," he said, warming to a subject for the first time that afternoon. "Those guys and gals work with those machines all the time.

Some of them are on only one machine all day, every day. Others may operate a variety of machines but they do it day after day. They learn what every little sound means. They know those machines inside and out."

"Hmmm, would you say they pay close attention to how the machines react to different interventions? That they listen for responses as well as watching output and monitoring the SPC [Statistical Process Control] charts?"

"Of course. They have to know what works and what doesn't. It's not rocket science, Jeanie. It's just paying close attention."

"So, Harry, if you paid that kind of attention to the people who report to you, do you think you'd learn how to help them reach optimal output?" He seemed struck by the thought.

Harry had experienced the kind of personal crisis that provides an opportunity for reassessment and major change. We continued to work together for the next three months, during which time Harry became living proof of one of my beliefs about change: "If it doesn't hurt you at some point, you probably aren't doing it." Not everyone takes advantage of those painful opportunities, but Harry did. He started focusing on the people around him: their particular skills and needs, their primary attributes, and how they could best contribute. He worked to help them perform optimally. His style evolved from the stern taskmaster and authority figure to learner, coach, and teacher. It wasn't quick and it wasn't easy. We spent a lot of time debriefing after meetings and thinking through what he could have done better. He actively sought feedback from his peers and subordinates. He had to find new ways to channel his smart aleck streak and learn to think before he reacted.

Learning a whole new way to work energized Harry, as did learning to relate differently. And the results pleased him no end. Not only did his boss notice and affirm the effort he was making, he and his managers became a cohesive team that actually had fun working together. They were highly innovative and started a renaissance within manufacturing. Best of all, he and his wife experienced a renaissance within their marriage.

Three years later, when Harry was promoted to a job in another division, his team gave him an award that said, "With appreciation to Harry Winston—Diplomat, Teacher, Leader—We will miss you."

Organizational change always involves personal change.

10

Keep Talking

Formal and Informal Networks of Communication

COMMUNICATION TAKES ON new importance during Implementation; in its own way, it becomes an operational issue, absolutely necessary to keeping the change effort on track and to ensuring that each part knows what the other is doing so the work stays coordinated and mutually reinforcing.

An organization communicates through many channels and streams, some formal and many informal. Most of the everyday work of an organization gets done primarily through the informal networks—a labyrinth of conversations between individuals and among groups who talk with each other on the telephone, via e-mail, and in ad hoc meetings and hallway chats. These networks get built over time. Each individual creates relationships with other individuals with whom they work, share information, and, ideally, trust.

WHEN NETWORKS ARE DISRUPTED OR MISALIGNED

In many change initiatives, particularly mergers and reorganizations, these informal networks are disrupted or even destroyed. Susan in marketing can no longer call Astrid in legal when she has a copyright question, because Astrid has been laid off. Bill in manufacturing can no longer meet with Joerg in engineering, because Joerg's group has been integrated with three other engineering groups and moved to a central facility 2,000 miles away. Many of the "go-to guys" are gone and many of the "life lines" have been severed. I talked with a retiree from General Motors who was convinced that this was one of the problems with GM. "After repeated layoffs and early retirement programs, all the informal knowledge had walked out the door. The old networks had been obliterated and now there was no one left who could tell the others how to get stuff done."

When informal networks are disrupted, it takes longer for people to accomplish their work because they must spend more time figuring out whom to talk to about what, and rebuilding their informal networks. When informal networks are functioning well, news can travel with lightning speed through a company, and people know which sources to trust and which to take with a grain of salt. But when networks are disrupted, there are gaps between groups and individuals. People get messages from other people whom they don't know well; they may not be sure how to interpret them. Was he kidding? Was she exaggerating? During times of change, when people are hungry for news, alarmists have a field day; rumors and misinformation proliferate. Leaders who learn how to use informal networks well can gain a huge advantage.

THREE TYPES OF INFORMAL CHANNELS:
CASSANDRAS, NETWORKERS, AND INFLUENCERS

The leaders should listen to and communicate with and through three key kinds of networks during the change process. Each group has a different role; all can be employed to great effect. I call them Cassandras, Networkers, and Influencers.

A Cassandra—a name borrowed from classical mythology by Intel CEO Andrew Grove—is a person Grove describes as "quick to recognize impending change and cry out an early warning." Cassandras are often middle managers and line supervisors—the men and women who, every day, are in the thick of operational action and in close touch with people throughout the organization. As Grove puts it in his book, *Only the Paranoid Survive:*

> They usually know more about upcoming change than the senior management because they spend so much time "outdoors" where the winds of the real world blow in their faces. Because they are on the front lines of the company, the Cassandras also feel much more vulnerable to danger than do senior managers in their more or less bolstered corporate headquarters. Bad news has a much more immediate impact on them personally. Lost sales affect a salesperson's commission, technology that never makes it to the marketplace disrupts an engineer's career. Therefore, they take the warning signs more seriously.

Cassandras tend to be individuals with an intuitive sense of what might happen in the future; they can see what others do not. As a result, Cassandras may be annoying to some leaders; they may sound like complainers or may seem prone to brewing a tempest in a teapot. But a reliable Cassandra is a very helpful conduit—a person who can give an early warning and possibly cause the leaders to rethink their actions or plans before everybody in the organization gets riled up.

In addition to Cassandras, leaders should avail themselves of the type of people I call Networkers. As a result of their position, personality, or natural inclination, they are particularly attuned to the organization, know what's happening and what people are saying, and are able and willing to articulate current attitudes and interpretations. They are well known around the many different groups within the organization, and can move easily in and out of them. I think of these people as "thermometers," because they accurately register the current emotional temperature of the organization around them. Some of them are first-line supervisors or middle managers. Often, they are in positions that might be described as "horizontal." They regularly interact with a wide variety of people across disciplines or departments within the company—a group administrative assistant, a marketing research person, a laboratory manager, a maintenance engineer. Rarely do they work alone or in a relatively autonomous "vertical" work group. Identify the Networkers early in Implementation, and enlist them in gathering feedback; they can be enormously helpful in identifying what is working and what isn't, where each condition can be found, and which people are excited or distraught. With continuous input from all levels of the workforce, it's possible to have a sense of the gestalt of the organization and to know which areas can be leveraged and which ones need more attention.

The third group, Influencers, are people with an ability that the Cassandras and Networkers may not have: They can adjust and change the attitudes and opinions of the organization. These opinion leaders are analogous to thermostats because they can cool a place down or fire it up. At every level of the hierarchy, they exert a strong influence over others. Influencers usually constitute about 10 percent of the organization. Other people seek their opinions and often base their own attitudes and actions on what the opinion leaders say and do. (Some people are expert at managing up, but have little influence with their peers or subordinates, so it's a good idea to get your list of Influencers vetted by the Networkers.)

I once worked with an Influencer who drove me crazy. Every time I reviewed our action plan, he would screw up his face and start shaking his head from side to side. That was a sure sign that I would have to spend fifteen to twenty minutes explaining why we were doing each item and how it would help in the long run. I resented the extra time he took, and I hated it when he started shaking his head. Gradually, I learned that when he was satisfied with the answers he got, he would go out and do what we'd agreed, and then bring the rest of the team and his department with him. I learned that he was indeed an Influencer with a huge following (although I never could figure out why). I realized that investing time with him meant I didn't have to repeat myself with other groups. Although he required more of my time in the beginning, he saved me time and effort in the long run.

Leaders need to identify these opinion leaders, get to know them, enlist their support and help in the change efforts, and work through them to influence the rest of the organization. At Micro Switch, many Influencers were in the Eagle Visionaries group. At CoVen, Dr. Margolis was important not only to the drug development effort but also as a key opinion leader. Marco made the mistake of valuing her for her operational role, but not for her ability to affect the thoughts and actions of others.

THE WALLS CAN TALK: COMMUNICATE AND CELEBRATE WINS

People need success. They want to experience it themselves, and they want to be associated with it. Especially as Implementation begins, Fruition may seem a long way off, and many will wonder, "Will I live long enough to see this succeed?" There may be small daily successes—a productive meeting, an order from a new customer, a word of encouragement, the completion of some tangible deliverable—but people may consider them to be too small to count. At the same time, the big organizational successes—growth in sales, launch of a new product, a rise in share price—may be months or years away. The workforce, lacking nourishment from any kind of success, is stuck between "too small to count" and "too big to see."

It is extremely important to find ways to celebrate wins and successes, no matter how small, as early as possible during Implementation.

People take heart when they see that success is possible with the new requirements, and they gain pride and energy from the success of others.

I saw one of the most unusual and effective methods of celebration at a manufacturing company based in North Carolina. We were working with them to develop a change initiative that would require a series of operational and behavioral changes over a period of several years. The folks in the factory entered their Implementation phase filled with excitement and expectation. They made a number of changes more quickly than the leaders had anticipated. But, after several months of work, it seemed as if there was nothing new to show for their efforts. There was virtually no measurable improvement in overall factory performance, nor had the predicted synergies produced much in the way of time or cost savings. In fact, the workforce had accomplished a great deal, but nobody was talking about the little wins and small successes along the way.

The early enthusiasm was fast waning, and we worried that the workers were headed into an early Determination phase. We encouraged the leaders to talk with the workforce, to recognize their good work to date, and to challenge the group to come up with their own ways of maintaining their enthusiasm. Subsequently, a number of recognition and brainstorming sessions were held. At one of them, a line worker came up with a surprising observation. "The walls aren't doing anything," she said. This rather cryptic statement met with silence, until she went on to explain what she meant. "What if," she said, "whenever a team accomplishes something good, they get to paint it on the factory wall, so everybody else will know about it." After a moment of silence, another worker chimed in. "Hey, that's a great idea," he said. "The size of the writing could match the size of the accomplishment. So if you had a really big goal, you get to write the accomplishment really big. If the goal was small, you write small." The idea caught hold immediately. People lit up, started to laugh, and added other refinements. "We could put a date on every one of the accomplishments. It will

be like a history of the change process," shouted a machine operator. "We'll be able to see how far we've come, and how far we have
to go." Now everyone got excited, including the leaders. The
group decided to go ahead, without any vote or need to get approval from some steering committee. Within a few minutes, the
discussion turned to whether the walls should be painted some neutral color first, to serve as a pleasing background for the headlines to
come. They decided yes, and chose light blue, the color of the University of North Carolina.

The blank wall, with its bright color and silent challenge, perked
people up. Within the first week, the first headline appeared. It was
written in white letters about six inches high: PICNIC AREA
PLANTINGS AND CLEAN-UP COMPLETE. No big deal, and no
great contribution to the ultimate goal of a factory turnaround. But
the size of the accomplishment didn't matter. It showed that a task had
been undertaken and successfully completed. People could go to the
picnic area to look at the plantings, and praise their colleagues for their
work (as well as enjoy an enhanced lunch site). The positive energy
that simple phrase released flowed through the factory. Over the next
several months, the wall gradually became filled with small and
medium-size accomplishments. Every time a team appeared at the wall
with paintbrushes, people came to watch the painting and congratu-
late the members of the team. Sometimes the team hosted a little
party. The company executives and factory visitors often came to see
the wall and admire the creativity and results of the teams' efforts. No
approval process was required to post an accomplishment on the wall,
and no official committee determined how big the letters should be.
The teams assessed the value of their own accomplishments and no one
ever complained about their self-judgments. The most memorable day
at the wall came when a team painted, in bright purple letters two feet
high: FABRICATION CUTS CYCLE TIME BY 40%. A cheer re-
sounded throughout the factory. After four months, the wall was so
crammed with accomplishments it became necessary to paint a
second wall.

The Determination phase did come, due to a regulatory change that stalled a major new product introduction. It meant that the reinvestment funds the factory was expecting would be delayed for at least six months, if not longer. In touring the factory, I expected to see a real downturn in morale but, although they were unhappy about the turn of events, the workers were more committed than ever to "filling the walls." They understood what was happening to them, and they admitted how tired they were and how difficult it was to transform an organization without the money they needed. But when asked if they wanted to stop, the factory workers reacted with shock and immediately started reciting activities that would soon have a big payoff. They had come so far, they had no desire to quit. The proof of their success was on the walls.

ACKNOWLEDGE AND EXAMINE THE FAILURES

As rewarding as it is to bask in the successes, it is also important to acknowledge and learn from the failures. And there will be failures: teams that fall apart or never gel, initiatives that wither, ideas that lead to reverses, structures that need to be reconfigured, training that misses the mark, meetings that end in deadlock, decisions that never get made.

Many leaders feel a natural urge to avoid talking about the failures. However, most of the workforce will know when something hasn't worked, so not talking about the problems doesn't buy any credibility. On the other hand, how failures are addressed can make a big impact. The most impressive example I have ever witnessed was at a division-wide meeting called by the leader to review a recent operational failure. He talked briefly about the failure and then said that he had identified the person responsible for it, and wished to hold that person publicly accountable. The crowd went still and silent; you could feel the tension and discomfort. The leader continued, "And I am going to reveal the identity of the person responsible right now." With that, he pointed to the screen. A picture of himself appeared. Gasps were heard throughout the audience. He paused, then explained the mistakes he had made that had contributed to the disaster, and what he would do differently next time. He wasn't the only person who had participated in the failure, but he was the only one who was going to be publicly identified. At the end of the meeting, as people filed out of the auditorium, they were impressed and challenged by the leader's presentation. His admission set a new standard for candor and for taking personal responsibility. It was not forgotten.

By examining failures in a straightforward and intelligent manner, people come to understand that failure can be survived—personally and organizationally. Given that realization, those experiencing difficulties will be more willing to ask for help, and those whose initiatives have failed will be more willing to share their experiences so that other people can avoid similar problems. The focus needs to be on discovering what went wrong and how to fix it, rather than on giving time and attention to the assignment of blame.

KEEP YOUR PERSPECTIVE

The challenge of Implementation is to form new habits. Today, there is a popular notion that admitting you have a problem is almost the equivalent of solving it. Clearly, if you don't admit there is a problem, you won't be able to solve it—that's the challenge of Stagnation. But anyone who has ever tried to replace a bad habit with a good one will tell you that solving a problem—especially one requiring new thinking and actions—takes a lot of work. I may know what good eating habits are, for example, but that doesn't mean I'll think of them *before* I accept a piece of birthday cake. I may be diligently trying to change my eating habits but it takes a long time and a lot of practice before I automatically think "Snack equals apple" instead of popcorn or cookies—and I doubt I'll ever achieve "Tofu is yummy." When you are trying to implement all the changes required, remember that it takes a lot of practice and explicit effort to create new habits.

PART FIVE

DETERMINATION

WHEN THE MONSTER
RULES THE HALLWAYS

11

The Land In-Between

Asking the Hard Questions About the Organization and Its Future

THIS PHASE IS called Determination because the fate of the change initiative is most truly determined here, and because a great deal of grit is required to get through this phase and begin to experience Fruition. During Preparation, people picture their new business world as a goal, an ideal. In Implementation, they may work feverishly to create the new entity. Then, at some point, they begin to realize that they must actually live and work in this new world. And that is when Determination sets in.

In this phase, people ask themselves the hard questions about their current place and their future within the organization. Can I do this job? Do I want to do this job? Do I trust our leaders? Do I like where the company is heading? How does my new life compare to my old one? What is my future here? Am I being adequately compensated, rewarded, and recognized for the seemingly endless pain and hassle we have been through—and may still have to go through? Would it be easier/faster/smarter to start over somewhere else? Would I be better off in a totally different situation? As the reality of the changes sinks in, people gradually (or, sometimes, suddenly) understand that their working lives have been profoundly altered and things will not return to "normal" or to the way they "used to be."

When people answer the hard questions for themselves in a positive way, they can see the value of digging in, redoubling their efforts, and enduring the trials and challenges that are part of embedding the change. When they don't know the answers to the questions or assume they're negative, their effort to change loses momentum, and every action is viewed with skepticism or distrust. Sometimes the first indication of determination is an isolated operational problem. Service levels seem to be getting worse rather than better. The new IT system takes too long to install and costs much more than the budgeted amount. A key executive abruptly leaves. A mysterious production problem in the plant can't be solved.

Such operational problems are easy to see, and people pay attention to them; teams may be assigned to resolve them and to monitor their progress regularly. But such problems may actually be symptoms of underlying emotional problems. Some people are unable to agree with the new goals and won't support them. The behavior of others is inconsistent with the new business model. People who should be working together won't. The original vision may also come into question. The leaders' credibility can get shaky and the followers then become worried. Early successes seem to have evaporated. Getting people to think and act differently is slow and painful. As one manager put it, "Getting our people to appropriately apply the new thinking and come up with the right answers and actions is a real stretch. And to get them to do that over and over again in a wide variety of situations now seems like 'The Impossible Dream!'"

These scenarios are symptomatic of what I call "retroactive resistance." It's not uncommon for people to balk at inhabiting the new world now that it's right in front of them. Suddenly, all sorts of concerns start to surface from the very people who have been champions and sponsors. People who were part of the new e-commerce initiative now worry that the e-venture will harm the traditional business in ways that are totally unacceptable. They start backing away from their own recommendations. One client said, "Actually, Jeanie, I think this situation is so toxic it should be called 'radioactive resistance!'"

The emotional and behavioral issues can prove to be the deadliest because leaders often misdiagnose them or see them as trivial or temporary. But ignoring concerns and feelings won't make them go away, and discounting their importance is likely to inflame the sore places rather than soothe them. As a result, the problems grow worse and the issues gradually permeate the organization. Often, the leaders do not recognize that the organization is in the monster's grip until they are just about to declare victory or have already done so.

The likely result is a plunge into a prolonged and difficult Determination phase that stalls the organization as it strives for Fruition. The change effort may even come apart altogether and take up residence in the graveyard of corporate initiatives—just another one of those things that "never really took off."

The Determination phase, because it is the true test of change, can be an extremely painful experience or can yield the most challenging and rewarding work of a lifetime. Many will say, "I've never worked so hard or learned so much." No one who has lived through Determination forgets it.

COVEN:
A TELLING REACTION TO AN UNTIMELY ANNOUNCEMENT

At CoVen, just as people were beginning to deal with their new working structure, the R&D Functional Integration Team (FIT) announced that the Venerable Labs in Amsterdam would be closed and the facility demolished. All research activities would be moved to the new $200 million DevCenter in New Jersey. This was the right business decision for CoVen—The Labs were inefficient and their equipment and IT systems were outdated.

We had tested this decision with key Venerable R&D opinion leaders at a meeting about a month earlier. They had told us, "This will have a disastrous effect on morale. The Labs are a revered symbol of Venerable! If you demolish them, Venerable people will be extremely upset. You're sure to lose people—if only because you're asking them to move from one of the most livable cities in Europe to the wastelands of New Jersey. Why not keep a skeleton staff at The Labs? Or at least wait a while to demolish the place. What's the rush?"

Marco replied that one of the objectives of the merger was to cut costs. "By demolishing The Labs, the company can save at least $3 million in operating expenses," he said. "What's more, The Labs sit on a valuable piece of property. It could easily be sold for millions more. This single action could have a positive effect on our first-year bottom line of $10 million or more. I can't ignore that," he concluded. Then, almost as an afterthought, he added, "That's money we can invest in drug development programs and equipment. We want to invest in those things that will make us more successful in the future—not in artifacts of the past." Silence. Marco had discounted an emotional issue and trumped it with a financial argument.

Finally, Dr. Margolis spoke up. "Well, Marco, you've converted a question of history, affiliation, company loyalty, and values into a question of money. No one disagrees that the Labs are inefficient, especially in comparison to the new DevCenter. But, by demolishing The Labs now, you demolish a little bit of the company's soul. How do you go about putting a value on that?" A few people actually clapped at Elena's comment; most nodded in agreement.

Marco, however, got annoyed and answered, "Listen, I accept that people have a strong emotional attachment to The Labs. But the move to the DevCenter is inevitable. I understand that some won't want to go because of their personal commitments in Amsterdam. But there are other places they can go within Europe, and an assignment to New Jersey is not forever. I think it's best to make the move immediately and all at once and get the pain behind us, rather than drag it out. I think *that* would cost us more, both emotionally and financially." He spoke with finality, and made it clear that there was to be no further discussion.

Just after the meeting, the FIT team had a closed-door session with Marco to discuss a variety of ways to ease the news of The Labs' closing or at least to gain more buy-in ahead of time. One recommendation was to have a strategy session with the key opinion leaders and enlist their help in preparing the organization. Marco's perspective closed off all discussion. "This is silly. Really, this talk about reverence and loyalty and morale plummeting is 'much ado about nothing.' All this chatter will evaporate just as soon as people see their new space at the DevCenter. What researchers care about is a good facility and fancy new research toys—and this one is definitely state-of-the-art! When they see how attractive the new building is and all the amenities it offers, they'll forget about the Labs completely. Just watch."

Marco decided to announce the closing of the Labs via a memo from him to the entire R&D organization, on a Friday afternoon. The idea was that people could digest the news over the weekend so that it wouldn't overly disrupt the work environment during business hours. On Monday, a follow-up notice, including an article in the weekly newsletter, would be posted on the CoVen intranet site. The plan, however, went more than a bit awry. Marco, who had been trying to improve his relationship with the press, had scheduled an interview to be taped Thursday evening. The interviewer, Piet Jansen, had a local radio business program in addition to his newspaper column. During the interview, Jansen asked about the rumor that The Labs would be vacated. Thinking the show would not be aired until Monday, Marco confirmed the rumor and added that The Labs would be demolished and the land put up for sale. The radio station, realizing that it had a scoop, aired parts of the interview Friday morning. Hundreds of CoVen employees heard it on their way to work. All that day, and through the weekend, telephone lines were jammed with voice- and e-mail traffic. Employees talked with shock and disbelief about the action and the crude way in which it had been announced.

Marco and his direct reports were surprised by the early release of the radio interview on Friday and the reaction to it; they were shocked when the announcement of the closing made front-page news on Monday, not only in the Dutch newspapers, but in the international press as well. It was as if Lucent had decided to shutter Bell Labs, or Disney had abruptly demolished DisneyWorld. The demise of The Labs quickly became a symbol for corporate ruthlessness, insensitivity, and bungling. When the management could close The Labs like that, what else wouldn't they do? Venerable employees outside R&D saw the closing of The Labs as an ominous sign. Marco was furious at the radio station, and especially Piet Jansen, for airing the interview too early.

The Labs incident left its mark on the organization. It was most evident in the work of the task forces and subteams that had been chartered during Implementation by the R&D FIT to redesign processes and develop new systems. After the announcement, task force leaders found it difficult to schedule a time when all the members could meet. When they did meet, not everybody showed up. When they met and tried to get some work done, some members reopened the discussion about their objectives. A few team members quit. When we talked privately with people about their feelings and attitudes, many said they felt like traitors to Venerable; others stated flatly that they thought the integration was going to fail and didn't want to work hard for nothing. One task force leader commented, "I don't understand what's happening. It seems to me people should be jumping on the opportunity to show leadership at a time like this. Instead, I get very little cooperation. I feel like everybody knows something but me."

"Have you asked what's going on?" I asked.

"No," he said.

Despite the turmoil in R&D, however, CoVen continued—successfully—to manufacture, sell, and distribute drugs. The sales force met and then exceeded the quotas for the first six months postclosure, and they were rewarded with cash bonuses. A new drug (albeit, a minor one) was launched, as planned, and was well received by the market. The CoVen share price rose by a couple of points. The new CoVen DevCenter was opened, with appropriate fanfare and publicity, and people began to move in from various parts of the world.

It was possible, during that period, for the change leaders to think that the R&D organization was functioning quite adequately. My suspicions were that it only seemed placid on the surface and, underneath, unresolved issues were churning and waiting to surface again. Knowing how to react at times like this is hard, for both the leaders and their advisers. On the one hand, you don't want to be an alarmist, causing problems where there aren't any or where they're healing successfully; on the other hand, you don't want to bury your head in the sand and pretend that all is well when it isn't. We suggested to Marco that he and his FIT team make discreet inquiries among their own trusted contacts—particularly the networkers and the opinion leaders—to learn their perspectives on how things were going. This simple idea was seen as not only unnecessary but dangerous. "If there isn't a problem, we don't want to create one by asking questions."

Six months after the merger had been announced, we had a review meeting with Marco. He looked tired, but pleased, as he reviewed the accomplishments to date. "I would say the change process is nearly complete," he said. "We've fairly well accomplished the primary tasks we set out to do. Almost everyone has moved into the new DevCenter. Most of the senior scientists have all moved or are on schedule to move. Obviously, they've stayed with the company. The reappointment process is mostly complete. The rest is just details of execution. The bad news is: My team is exhausted from six months of nonstop work. We all have mountains of regular work stacked up, and other commitments we need to respond to. The primary responsibility for the change process now shifts to the line managers. It's time to disband the FIT and most of the other sub-teams and say good-bye to the consultants."

I agreed with Marco's assessment, but not his plan. It was certainly time to give primary responsibility for implementing the new structure and processes to the line organization, now that it was in place. I could see that the leaders needed to refresh themselves and were eager to limit their focus to the business of discovering and developing drugs. I understood that they believed that the Implementation phase was complete and that Fruition was right around the corner. But I also knew that, with so many unresolved issues, it was too early for the leaders to shift their focus away from the change process. Disbanding the FIT and the infrastructure that was driving Implementation would be a big mistake, albeit a common one. Just as Marco and his direct reports wanted to focus on day-to-day work, so did every other manager. But too many details were still incomplete, and no one would own them:

- Whose job would it be to ensure that the measurements being put in place throughout the R&D organization were mutually reinforcing and consistent with compensation?
- Who would oversee the design of the new compensation scheme and make sure that it reinforced the desired behaviors?
- Who would be putting the details on the new key processes to ensure they were compatible with the new structure and business model? Where was the oversight needed to ensure that the new processes were being used and were working as designed?
- Who was going to make sure that all the appointments were made with all deliberate speed? Most people had been reappointed or reassigned, but a significant number were still waiting to hear about their applications. Over 30 percent of the people who had positions didn't know the ranking of the job or its salary structure. Had they moved up, down, or sideways? Who would complete the descriptions of their roles and responsibilities?

- The strategic plan for R&D and the therapeutic areas had not been done, nor had the selection of projects within those areas, so scientists were uncertain about their specific assignments. Who would develop the plan? How would the project decisions be made?

- A few key positions remained unfilled, so some groups were reporting to interim bosses, or had no manager at all. Who would determine the requirements for the new people? Who would lead the leaderless in the interim?

- Although areas for cost cutting had been identified, the savings had not yet appeared on the bottom line. Who would be responsible for ensuring that the efficiencies were realized?

Feedback from the organization showed growing discontent within the workforce, and a lack of confidence in management. If the leaders began to remove themselves from the change process, my concern was that a cynical interpretation would prevail. I could imagine people saying: "Great. Now that the senior managers have axed all the people they're going to axe, and are secure in their own jobs, they're off to other things. Meanwhile, the rest of just have to tread water without really knowing what we're supposed to do, who we report to, and what effect all this will have on our careers." Worse yet, if Implementation was not seen as a top priority of the leaders, forward progress would decline and the obstructionists would have free reign.

I advised Marco that it was time to recruit some fresh troops—involve some new directors and managers to replace some of the members of the FIT—and have them oversee the completion of Implementation. He could appoint a few high-talent individuals to start work on the vision and long-term strategy and have them report directly to him. Then, when he thought the work had developed to a point where it needed further input, he could involve his executive team.

"That way," I argued, " you and your team can get some much-needed rest and focus on other issues without losing momentum, or risk stalling-out, before integration is complete. It has the added benefit of recruiting more people to lead Implementation, which you need. It's very important to change the dynamic from 'Don't be associated with this' to 'All the stars are on board; they're leading the charge.' Plus, there is a hunger within this organization for direction and inspiration and a sense of the future. People really want a reason to get excited and feel good about being here. My concern is that without it they won't make a long-term commitment to CoVen and you might face a second wave of talent drain, far worse than the one we had when the merger was first announced."

Marco believed that everyone in the R&D organization was as sick of the transition as he was, and just wanted to "get back to business." I kept thinking of what a wise client once said to me, "You can't cut your way to greatness. Greatness has to be built by talented people who are dedicated to achieving a shared vision." Talented people always have options. During a merger, the run on talent accelerates as competitors see an opportunity for cherry-picking the best and brightest. Marco disagreed that talent drain was a risk. He felt sure the worst was over.

"You may be nearing the end of the Implementation phase," I said. "But you've got another phase to get through before you reach Fruition, and it's called Determination. The next weeks and months will determine how successful this change process will be. You need to create an army of champions who are willing and able to embody the new R&D organization. Today, you don't have an army; you just have a few scattered officers."

Marco replied, "I appreciate the work you have done so far. And I think you have done it well enough that you have put yourselves out of a job. I plan to transfer all responsibilities to the line managers. We will disband the FIT and most of the subteams and my executive group will spend their time running the business."

And that was that.

12

The Leaders' Behavior

The Importance of Sustaining Energy

Every change initiative will inevitably have a Determination phase, but every occurrence of the phase is different. Some occur early on; others come so late that people had assumed they'd escaped Determination altogether. Some are relatively painless and brief where organizations pull together to "live the change." Some seem prolonged and tortuous, as people thrash around, trying to figure out how to perform and succeed in the new organization. In every case, the actions and behaviors of the leaders have a tremendous impact on the nature and duration of the Determination phase.

EXPECT THAT CHANGE WILL CONSUME HUGE QUANTITIES OF ENERGY

I cannot overemphasize the amount of energy it takes to lead an organization through a major change. The leaders are asked to develop the change plan, model the desired beliefs and behaviors, recruit champions, overcome resistance and inertia, and get people moving in new ways—all while keeping the rest of the business afloat.

"One of the first things that hits you about turning around a company," says Sir Graham Day, former CEO of British Shipbuilders, British Aerospace Plc, and Cadbury Schweppes, "is the sheer energy it takes. In the beginning, all the energy is yours. It feels as if you're dragging the entire organization along, just trying to create some movement, some momentum. Finally, when everyone else is working hard and they're wondering what I'm doing, I know I've done my job."

Ray Alvarez understood the amount of energy that would be required to change Micro Switch. He kept himself from burning out by constantly seeking to engage others in the process, by managing his own expectations of how much could be accomplished in what amount of time, and by staying physically healthy. Marco and his team at CoVen applied tremendous amounts of energy to the initial phases of integration, expecting that they would be able to throttle back within a month or two postclosure and take a rest. When the organization needed them most—during Determination—they were too tired to rise to the challenge and too disengaged. The CoVen R&D executives could have prevented a difficult Determination phase, but they failed to recognize the threat. They assumed that they only had to manage operational issues. They failed to recognize that creating a new organization is essentially an emotional proposition.

DON'T DEFINE REALITY BY YOUR EXPERIENCE ALONE

Change leaders, like most of us, tend to project their own perspectives onto the situation at hand. However, they must be extremely careful to assess what is going on by listening to the "reality" experienced by other people, and not dismissing the perceptions of others. This is an especially important skill during a major change, because the reality of the organization shifts constantly. Particularly in mergers, the different groups of people who are coming together in the new organization bring a variety of assumptions, histories, and experiences that the leaders may not understand or may not have encountered before. Some managers make it a daily practice to listen for others' reality and to take that information into consideration.

It sounds obvious to say that listening to and understanding others' perspectives is a fundamental skill for effective leaders, but that skill is often ignored. I recall a managing director who had regular meetings with his team to talk about issues that were bothering the workforce. For a while, he would listen to their lively and intelligent discussions about how best to respond to this or that issue. Then he couldn't stand it anymore and would bluntly interrupt: "No! That's not what happened. That's not the way it is. Here's what *really* happened. And here's what we should do about it." For him, his personal experience was unquestionably "the truth." Although he got plenty of intense feedback from his peers, he simply could not grasp that different people experience the same events differently, leading to multiple interpretations, and, in fact, multiple valid solutions. Rather than accept this, he felt sorry for those who were unable to see things "correctly," as he did. Believing that one's own experience equals *the reality* is a triumph of the monster.

It was difficult for the CoVen leaders to understand how radically their experience—their reality—differed from that of the majority of the workforce of both companies. Many of the executives dismissed the objections and doubts of others as whining that would soon fade away. "I know people are unhappy now, that's to be expected, but once they are secure in their new jobs, all this will blow over." Because the executives' concerns in the beginning had been focused on which of them would run the company and how their compensation would be structured, they expected others' concerns to be centered on those same issues. It never occurred to them that their prized and highly educated scientists might be more bothered by other issues. They did not recognize that people could sincerely question the rationale for the merger, doubt the motives of the board and the executives, and be unable to see—or maybe even care about—how much stronger and more successful CoVen would be as a combined entity. Nor did they realize that these concerns can linger for months and even years. They may not surface immediately, but that doesn't mean they have gone away.

TEST YOUR ASSUMPTIONS

Leaders often operate according to assumptions that seem logical to them but are not logical to others. I have repeatedly seen that individuals construct logic chains that fit their own beliefs or agenda. Arguing on the basis of logic rarely convinces anyone of anything. Without an understanding of the other person's perspective, there is no ability to present a persuasive argument or to understand the other person's continued resistance.

Marco Trask assumed that the senior scientists at Venerable would relish the opportunity to work at the new CoVen DevCenter. That inaccurate assumption led him to make a serious error. Even when the assumption was tested among key opinion leaders from Venerable R&D, Marco was unable to take their view as valid. The closure of the Venerable Labs was announced prematurely, without preparing the organization for the announcement, explaining the rationale for the closure, or acknowledging the historic importance and significance of The Labs. Marco and his team didn't listen to the concerns of the R&D Influencers, nor did they ask for their help in preparing the organization.

Making assumptions such as these is natural; refusing to test them, however, is a mistake. A change leader who makes plans based on untested assumptions runs a high risk that those plans will go astray—and that he or she, and the assumptions, will seem stupid or naïve in hindsight.

KEEP THE COMMUNICATION GOING

I once worked with a CEO who well understood the importance of communications. He was leading his third successful turnaround and kept trying to get his director-level executives to recognize the necessity of personally and continuously communicating with their organizations, especially during the challenges of the Determination phase. They kept resisting. Finally, he informed the directors that 50 percent of their bonus for the upcoming year would be based on their communication effectiveness. The directors were stunned and immediately began arguing about other issues they considered to be more critical.

The CEO stood firm. "I'm tired of trying to get you to take this seriously. I know that altering your compensation will get your attention. Until you realize that all the people who report to you must understand and buy into what we are trying to do, none of us will succeed. And your people won't understand, let alone give their all to turning around this organization, until they are convinced that we mean business and that we both need and want their participation. We can send out videos and post new messages on the intranet site until the cows come home, but it won't do any good. They have to see you personally, and experience your commitment firsthand, before they'll believe a word we're saying." His VPs grumbled and wondered aloud about his sanity, but they did what they were told. A couple of them were converted quickly; others took more time. The VP of technology said, "Originally, I joined this company because I wanted interesting intellectual problems to solve. Now, I want to have a real impact. I lie awake at night thinking about what I can do to make sure our technology has an impact on people's lives and in the marketplace. I've moved away from direct design so now I have to work through others. I've realized that the CEO is right; if people don't hear from me directly, don't see my commitment firsthand, they won't believe and they won't do what needs to be done."

Knowing what to say, and when, is as critical during Determination as it is during the preceding phases. What those "in the know" usually don't realize is how much they do know that others don't, and how much of that knowledge is legitimate to share. In Implementation, people tend to burrow into their own work lives, teams, and projects, and lose sight of what's happening in the rest of the organization. It's important to provide regular updates, even when there isn't any "hard" news to deliver, to help people make connections to others outside their own spheres.

MANAGE THE DYNAMICS, NOT THE PIECES

The need for oversight and regular progress reviews continues. It may best be provided, however, by a board or committee that reports to the executives. The executive team itself should focus on the gestalt of the change. They need to be aware of the dynamics: how changes in one dimension impact another. Is the compensation scheme driving the desired behavior in the sales organization and in the technology group? Are the strategy discussions resulting in better cooperation between procurement and the e-commerce initiatives? Do the director-level people understand the strategy and desired culture well enough to drive it within their groups?

During Determination, if the change leaders talk less with each other than in the earlier phases, it can get harder to ascertain whether the changes are mutually reinforcing. This is the natural result of shifting focus. The intense weekly meetings have stopped. Managers and directors are concentrating on their own parts of the organization, so they schedule fewer meetings with each other. They see each other only during monthly or quarterly reviews, but even then the agenda is so packed that they don't have enough time to talk about what's going on in their own organizations—what's working, what they're worried about. The change effort may then start to fragment. Teams or groups may even begin to work at cross-purposes. In most organizations, the executive layer is the only place where all the functions come together. If the executives aren't watching the overall dynamics, no one is.

The leaders may also start to tire of the core change messages. It takes a long time, and repeated deliveries, for a message to be heard and understood, even during the best of stable times. Executives who are "on message" are seldom prepared for how often they must repeat themselves before the ideas truly penetrate. They get so sick of talking about the objectives, the strategy, how the main processes work, and what the desired outcomes are, they can hardly speak the words. They get annoyed, begin to assume that people must be stupid or inattentive. Sometimes they will change the message just to keep it fresh for themselves. Worse, they may skip it altogether.

If the organization gets different messages from the leaders, it can choose to believe the message it likes best or to "shop around" for the answers that most closely conform to what they want us hear—just like a child, after hearing "No" from one parent, will ask the other parent the same question, hoping for a better response. The difference between a large organization and a functional family is that the parents are likely to talk to each other every day and compare notes on what's happening. Leaders are not in such close contact with each other; some only see each other in meetings, and they seldom compare notes on the organization's dynamics. Conflicting messages and uncoordinated efforts then continue and become more extreme over time.

CONNECT WITH PEOPLE AT ALL LEVELS OF THE ORGANIZATION

When leaders display a self-centered sense of reality, or make inaccurate assumptions, it is rarely because they are unintelligent, uncommitted, or uncaring. Generally, they do not have enough vertical contact with others in the organization or enough time to stay in touch. They simply are unconnected. They're not actively using informal networks that keep them up-to-date on what's happening and who's saying what. They don't walk the halls enough, share lunch in the cafeteria, drop into other's offices, or invite people to visit theirs. Again, this is not evidence that the leaders are loners, misanthropes, or shy. Rather, they are extremely busy, preoccupied, and trying to balance too many demands against too little time. Most leaders recognize the value of being connected with people at every level and of getting unfiltered information, but very few know how to make it happen without investing more time than they feel they have available.

Making connections does not necessarily require an elaborate communications structure, nor does it automatically consume much time. We've already discussed the use of networkers to improve an executive's "read" of the organization. It is also possible to get "the feel" of a facility rather quickly by visiting. Pay careful attention. Don't zip through with the intention of crossing it off your mental "To Do" list.

Walk into an office building or factory and you'll get an almost immediate sense of the general morale there. Is there interaction, laughter, a sense of purpose, a buzz of activity? Talk with employees in the elevator or on your way to a meeting. Within a few moments, you'll get a sense of their attitude toward their work and/or toward you. Are they relaxed as they talk with you, or guarded and tense? Are they willing to share their views on the state of affairs in the company, or totally mortified that you asked?

I know one executive who used to ask his employees, with a real sense of expectation, "What do you have to tell me today?" He did this at every opportunity. As I watched him, I noticed that some individuals were a little surprised by his question, but immediately started thinking of what they could tell him. Once, a young woman, new to the company, just stared at him and stammered, "Gee, sir, I don't know." He said in a very reassuring voice, "That's OK. When you think of something I might like to know, just give me a call. If I'm not there, leave it on my voice-mail and I'll get it. Thanks for thinking about it." And then he handed her his card. I asked him about his questioning. He explained to me that he had been doing this for years. He had experimented with the wording of the question. "If I ask, 'How are things going?' or something like that, the natural response is for people to say 'Fine,' or some other banality. They don't hear that as a real question. But when I say, 'What do you have to tell me today?' it shows that I believe they have information that I should have, and that I want it, and that I'm not necessarily looking for a 'nice' reply. All of which is true. I need to know the opinions and ideas and general feedback from employees throughout the organization. If I don't ask, I won't get it. And when I do ask, I'm often rewarded with insights or ideas I never would have dreamed of."

In their book *In Search of Excellence,* Bob Waterman and Tom Peters defined a practice they called "management by walking around." Walking around is useful, as long as you stop and talk, and, most important, listen to what people have to say. I had one client, a VP of engineering, who was rather shy. When he was told by his boss that he had to practice management by walking around, he dutifully made the rounds of his department once a month—only it was more like a run through, with *run* being the operative word. He was uncomfortable talking to people, he didn't know how to break the ice or why he was out there. Meanwhile, the engineers wondered why he was constantly patrolling their work areas. They posted a "Spot the Boss" tally sheet on their computers. Anyone who caught a glimpse of the VP got five points, anyone who spoke with him got ten points. If he discussed anything other than sports or the weather, you got 100 points. Leaders need to realize that conversations and evaluations of their actions are happening all the time, whether they're participating or not.

13

The Followers' Experience

Getting People Involved in the Issues

MICRO SWITCH:
THE BUILDING BLOCK COUNCILS

DURING IMPLEMENTATION, Ray Alvarez had formed six teams that he called Building Block Councils. Each was to focus on a specific area: customer satisfaction, quality, goals and measurements, awareness, training, and recognition. Part of the charter for these councils was to get people involved in the issues, and to develop learning tools and approaches for everyone to share. Each Building Block Council was sponsored by one of Ray's direct reports, was led by a manager, and included people from different functions and levels. "We picked high-talent people who would contribute," Tom Ingman, director of Human Resources, recalled. "We wanted them to be excited about the revitalization. We wanted each of them to *lead*, in an individual and creative way."

The Council leaders were given enough freedom to shape the work in a way that best suited themselves and their teams, and to bring their own individual passions to the cause of change. The leader of the Customer Satisfaction Council said that Ray had been "very clear about his expectations" and yet had not been dictatorial. "He depends on a lot of different people to come up with the right solutions. He doesn't try to control us. In fact, I feel I have so much leeway that I always feel guilty that we're not doing enough." The leader of the Training Council had long been a student of management and business change. For the first time, he felt he was able to bring his wealth of knowledge to his job and share it with others.

The leader of the Recognition Council, Rick Rowe, went at his assignment differently—he interviewed more than 300 Micro Switch employees, gathering their views and ideas about recognition. While learning a great deal about the recognition people wanted (mostly, a simple "Thank you"), he uncovered issues that did not pertain directly to his charge. "A lot of people were saying, 'Just tell us what to do, and we'll do it.' But we were saying, 'We want to empower you to figure out what to do.' People get very unhappy and confused when Ray or their group leader won't simply hand over the Master Plan. This tends to slow us down. But I think the only way to get real engagement is to get people involved in developing the plan they will follow."

Often, a specific project within the broader change initiative can experience the phases of the Change Curve in its own way—separate from the rest of the organization—and thus provide a model for other teams and for the organization as a whole. Such was the case with the Goals and Measurements Council. It took three months of work during Implementation for the Council to define six key performance metrics: (1) parts per million (PPM); (2) administrative errors per million (EPM); (3) on-time delivery (OTD); (4) customer lead time; (5) sales growth; and (6) gross profit.

The Council presented its work to the VPs and directors, and said, in essence: "Here are the metrics. Now, go out into your areas and start delivering the results!" As is often the case, the Council assumed that its work was finished once the metrics had been "delivered." They felt they had reached Fruition. But, as time went on, the Council began getting feedback that each director was interpreting the measurements in his or her own way; there was little consistency across subgroups and businesses. The Goals and Measurements Council, which had been on the verge of disbanding, then plunged into its own Determination phase. The Council had to go back to work. "It took the better part of a year, and it was an intense process," said the Council leader, Judy Fox. "Each member of the Council took a segment of the company and worked with them directly until people really understood how their work precisely linked to the metrics. Each team member made informal visits, led brainstorming sessions, participated in presentations—whatever it took to make sure people really got it."

But understanding the metrics proved not to be enough. "We found that people would use the metrics, but—if they missed the targets—didn't do anything to take corrective action," Judy said. "They didn't understand that the point of the measurement was not just to come up with interesting information. It was to identify areas that needed improvement and then find a way to measure progress in fixing the problems."

Such are the trials and tribulations of Determination! What leader would have predicted that people would miss this seemingly obvious purpose of measurement? This realization required that the Council members go out again to talk, teach, and listen, until people understood their personal role in responding to the measurements. At last, a year or more after the Council thought its work was done, evidence of success began to appear. "You could travel anywhere in the company and see the local measurements posted on the walls," said Judy. "You could talk to people and it was clear that they were aware of how their individual actions affected the measurements, and thus the performance of the Micro Switch division. They really got it through their heads that goals and measurements are how we drive performance and that everyone owns a piece of the results." The

Council had, in fact, reached Fruition while other Councils were at different stages of the process—some in Implementation, some in Determination, some still in Preparation, waiting to get started.

At the beginning of Implementation, the Building Block Councils were highly visible and their work attracted attention across the division. Sometimes the Councils met in the cafeteria, to brainstorm ideas and hash out issues. They discovered that other people would watch and listen to their meetings, observe how they worked together as a team, and then pass on the learning to their own teams and Councils. One team leader observed, "Teamwork was our biggest challenge. We had some folks who believed they couldn't succeed if they didn't do everything their own way. But, after a few months, we really started sharing learning across the Councils." This helped as new teams were formed. They could move faster and make fewer mistakes.

Individuals, too, have very different experiences of Determination. Rick Rowe said, "Before we started this process, I think I was seen as kind of a renegade. I always wanted to shake up things, and that was frowned upon. I wasn't having much fun. Now, it's like I've died and gone to heaven. Shaking things up is valued. I don't ever want this to end!" Judy Fox, too, personally enjoyed the new environment. "When I joined Micro Switch, I was shocked to find out that I had joined a company that I came to see as a loser. Now I think of it as the most exciting place I've ever worked. I have lots of flexibility. I can be creative and really stretch myself. Micro Switch is not just changing, it has become an environment where change is a way of life. Changing enables us to change more."

But many other people at Micro Switch felt threatened by the pace of change and by the ambiguity and uncertainty they felt in the workplace. "Some of my people asked to be allowed to leave the Council," said Judy Fox. "They wanted to know exactly what we were going to do and how we were going to do it. They didn't want to be part of figuring it out. I didn't force them to stay; I didn't even try very hard to convince them. Other members of the team did their work, but didn't really get into it the way I did. For them, the experience wasn't rejuvenating—it was just another assignment. You will always have some folks like that, and you need to get them involved, but you can't expect them to get all fired up and leaping out of their chairs with excitement. So you find ways to recognize and reward them, listen to them and talk with them, but don't make them feel second rate because they don't have the enthusiasm you do."

A specialist in organizational development at Micro Switch described the environment. "Some folks believe that the pace of change is dizzying. They can't keep up and they don't even try to pay attention. Other folks feel that the process is pretty chaotic, and they have no personal control over it, but figure that the leaders know what they're doing, more or less. A third group of people focus on the little bit of the process they can control and don't think much about the rest." An engineer talked about the effect of change on individual contributors. "When Ray decides to make a change in the organization or how we do things, it looks to him like a little nudge from the top. But as that nudge moves through the organization it becomes a push, then a shove, and when it gets to me—somewhere near the bottom—it feels like I'm getting crushed."

To understand how people were faring during the change process, Ray sent out a second General Manager's Survey to a sampling of managers, supervisors, and individual contributors—84 people in different groups and at different levels throughout the organization. The survey included questions about the vision, values, strategy, strategic review process, resource allocation, and organizational structure. Most of the respondents believed that management was doing the right things: changing the culture, improving the physical work environment, and streamlining and improving the key processes. Two concerns also emerged: the need to become faster at new product creation and more aggressive in globalizing the business.

Ray was wrestling with his own feelings about the change process and was concerned that the organization might be overwhelmed if it tried to take on the new challenges identified in the most recent survey. He was also worried about the economic climate—his predictions about a looming recession were coming true. And, he felt that he was still not getting enough support and involvement from his people, typical for a leader in Determination.

At a regular meeting of his direct reports, Ray asked everyone to mark, on a big Change Curve chart, the phase they thought the organization was in. He also asked them to write their initials in the phase where they were personally. Most of the group put their initials in early Implementation. Ray then scribbled his initials on the deep trough of Determination. The others were stunned.

The tone of the meeting quickly changed as Ray began to express his frustration with the current situation. "I've busted my chops for over two years trying to get this place shaped up. But a lot of you act as if you're just along for the ride! And your direct reports keep waiting to be told what to do. People seem to think that our strategic reviews are just for entertainment. I've heard people say, 'Let's go watch Ray; it's so much fun to hear him talk and watch what he does.' Well, I didn't start this change process so I could show off. I did it so you and the rest of the employees could learn how to think and act strategically. I already know how to do this stuff! This isn't about *me*. It's about *us* and how *we* rebuild Micro Switch. I can't do this alone. Maybe that's the problem: Maybe you think I can. Maybe I've been too strong, too out-in-front, too forceful. Maybe if I leave, you will really step up and make this happen. Maybe the best thing for Micro Switch would be for me to quit!" With that, he abruptly left the room.

Ray's action had the desired effect. People realized that the worst thing for Micro Switch would be for Ray to quit; if he left now, the whole effort would go down the tubes. They'd always known that Ray could easily get another job, but now, suddenly, they realized that he might actually be thinking about it. They finally got it—that they had to seriously step up their energy and involvement. Ray really did need their help, and if he didn't get it, the change process at Micro Switch would likely come to nothing. Most of them had come to believe that Micro Switch had to change or die, and they had no desire to go back to the old ways. Ray's fusillade made them understand their responsibility in a new way. This change was not just an exercise, it was in deadly earnest and they would have to give themselves to it wholeheartedly. I could see a new seriousness and sense of commitment in their faces as they left that meeting—and in the following months, which Micro Switch spent in Determination.

Later Ray told me, "About halfway through the meeting, I realized that I had to do something dramatic to wake people up and get more of them on board. I was serious about my intent, but it was also a calculated move." Fortunately, the move paid off.

COVEN:
DEMOLITION SPARKS DETERMINATION

Some weeks after Marco's radio interview, demolition of The Venerable Labs began. I mark the day as the beginning of Determination for CoVen R&D. The actual date of demolition had not been announced, but, on the way to a meeting at the administrative offices that morning, one of the scientists noticed a crane and backhoe at The Labs site. He sent an e-mail to the entire company, notifying them of what was happening. A technician drove to the scene, set up a video camera, hooked it up to his notebook computer, which had a powerful wireless modem, and posted frames of the destruction on the CoVen intranet site every few seconds. Word got out around the world, and soon people began posting comments and Labs-related memorabilia on the intranet bulletin board. By midday, when people were at work in both Europe and North America, intranet traffic got so heavy that the system crashed, causing disruptions to business throughout the company. The next morning, the on-site technician reported that he had rescued The Venerable Labs sign and solicited suggestions for what should be done with it. The rush of e-mail and bulletin board postings, containing all manner of ideas, was so enormous that the system crashed again.

When Marco and the R&D Functional Integration Team (FIT) members learned what was causing the network failure, they were shocked. They thought The Venerable Labs had been forgotten. But the influence of The Labs extended well beyond those who had been physically located at the site. In the sixty-seven years of its existence, The Labs had served as a training ground and intellectual center for thousands of talented people. Even those who had left Venerable over the years continued to feel loyalty to The Labs. They knew that being recognized as alumni had made it easier for them to secure new positions elsewhere.

Marco posted a terse statement on the intranet site. It said, in effect, that The Venerable Labs had played an important role in the history of the pharmaceutical industry, but The Labs had outlived its usefulness. The new DevCenter would continue on in the great tradition, blah, blah, blah. The local, then the national press learned of the demolition and the intense internal reaction to it. Marco spent his day fielding calls. He was on his best behavior, talking about the meaning of The Labs and how excited everybody was by the new DevCenter.

Marco ended the day with an interview with the local reporter, Piet Jansen, who, it seemed, was trying to put the worst possible interpretation on the situation. Marco clearly saw Jansen as an enemy who was seeking only dramatic headlines. To counter this, he tried to make light of the whole situation. "Well, you know," he said, "there was a lot of beautiful wood paneling in that building. I hope we can save that and maybe I'll have it installed in the dining room at my summer home, to remind me of the great work of Venerable Labs." This was, of course, exactly the kind of fodder the reporter was looking for, and he used it to the max in his report. The comment was picked up by people in the company and became a rich source for grim humor. People began exchanging e-mails, faxes, and phone calls, and creating elaborate color printouts on the subject of new uses for items and materials taken from the demolished Labs. Many messages referred to Marco's summer home. Many were angry; all were rude and cynical.

Who knows how much time and company resource went into creating and maintaining that barrage of communication—all prompted by one miscalculated remark from Marco.

This was an extreme but not an unusual case. People need to vent their emotions during a change initiative, and wise teams provide a method or forum for them to do so. They also develop contingency plans for bad news (before it happens) because something bad *will* happen.

Although Marco's executive team was surprised by the severe reaction to the demolition of The Labs and the ensuing barrage of e-mails, they did nothing about it. They kept their focus on operational issues, assuming that this too would blow over. Instead, the reaction should have been a clear warning to them. They should have been able to see that The Labs was highly symbolic. People lamented the demolition not so much because they were upset about its physical demise, but because it symbolized their feelings about their own importance and their questionable futures. The scientists and physicians were distracted, disturbed, and uncommitted to the new organization. In essence, they were telling the leaders: "We're not with you. Don't you understand?" Marco and his team did not understand.

Slowly, the furor over the demolition of The Labs abated. People tried to focus on the new tasks they had been assigned, but felt little excitement or interest in the work. The teams that were still in existence became less and less productive. The tasks seemed to exist in a vacuum—no one had a real sense of purpose or a robust sense of what they were trying to build.

Then, a few weeks after the leaders had announced that the change was "complete"—and only a few days after The Labs' demolition—came a bombshell: Dr. Elena Margolis quit and took a job with CoVen's chief rival, a Swiss-based conglomerate called Kloorg. Several of her coworkers called to tell me the news. It seems that she had been approached by Kloorg as soon as the merger had been announced and had refused their first offer, citing her loyalty to her team and her projects. But Kloorg stayed in contact, wooing her, and had finally made an offer so attractive that—coupled with Marco's lack of vision and his insensitive handling of The Labs demolition—she accepted. She took two colleagues with her, was set up in a new lab, and was told that her projects would be fully funded.

Interviews quoted Dr. Margolis as saying, "I left CoVen because the management has failed to articulate a vision for R&D and a plan for achieving it. They are so focused on operational details, they have forgotten to look ahead. I was working on a very exciting new medicine, but I couldn't get reassurance that I would get the funding or attention we needed. Additionally, the relationships between R&D and marketing, and R&D and manufacturing have not solidified. I lost confidence that when we completed our work, the rest of CoVen would get the product to market in a time frame that would make it competitive. I'd rather abandon a project than devote years of my life to a useless effort." Business observers shook their heads at this distressing development. CoVen's share price fell three points.

Marco was upset and even affronted by Elena's remarks and actions. He felt that she had behaved in an unprofessional manner. But, for many of the physicians and scientists, her comments legitimized

Figure 13.1 Major milestones in Coven's R&D Determination phase (elapsed time: 12 months).

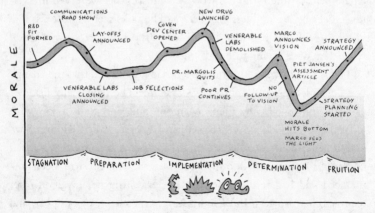

their feelings about the lack of leadership. For the first time, they began to see that their task forces were spinning their wheels because they had no clear objectives; they personally felt adrift because, in fact, they were. They took another look at the information we had supplied about the Change Curve, and recognized that they were deep in the Determination phase.

Within three weeks of Elena's departure, two more key scientists and a senior researcher followed her example and announced their resignations. Marco Trask did his best to persuade them to stay, but it was too late. The scientists founded a new firm together, with substantial financial backing. The researcher went to a competitor. The change leaders, although disturbed by the departure of Dr. Margolis and the others, chalked it up as an inevitable loss. Once again, they failed to recognize an obvious sign of one of the most serious problems in the Determination phase: talent drain. Not only is this a short-term concern—"With jobs vacant, how do we get our work done?"—it has very serious long-term implications as well. If there is a mass exodus of key people, recruiting others will become painfully difficult. No one who sees himself or herself as a star wants to join a loser. If not well managed, the talent drain can put the new products in the pipeline at risk. The pipeline may run disastrously dry a few years hence, or, as Margolis pointed out, the products may be so late to market that they will be noncompetitive.

14

The Importance of Commitment and Values

Developing New Ways of Thinking and Acting

THE COVEN R&D leaders did what many leaders do in Determination; they assumed that they already had the hearts and minds of individual contributors, and therefore made little overt effort to enlist their support or ensure their understanding and buy-in. They announced the new structures, methods, and processes and simply assumed compliance and understanding.

Remember the communication myth: "It may have taken us months to figure this out, but you can get it in an hour." People need the opportunity to try on new ways of thinking. If one part doesn't fit a scheme, the whole scheme is thrown into question. Some managers

are terrific at explaining to their organizations, the context, rationale, and meaning of new structures and processes. But a surprising
number aren't. Maybe they just do unto others as was done to them.
After all, if no one has taken the time to make sure they understand,
they probably don't; the last thing they want to do is try to explain it
to the people reporting to them.

GET COMMITMENT OR YOU WILL GET BACKSLIDING

When the going gets rough—when symbolic actions are negative,
when leadership falters, when top talent leaves—people start to think
about retreat. Maybe this whole thing is not such a great idea, after
all. Maybe it hasn't been thought through; maybe it'll always be this
painful; maybe it simply won't work; maybe now is the good time to
go. What happens if the leaders are wrong about the new plan? What
happens if all the big stars leave? What if we start missing critical
deadlines? How safe are we?

Backsliding has a disastrous effect on the change effort. Allowing
people to gradually return to doing things the way they used to be
done, or to measuring their performance by old benchmarks and
standards, undermines the overall effort and the leaders' credibility. I
worked with a pilot team that had phenomenal success in implementing the new process, only to have their learnings rejected by the rest
of the organization. When the time came to "go live" with these
proven best practices, the rest of the organization was allowed to do
things their own way, on their own timetable. Not surprisingly, they
chose to stick to the way things had been done in the past and introduce only minor tweaks. Not only did their results fall far short of
those of the pilot team, but because each location did things inde-
pendently, there was no way to compare approaches or results across
the system. The worst part of it was, no one seemed to care.

When people work hard during the Implementation phase and
then see their progress dissipate, morale drops like a stone. They invested time, sweat, and sleepless nights in the effort, came close to
achieving their objectives, and then have to watch it all slip away. As

a result, they feel their sacrifices and accomplishments have been marginalized. They lose faith in the overall change initiative and, worse, lose trust and respect for the leaders. They become wary of committing themselves again; they grow cynical and jaded. Often, people begin to exhibit a "righteous passivity"—they feel victimized by their treatment but are not actively working to change it. They go through the motions in a state of suspended animation, not overtly resisting change but not truly participating in it either. Visiting such an organization is like spending time with the undead: you know there are brains and souls inside those bodies, but you can't get them to respond.

STAY INVOLVED

The most dramatic lesson that we learned (once again) from the Determination phase at CoVen was that it is vitally important for the leaders to remain involved long after they think they have set things well on the way to Fruition. It is no good to delegate, to "check in" now and again, or to receive an occasional report. In fact, the withdrawal of the scrutiny and support of the leaders is one of the most common causes of a rocky or even fatal Determination phase.

A similar situation occurred with a well established company, TechnoProducts Inc., which wanted to decrease the time and cost of launching complex new technology products. Although the company had developed many successful products in the past decade, a start-up had recently beaten it to market with newer technologies. The competitor had targeted the premium segment of the market, developed a new product, brought it to market in a period of fourteen months, and gained a major chunk of market share in this new product area. It damaged the prospects for Techno's own new product, which had been in development for more than three years and was unveiled five months after the launch of the start-up competitor's entry.

We worked with Techno for several months to redesign its new-product development process, and we succeeded in decreasing the time-to-launch—on paper—to twelve months. We knew that we would ultimately have to do much better to match the new competitor, but realizing even this time reduction would take major effort. It would require continuous coordination across various functions and geographies—behavior that the organization was not accustomed to.

Our direct client, Robert Ambrose, the chief operating officer, was extremely enthusiastic about the plan and appointed himself chief change leader. After the CEO and executive committee approved the recommendations, Robert moved rapidly and decisively to implement them. His energy was awesome and his commitment was absolute; in fact, his singleminded devotion to the change effort bordered on being manic and was definitely obsessive. He worked seventy-hour weeks, traveled constantly, and was on the telephone or at the computer throughout his rare weekends and evenings at home.

Within six weeks, Robert announced that the changes had been implemented and the transition was finished. When I asked him to explain what he meant by "finished," he listed an impressive set of completed actions: new organization structure, new reporting lines, new job descriptions and evaluation criteria, and a reconfiguration of where people were located. An intranet site had been created for the new process—complete with guidelines, frequently asked questions, and easy-to-understand schematics. It was so complete that everyone in the organization could locate his or her function and specific requirements. We congratulated him on all that he and his team had accomplished.

Then I said, "Now comes the hard part. Now you have to manage the dynamics and align the beliefs and behaviors so that it all works and you get the results you're after. You have to keep up with the changes, to make sure that everyone knows you're paying attention and that you care about the outcomes. You want to be watching the behaviors to be sure that what you've designed actually works in practice."

I was thinking, in particular, of the program managers. In our assessment of the subgroups that would be affected by the new design, we observed that the program managers had historically been "kings of their own fiefdoms." With the new process, they would lose both formal and informal power and authority. The program managers would have to change more than any other subgroup. And while they still remained critical to its success, they saw themselves as having the most to lose. We knew it was imperative for the Change Team to spend a lot of time with the program managers to help them see the benefits of the new process to themselves as well as how they could succeed by supporting it.

Robert did not agree that there was more work to be done. Just like Marco, he strongly believed that the operational changes would automatically drive any needed changes in beliefs and behaviors. He seemed astonished, even a little hurt, that we could doubt the soundness of his efforts. After much discussion, we agreed that we would come back in six months to audit the results of the new process and assess the morale and confidence of the organization.

Six months later, we returned and found that the overwhelming opinion of the employees throughout the organization was that nothing had changed at TechnoProducts. Robert had completely withdrawn from the effort, focusing instead on his COO responsibilities, and one of the old-guard program managers had replaced him—informally—as the primary communicator and nominal change leader. He was, in actuality, an anti-change leader. This program manager's real commitment was to resisting change and preserving or reinstating the previous balance of power. As a result, the other program managers were performing just as they always had. The old informal power structure was running the show, and there seemed to be no negative consequences.

We made our report to Robert. He was surprised, annoyed, and not particularly receptive. Given that he operated in a logical and straightforward way, he had difficulty understanding why the changes he had put in place were inadequate. "This isn't rational," Robert fumed. "The new structure and processes are sound, they will work and they're good for the business. I don't understand this resistance."

"The problem is that 'good for the business' does not necessarily mean good for the individuals," I explained. "The program managers are acting rationally when you look at it from their perspective. Under the new rules, they lose their power and influence. The criteria for project funding, for example, are far more stringent now than in the past. Individual projects have to compete with other projects from other divisions. Now they all share one common resource pool and have to adhere to a common set of requirements to ensure that the overall strategic and profitability goals will be met. The program managers used to have their own budgets; they made all the funding decisions by themselves; they were top dog. Now they could end up with very limited budgets because someone else's projects come out as a higher priority. The program managers are also expected to play a support role to the product design teams, rather than having authority over them. No wonder they're resisting. They only see losses." No one had worked with the program managers to help them see how they could be successful and find satisfaction in their new roles. Nor had anyone made it clear that they would not be allowed to backslide. There were no serious consequences for not making the new process work.

To verify our findings, Robert conducted his own informal investigation, tapping into his trusted network throughout the organization. He heard the same messages from them—that the program managers were intimidating the new product design teams, withholding resources, and generally refusing to acknowledge that anything had changed. Robert also started attending the program funding reviews and had intensive interviews with a number of the program managers themselves. He now had a robust understanding of how individual beliefs and behaviors were directly impacting performance. This caused him to reassess his own role in the change process, and he resolved to work with the program managers to make their transition easier and to take actions that no one could ignore.

Robert set up weekly closed-door sessions with the program managers. They had assumed that he was not really paying attention and that, even if he was aware of what was going on, he wouldn't do anything about it. He wanted to have candid conversations with them about any problems they were experiencing and what could be done to help them. He made it perfectly clear that going back to the old ways was not an option but that he did want to work with them to craft roles the program managers could be proud of.

Additionally, Robert took back the role of chief change leader and chief communicator and he seemed to be everywhere at once, giving praise and sharp criticism. He made project funding dependent on process compliance and made sure monthly report cards were generated for each program. To ensure that the records were "public" and available for all to compare, he published them on the company intranet site. He promoted those who were role models and enlisted other champions throughout the organization. Some of the program managers quickly bowed to the inevitable and started implementing the new requirements. One just got sneakier about his resistance, but not sneaky enough—he was offered early retirement three months later.

All this activity, especially the funding exercise, caused the entire organization to snap awake. Hits on the intranet site skyrocketed, as did requests for training. Within four months, a difference could be felt; there was excitement, belief, and proof of forward momentum. The grumbling decreased as early results confirmed that the new processes did work and did produce the desired results. Our next checkup came nine months later. We found that the new organization and requirements were established and already being improved. People felt good about the new ways of working and the results. The first product created with the new process was launched in thirteen months. The second one took eleven. The next goal was set at eight months, and Techno felt confident that it could crush the upstart competitor within two years.

Keep Physically and Emotionally Fit

Staying involved for the many months needed to push an organization through a major transition takes a tremendous physical and emotional toll on the change leaders. That's one of the reasons why the CoVen leaders wanted to end their involvement with the change activities: they were mentally, physically, and emotionally spent. When athletes prepare for a challenging competition, they must have mental toughness, emotional balance, and superb physical conditioning to perform at their peak. Executives, however, seem to think they can run the corporate equivalent of the Iron Man Triathlon without paying much attention to their mental, emotional, or physical conditioning. I've often mused that brilliance is a terrific characteristic for the executive who is going to lead an organization through a major transition, but persistence and stamina are the true essentials.

Many executives reserve time for exercise—running, or basketball, or workouts of one type or another. But, in most corporate settings, it's taboo to talk about emotional needs; a strong will is often mistaken for mental toughness. Executives must realize that a major change initiative will severely disrupt their daily work routine, challenge their perceptions of themselves, and force them to rethink their future plans. It can also have a serious impact on their personal and family lives—and in the Determination phase, the challenge is toughest. Few executives or managers seem to recognize that taking care of themselves mentally and emotionally is part of becoming successful. Karl Menninger, founder of The Menninger Foundation, which is renowned for its work in counseling executives, encouraged his clients to ask themselves: With whom do I share myself? With whom do I celebrate? When I get sick of it all, whom can I vent to? Studies of people who go through periods of high stress have shown that those with a strong support system fare much better than those who try to make it on a strong will.

Taking care of oneself—physically, emotionally, and mentally—is a serious and legitimate task of change leaders. Leading others is a draining experience; all the energy seems to go out, and very little comes back in. As Richard E. Olsen, the CEO of Champion International, Inc., put it, "No one ever calls you at night to give you good news." Change leaders are expected to go the distance; they're expected to have the answers, to comfort and to lead, to change themselves while everyone else watches and judges. No one expects to take care of the leaders. They must take care of themselves. Thus, one of the critical job skills of leaders is knowing how to give, receive, and ask for emotional support. When we look at the emotional toll that leadership can take, we realize that trusted relationships are of bedrock importance. Rather than seeing personal or family time as something to be sacrificed during the transition, it becomes a stabilizing force that keeps the leaders nourished and grounded.

COMMUNICATE AND LEARN THROUGH MIDDLE MANAGERS

When Determination gets ugly and the urge to backslide sets in, the leaders will need a network of middle managers and first-line supervisors to help them through. As we have discussed, change leaders must create champions and leaders at every level of the organization. It isn't necessary to enlist everybody, but you do need critical mass. If other people are not engaged along the way, the chances are high that the leaders will give out before the momentum is strong enough to carry the organization over the rough spots. One master of change told me, "I'm salting the organization with believers. Every curmudgeon I convert to an enthusiast is worth his weight in gold." (Recall Harry Winston, the recalcitrant manufacturing manager who became a change leader.)

Especially during Determination, the leaders need feedback and dialogue to understand how messages are heard by the organization, whether people are inspired, and what, if anything, is changing as a result. Employees are generally more than willing to share their concerns and reactions with almost anyone who asks. Plus, they talk to each other, they "grumble," they speculate over what's *really* going on, and—as at CoVen after the destruction of The Labs—they're adept at using e-mail to vent their negative emotions.

Change leaders should be particularly sensitive to the morale of middle managers and first-line supervisors. They are like canaries in a coal mine. Not only are they good sensors, but their morale directly affects the morale of the "mass"—the people they manage and interact with. In large organizations, the senior executives typically are remote figures whom individual contributors rarely see and with whom they feel no personal connection. The middle managers and direct supervisors interpret the meaning of the executives' messages, translate the directives into specific work instructions, and, most significantly, do the personnel evaluations. A dispirited, angry, or disenfranchised middle manager or supervisor can have a profound effect on the performance of the people around him or her.

These first-line supervisors occupy a unique and pivotal position. They operate at the intersection between the senior executives and the individual employees. They act as a two-way valve through which information flows both up and down. Through them, most individual contributors learn what senior management is doing and thinking, and, in return, senior management learns about the thoughts, actions, and reactions of the employees. By keeping in regular contact with supervisors and middle managers, change leaders can quickly disseminate their messages and get a fast read on the morale of the organization.

Two Tests of Values; Two Different Outcomes

Determination has a way of getting to the root of what people truly believe—as opposed to what they say they believe. During Preparation or Implementation, the leaders should have agreed on a values statement. The process of developing the statement may have been comprehensive or it may have been cursory. Either way, when tough times arrive during Determination, the stated values may come in conflict with very powerful business instincts. Actions that are at odds with the stated values can lead to disillusionment and erosion of trust and momentum. If the actions taken—especially difficult ones—are in alignment with the values, they help to build morale and deepen trust.

The change process at a consumer goods manufacturer, FastMovingGoods Inc., was badly damaged by a values clash. The company, hoping to build sales and improve profits, undertook a major transformation to streamline its operations and improve customer service. Over the years, FastMoving had come to rely on a practice known as "loading." When its quarterly sales targets could not be achieved, the company would "make the numbers" by announcing discounts and special offers to its retail customers near the end of the quarter. The customers would buy more product than they needed, to take advantage of the good deal, and then store the excess inventory in their own warehouses, or even sell it off to "diverters." Diverters are independent distributors who buy and sell all manner of goods at discount, mark them up slightly, and resell them—but still at a discounted price in comparison to the price asked by the manufacturer.

The practice of loading can work for some time, but eventually it goes sour. The customers refuse to go along anymore—their warehouses are full, the market becomes glutted with goods—or analysts wise up and realize that the reported sales growth is not real. And, although the company's salespeople rely on loading, they also hate it—they know it's phony and it can hurt their profit margins.

FastMoving decided that, to improve its customer service and bottom line, it would have to stop loading. That meant taking a large sales "hit" in a single quarter. During that time, the customers would use up their stored inventory, and sales thereafter could more accurately reflect real sell-through. The CEO of FastMoving boldly stated to analysts and the senior management team that the practice of loading would stop because it was not consistent with the stated values of integrity and openness. Everyone applauded the decision. The company did, in fact, take a hit in the fourth quarter of its fiscal year but managed to reduce customer inventory substantially. The share price did not rise, however. In the following quarter, sales were below target. The CEO quietly demanded better sales and profits from his senior salespeople and implied that they should use any method necessary to get them. They knew what that meant: loading.

FastMoving went back to the old days of "playing games with the customer." They achieved their sales goals for the quarter, but at a terrible price—the CEO's credibility plummeted, as did people's respect for him. His reputation within the company was so badly damaged, it became standard practice to ridicule him in meetings and conversations. As a result, the Determination phase lingered on at FastMovingGoods, and people began to place bets on how long the CEO would last.

Micro Switch also faced a test of values, but with a very different result. The recession that Ray had predicted began to negatively affect Micro Switch sales. In the past, Micro Switch had dealt with any downturn in the economy by laying off workers. But, early in the change process, the management team had articulated a set of values, one of which was: "Our workforce is our strongest competitive advantage." There was obviously a very strong clash between that value and the practice of laying off workers as the first line of defense against weakening sales.

"When the business started to go south and the prospect of a lay-off hit us, we really had to fight it out," said Ray. "At one of our staff meetings, Tom Ingman brought out the values statement and said, 'If we believe these values, then we have to do some things to avoid a layoff.' That was a test, because the workforce was watching to see what we really believed. Even though we hadn't published the values, we had talked about them whenever we talked about change. We had talked about how we were going to improve the business and become a world-class company. They were watching to see what we were going to do."

There was dissension among the management team. Some thought layoffs were the only way out and saw no reason to hesitate; others believed that layoffs should be avoided if at all possible. Ray added to the tension by stating flatly that if there were layoffs, they would have to be done proportionately among management personnel and factory workers. In follow-up conversations, his direct reports came to him to argue their perspectives. In the end, they agreed with Ray and Tom Ingman that to take any action that would contradict the values would undermine everything they had done to date: all the agonizing, preparation, hard work, and building. They also hoped and believed that if they could respond to this challenge in ways that would dramatically demonstrate that they were upholding the stated values, the workforce would see the difference, appreciate it, and respond in kind. "That was our biggest test," said Ray, "the biggest test that we had."

All of this was well and good in theory, but something had to be done to cut costs, and personnel was, of course, the largest expense item. Tom Ingman took the issue to the Building Block Council, composed of the leaders of the six Building Block teams, for discussion. They came up with a number of ways to address personnel costs; one was called DWOP—Days Without Pay. Rather than lay off front-line workers, managers and directors would be asked to take a certain number of Days Without Pay during the year. "We did an analysis of how much savings we were looking for," recalled one Building Block Council member. "Then we divided it by the number of management people we thought we could include in the program. Then we worked out the number of payless days that would be required of each person. It came out to ten days a year."

Each person could decide when to take his or her DWOP days. "We could take them any time during the year and spread the hit, so you didn't feel it that much," said Deb Massof, director of marketing for one of the divisions. When the idea was presented to the directors and managers, they saw it as a reasonable solution. "We were pretty well 'bent for the barn' by then, so there was no resistance. It was the right thing to do so that we wouldn't hurt our front-line employees." Many people who participated in the program didn't even take the days off; they just worked a day for no pay. "I remember just being buried with work," said Deb. "I didn't even take my vacation days. How was I going to take DWOP days?"

Micro Switch also created a program called Voluntary Time Off (VTO) for nonmanagers; it allowed factory workers to take two or three days off without pay. Factory workers had been able to take VTO before, but the days had counted as absences. A certain number of absences led to dismissal. "So we said, OK, we won't count them as absences any more," said Ray. More people took advantage of the program, but only for a few days here and there. As the recession grew deeper, Ray and his team saw VTO as a good way to reduce costs further, still without cutting jobs. So, he encouraged people to take more VTO, for longer periods of time. There was little response. Finally, Ray discovered why. "Folks said, 'The reason we don't sign up for longer-term VTO is because we lose our benefits.' So we said, 'Gee, we can solve that. What if you could sign up for VTO of up to six months, and keep full benefits? When the six months, or whatever period you choose, is over, you come on back and do your job.' That got people interested, and helped us reduce costs and manage the workforce better."

Micro Switch found a third way to deal with idled front-line workers, whom they called the "Temporary Available Personnel pool" (TAP). If VTO wasn't appropriate, they would assign a worker to the TAP pool. "We used those folks for all the little things that were on everybody's punch list, but which you can never resource," said Ray. "Some people found new careers out of that. One guy filled in for our photographer when he was on vacation and got so into it that he started up his own photography business in Freeport."

Unlike FastMovingGoods, which suffered from the values clash (and CoVen, which lost Dr. Margolis and others), Micro Switch benefited from its response:

- It showed that the leaders had the courage of their convictions. They were not willing to sacrifice their long-term values when placed under short-term business pressures.
- "Put your money where your mouth is." Their actions showed that the leaders—in fact, the entire management group—were willing to go a long way to protect and support the line workers.

They even sacrificed some of their own pay. This was a dramatic demonstration of how the management team valued the workforce. Instead of empty rhetoric ("People are our greatest asset"), they lived it far more effectively than any of their recognition or reward programs could.

- Managers felt good about themselves: they had been given an opportunity to "do the right thing," and they had done it without complaint and without undue hardship. It improved their morale.

- It showed that management and line workers could work together to meet a very difficult and serious challenge and could do so with creativity and good will.

- It was a palpable and radical change from the past. In the old days, factory jobs were in jeopardy with every gyration of the market. In the new world of Micro Switch, all jobs were as secure as a job can be. All jobs were valued. Everyone worked together for the common good.

The programs worked. Micro Switch was able to avoid layoffs, cut costs significantly, and meet its profit targets. Rick Rowe commented on the success in surviving Determination by saying, "Ray never gave up and he never gave in."

COVEN:
A VISION AND A REVELATION

Not long after Dr. Margolis departed CoVen, Marco gathered his 200 top managers together at the DevCenter to describe his vision for the R&D organization. He came close to apologizing for the clumsy handling of the demolition of The Labs, and promised there would be no more such surprises. He talked passionately about the role R&D had to play, not only for CoVen but for humanity. He talked eloquently about the values shared by all pharmaceuticals people—providing drugs that relieve suffering and improve the quality of life.

His comments were so welcome and so encouraging that morale jumped dramatically. It seemed to the staff that the R&D leaders had learned from their errors, and that the "defection" of Dr. Margolis had spurred them to action. Over the next few days, the leaders noticed an enthusiasm and buoyancy among the managers and individual contributors that had been absent since the earliest days of the merger. Everyone was cheered by the prospect of renewed clarity of purpose for their careers and for R&D. It seemed that Marco was ready to lead them out of the doldrums of Determination and onto the high ground of Fruition.

But it was not to be. People throughout R&D expected that they would soon be apprised of the strategy and overall plan for realizing the new R&D vision. Instead, daily interactions were the same as before Marco's meeting. He and the members of his team had nothing additional to say. They had planned no new announcements, and no one was assigned to detail the vision or prepare the accompanying strategy. The organization's assumption was that the leaders would come back with a more robust explanation of the vision and strategy and at least an outline of a plan for how the vision would be realized. This assumption proved false.

Meanwhile, Marco had assumed that the organization could and would translate the vision into action plans at the local level; he said, "People in R&D are smart people, they don't need us to hold their hands." As a result, middle managers and first-line supervisors felt confused and uncertain about what to do. There is nothing more disheartening than thinking that things are about to get substantially better—after months of misery—and then having them get worse. It is like that standard scene in adventure movies, when the stranded explorers/mountain climbers/marooned sailors see the rescue plane, after weeks of hoping and watching. They cheer and wave frantically at the plane, but it does not see them and flies away. No rescue. At that point, the lost ones fall into despair. They grow sullen. They turn on each other. Someone may get eaten. The same was true at

CoVen (although no one was eaten, as far as I know)—the buoyancy collapsed, and the entire R&D organization fell into a dismal mood.

At this lowest point, we returned to CoVen to assess progress and morale. We did so, and then made our report to Marco and his team. Morale was at its lowest point since the merger had been announced. Among the key knowledge workers, confidence in the future of the organization had dropped from 93 percent to 43 percent. Members of the R&D organization also felt little confidence in their leaders. As much as 35 percent of the employees were thinking about leaving within the next two years. We conducted interviews with several scientists who had left the company. They cited lack of leadership as a major factor in their departure. The problems at CoVen were not simply the result of exhaustion or burnout. People in every discipline and location throughout the R&D organization told us they felt no esprit de corps; they were working with no sense of purpose or direction. They felt leaderless and rudderless. Rumors of more resignations circulated daily.

At last, a breakthrough—from an unexpected source: the press. Piet Jansen, the reporter who had caused Marco nothing but trouble (from Marco's point of view), published a feature article about the troubles at CoVen. Jansen argued that CoVen was in a very tenuous position, and its biggest problem was the R&D organization. The article was so well researched and full of detail (Jansen had found information that even Marco didn't know about his own organization, and had collected lots of analyses from well-respected experts and observers) that it was hard to dispute.

What's more, it got personal. One of the interviewees was an executive who had once been Marco's boss at the biotech start-up, and was the closest thing Marco had ever had to a mentor. "Marco Trask has tremendous operational skills and admirable energy," the executive was quoted as saying. "But he may not be the best man for the job of integration at CoVen. That job is all about inspiring people; establishing a vision. Mood and tone count when organizations are coming together. Marco likes tangibles. CoVen R&D needs a leader, and Marco is a manager." The article quoted some of the scientists who had left, and they, too, were critical of Marco and his management style.

When I read the article, I thought, "Uh-oh, Marco is going to go ballistic. He'll want to crucify Mr. Jansen." I was right and wrong. Marco called and asked to meet with me. He was uncharacteristically subdued when I came into his office. "Jeanie," he said. "What is your reaction to that article?" A difficult question to answer, but one thing a consultant must do is tell the truth and tell it, as best one can, in a way it can be heard and acted upon. "Well, Marco," I said. "I think that it accurately describes the perceptions of many people on how things have gone, up until now. But it doesn't have to be a prediction of how things will go from here on out. Every change process I've been through has been messy and painful, at least at some point. But I know that there can be a turning point in even the deepest Determination phase. And one of the most dramatic turning points is when the leader goes through a change himself. Maybe that's what this article will do for you." We talked for a while longer and it was clear to me that Marco had been profoundly affected by what he had read.

The next afternoon, Marco called the R&D FIT back together. They met into the evening, adjourned for dinner, and talked over the table well into the night. They canceled all their appointments for the next day, and, by the close of business, they had crafted an action plan and the beginnings of a long-range strategy. The following day, they posted a message on the intranet site and sent personal e-mails to every member of the R&D organization. They promised the delivery of a detailed, long-range strategy, vision, values statement, and description of the desired state within three months. They began the work the day after that, and were careful to enlist opinion leaders from all areas, gather input for developing the values and strategic plan, and communicate regularly with their people.

The long-awaited strategy and accompanying vision were finally announced on October 1, eleven months after the announcement of the merger. It was comprehensive and intelligent, and even those who were to lose out as a result of it recognized its worth and thoroughness. The organization not only felt relief at finally having clarity about where it was going and how it was going to get there; it became positively energized. People now had a common purpose that they could believe in. They started working together to make the vision a reality. No longer did personal preferences and allegiances to one company or the other hold sway. The upswing in cooperation and energy was palpable.

THE LESSONS OF RAY AND MARCO

I have said it before, but it's worth saying again: In Determination, no organization can change until the individuals within it change. They have to think and act differently or nothing will be different. My favorite saying is, "A good way to go crazy is to expect different results from the same behavior." Think about it.

One frustrated manager told me, "I'm like the fanatic who redoubles his efforts when he realizes they aren't working. I desperately need a new way to think about and respond to the challenges I'm facing." We each have to see our situations and our responses to them in a fresh light. And we must be willing to change ourselves. When the leader demonstrates that he or she has changed, others will take that change challenge seriously and engage in their own change process. When the leader only exhorts others to change, the message falls on deaf ears and is, understandably, seen as "Do as I say, not as I do." OK, so I won't change either.

The newspaper article provided Marco with a shock of realization. His organization was stuck and could not move forward, and he was primarily responsible. Marco had to feel the threat to his own reputation and had to feel pain himself before he could feel the pain of those around him. It was an unusually clear and identifiable "Aha!"

moment, a realization of what Pogo said years ago: "We have met the enemy and it is us." Fortunately, like the moment when Ebenezer Scrooge opens his window and realizes that he can live a new life, Marco realized that he could turn things around. Personal change for most people is far more gradual. Fast or slow, dramatic or gradual, we all have to change.

Because so much is at stake—for the company and all the individuals within it—the Determination phase is an intensely emotional time, a time of hope and frustration, energy and exhaustion, excitement and dread for everyone involved, including the leaders. To successfully get people through this phase, leaders must develop an astute awareness of their own emotions, thoughts, and biases. By acknowledging and managing their own emotional assets and liabilities, they can better understand, guide, and leverage those of their followers. It is important for the leaders to constantly and honestly ask themselves, "What is going on with me right now? How does what I am feeling and doing help or hinder our progress? Is my experience tracking with that of my management team and with the rest of the organization?" The former mayor of New York City, Ed Koch, used to constantly ask, "How'm I doing?" Given that each individual has limited perspective, especially of self, it is helpful to ask trusted onlookers to give feedback as well.

When leaders really connect with their followers, the connection is forged from authenticity, as one human being to another. By taking responsibility for their own behavior, including their missteps, leaders can engage at a deeper level and demand from others a wholehearted response and genuine engagement, rather than a simple compliance with orders and rules. This means communicating regularly with people throughout the organization. It means acknowledging, at least to yourself, your own personal doubts, concerns, fears, and uncertainties about how things are going and how to proceed. It means sharing information—telling what you know and admitting what you don't. It means being accessible and available to talk. And it means caring about *people* as well as the outcome, being committed to the change, and being willing to show tangible commitment in actions and deeds.

For change to be real and long-lasting, it has to take place deeply and completely—emotionally, intellectually, and operationally. If the change leaders fail to address all three dimensions—the emotional aspect is often the most intense aspect during Determination—neither they nor the initiatives they are leading will reach their full potential. If they do achieve change in all three dimensions, they will emerge—in the Fruition phase—as better individuals, better leaders, and members of a far better organization.

PART SIX

FRUITION

THE MONSTER IS SUBDUED, AT LEAST FOR NOW

"We're just like one big happy family here."

15

Sweet and Dangerous Fruition

Reinforcing the Good

FRUITION ARRIVES AS a ray of light. It brings the realization that the efforts to change are—at last—having a genuine, tangible, and positive payoff. One or more of the goals set during Preparation is reached. The stock price goes up, the Web site goes live, new customers sign up, sales rise, profits improve, costs go down, productivity increases, people stop leaving the company, talented people start joining, the company wins the Webby award, a great new product or service is launched; *something* good happens, and hope grows that many good and measurable things will follow.

At the same time, it's clear that the intangibles have improved and the environment is brighter and more upbeat. People outside the organization—customers, analysts, the press, and the community—start saying nice things about it. Coming to work each day no longer seems like running the gauntlet or negotiating high-speed traffic; dealing with problems no longer feels like trying to drink from a fire hose. Things seem to work better and smoother. People are more confident; they take responsibility more quickly, and needed actions seem clearer. People may still be very busy, but they don't feel like they're underwater anymore, and the evidence of their accomplishments buoys them.

Fruition is the sweetest and most satisfying phase, a brief but golden time—a period of exultation, reflection, recognition, and congratulation. It is important to savor this time, to share the rewards and recognition generously, and to revel in the hard-earned gains the organization has made.

As the organization revels in Fruition, there are two great opportunities to be grasped. First, cement the trust and unity that have been gained throughout the organization. Second, embed the capabilities and attitudes that have produced the success. Now is the time to attend to these tasks, because they will be critical for accomplishing change faster and more easily in the future. They deserve explicit management attention. We have discussed how management's credibility is on the line whenever a major change initiative is undertaken. The population continually asks hard questions: Do the leaders know what they're doing? Can they pull it off? Can we trust them? Do they care about us? Will they make the hard decisions? Will they keep to the plan when the going gets tough? When the company arrives at Fruition, most of those questions will have been answered affirmatively. Now is the time to reinforce the fact that management not only designed a plan that worked, but also had: the chutzpah to recognize aspects that didn't work, the wherewithal to figure out new approaches, and the tenacity to persevere until success was achieved. In the best scenario, all this has been done in concert with the workforce, not "over their dead bodies." Given all that has happened, management has proven it is capable and trustworthy. The organization has learned, firsthand, the value of working together toward common goals, and has proven to itself that it can accomplish amazing feats. Cement this by reinforcing it over and over, in tangible and symbolic ways. Bestow awards, give performance bonuses, establish an incentive compensation plan. Reinforce the payoffs for goals accomplished, and motivate the entire workforce to achieve more such successes.

Planning celebrations and rewards is a complicated and often touchy enterprise. I worked for a bank that gave employees free turkeys for Thanksgiving and Christmas. People complained loudly that they'd rather have hams, so the management dutifully switched to hams. Then the Jewish employees screamed. When it comes to celebrations, don't be surprised if people "look a gift horse in the mouth." No matter what you do, you won't win unanimous approval.

Sometimes the best reward is an event that expresses a spirit of congratulation and celebration, in a tone that is appropriate to your company. Microsoft hosts a companywide party at which big-name rock and roll stars perform. The best BCG partners' meeting I've attended was the one at which the Beach Boys played. We all danced and just had fun together. (I should add that BCG gives an Exceptional Performance Bonus, cash awards to all staff members, in years of strong profit.)

Celebrations need not be elaborate; they can be small and personal. An office manager of a Chicago firm put in untold hours of overtime to ensure everything worked smoothly during the fourteen months it took to renovate the firm's offices. Not only did performance within the firm stay high during that time, her excellent project management skills and dedication saved the firm tens of thousands of dollars and cut three months off the time line. In recognition, the firm gave her (and her husband) a gift certificate for dinner at any restaurant they chose, anywhere in the world. Her two assistants got similar certificates to any restaurant in the United States, and the staff members who worked on the project got certificates to the restaurant of their choice in Chicago.

No matter what the reward, some people will grouse that it is too extravagant or not extravagant enough. I know of one manager who was given a gift certificate for dinner with no spending limit. The manager was angry with the company because he had been passed over for partner. He took his wife to the Ritz Carlton for dinner, and ordered several rare bottles of wine from the superb Ritz cellar. The dinner for two cost over $2,000. Next time the company gave the award, the gift certificate had a ceiling amount. Celebration and reward need to be managed as carefully and thoughtfully as every other aspect of change.

The goal of capturing the learning is to help the workforce internalize their experiences so that what has been learned and achieved during the change initiative is not lost. Rather, it is acknowledged, distilled, and used as a building block for the next change. By *learning* I mean the skills, approaches, and attitudes that have been employed and should be added to the organizational repertoire. They might include a wide variety of skills, from large-scale project planning and management, or superior internal morale measurements, to influencing tactics that help build support for new initiatives.

The more difficult the change process has been, the more critical it is to have the learning explicitly harvested and reviewed. In Fruition, people often say, "I never want to go through anything like that again!" It's important to help them understand that they have learned so much and gained so many new skills that, indeed, they never will have to go through the same experience again. You can't promise that they won't have to go through another major transition, but you can, and should, reassure them that the next experience will be better. They have learned how to handle the ambiguities and stress that major changes bring. They know what coping strategies work or don't work. They are more prepared for the next major hurdle. They will know what to expect next time.

This ability to accomplish change is especially important for companies that go through more than one merger. They need to lessen the trauma and stress of merging and to increase their confidence and expertise. An executive who headed two different postmerger integration efforts noticed a clear difference between the two mergers. "This [second] one feels so much smoother and easier because we know what to expect and how to proceed. With the other one, we were doing it for the first time so our anxiety was high and we had no way to know if our experiences were normal or a sure sign that something was wrong." In much the same way, the first new e-venture will painfully point out the company's inexperience, ignorance, technological weaknesses, and bad assumptions. An executive in charge of starting a joint venture in e-procurement said, "We were so naïve. We made practically every mistake possible, and they cost us plenty—in time, money, and sleepless nights. I, by God, want to make sure we learn from those mistakes!"

Grasping the learnings of change is also extremely important for startup e-ventures. Multiple Change Curves can be expected in such enterprises—one during the raising of venture capital, another in getting the Web site up and running, a third in securing the first customer. In striving to overcome each major hurdle, those involved go through a complete change cycle. Having accomplished each major milestone, they are emboldened to press on, knowing full well that Fruition in one cycle may not guarantee Fruition of the overall business—as the ever-expanding graveyard of e-ventures indicates.

In every type of organization, a danger awaits in Fruition: Celebration may turn into self-congratulation. Fruition can breed complacency and a belief that the Change Monster has been slain forever and will never return. In truth, the monster is always lurking, looking for ways to sneak back in and pull the company into Stagnation once again. Like the "paranoid" companies, organizations that reach Fruition must not rest on their laurels for long. They must restlessly continue to examine themselves and seek new ways to change and grow.

MICRO SWITCH:
SUCCEEDING FOR THEMSELVES AND FREEPORT

The tangible goals that Micro Switch attained in the Fruition phase were impressive. In four years, during a time when 50 percent of their products were sold into markets that were not growing, and with the economy only growing 2 to 3 percent, Micro Switch had an average compound growth rate of 7½ percent. The average operating profits improved over 16 percent annually. A healthy portion of the profit was reinvested in the Micro Switch business, but the division still managed to send the required profits "up the river" to the Honeywell headquarters each year. Operating expenses were also trimmed. Market share rose, and the company attracted new customers. During the same period, the management ranks were reduced by a third, but with no layoffs. The skill level of the factory workers was substantially improved in several areas, which made automation and other process improvements possible. And, within three years of Ray Alvarez's arrival, Micro Switch achieved a key objective by qualifying for an on-site review for the Malcolm Baldrige National Quality Award. The company also received over 127 supplier quality awards from customers. In the fourth year, Micro Switch achieved the highest level of manufacturing quality at any time in its history—according to the six metrics it had established for itself. And, instead of being sold, as the Honeywell CFO had proposed only a few years earlier, the division received multiple Honeywell Chairman's Awards. Micro Switch did not, of course, have its own stock, but Honeywell might have wished that it had created a tracking stock for the division. There is little doubt that it would have soared, especially in comparison to Honeywell's overall stock performance.

Even with Fruition so evident, Ray wanted to keep the organization motivated and ready for more. He said, "We can't rest on our laurels. We've come a long way, but keep in mind that this is just one step in a long road of progress." Given all the organization had been through, and the amount of emphasis placed on customers and responsiveness to customers, the workforce now understood that Micro Switch had to continue to work to stay out in front. "Now, when we tell the organization that the customers' expectations are changing and here's why, they understand it. We don't have to go through a lot to build healthy dissatisfaction."

A remarkable, and often unexpected, result of Fruition is that it can create success that has an impact far beyond the company itself. The town of Freeport, Illinois, benefited in many ways from the changes at Micro Switch, which was the largest employer in town. The company had traditionally used layoffs to counteract economic downturns, but that practice came to an end under Ray's tenure. The results were: less churn and more prosperity in both the job and housing markets. People felt more secure; they invested more in their homes and lives. Homes became more valuable. Freeport came to be seen as a more attractive market for retailers and other businesses. "Change in this community is being driven from the private sector, not the public sector," said one local leader.

Ray and his executive team got involved in community issues. They worked closely with the leaders of a number of civic groups, sharing with them their change management insights and methods. They utilized their strategic planning process to help develop five priorities for the Freeport area: (1) education and learning, (2) infrastructure, (3) public safety, (4) racial harmony, and (5) social services/health care. They challenged those groups to think big and to deliver. The community leaders responded to the challenge. Their organizations' performance improved and they successfully undertook a number of development projects of sizes and scales they had never believed possible. By bringing several different groups together, they were able to build the Martin Luther King, Jr. Community Center, which houses a number of agencies responsible for an array of services for the people of Freeport from affordable child care and after-school tutoring to job training for adults.

Community leaders credit Ray Alvarez with helping to revitalize the city. "He is a very strong personality. He used leverage and he used threats. But he got things done," said one. "There are people who have power and there are people who have influence. Some of them have power and influence simply because of the position they hold. When they retire, they no longer have either. But if Ray were to retire tomorrow, I would still return his phone calls. His influence transcends the political position he holds. I will always have time for Ray Alvarez."

Ray retired from Micro Switch in 1998 and did a short stint as interim President of Honeywell's Consumer Products Division. He and Mary now live in Shepherdstown, West Virginia. Thinking back on his experience, one of the aspects that struck him was the holistic nature of change. "A big change effort is holistic; that's what startled me the most. When I was first trying to decide what we were going to do, I really didn't see it as holistic. That's probably the biggest lesson—that you can't just go and fix sales, independent of fixing the factory, independent of fixing the morale and self-respect of the workforce. All these aspects impact each other. You have to make sure the people part comes together with the operational parts, but boy! when they do come together, it's pretty!"

Those who worked closely with Ray—especially the Eagle Visionaries—have continued to have successful careers. Most of them credit their experience in transforming Micro Switch as a major part of their professional development. Rick Rowe, who is now CEO of MCMS, says, "I took the Change Curve and I showed my staff from the very beginning. This is what we're doing, this is where you are. You're going to have these disconnects. You're going to be up here personally in the chart, while your people are all way the hell back here. You might have to slow down from time to time. I've taken them through the cycles, and they understand it intellectually, but the hard part will be their understanding it emotionally. You just can't understand it until you live it."

Another alumnus said, "The Change Curve is just common sense. I see it everywhere and I use it constantly—in my personal and professional life. Having lived through the Micro Switch experience, I now have a whole new awareness and a different set of skills than I did before. I'm going to need them now if I'm going to deliver."

COVEN:
MARCO SUCCEEDS TO MERGE AGAIN

Within four months of the announcement of its long-range strategy, the CoVen R&D organization had stabilized. The energy of the staff was now focused on the areas of development that had been identified in the strategy. There had been no further merger-related resignations; in fact, several talented scientists had joined the company. When CoVen brought a new diabetes treatment to market—slightly ahead of schedule and within budget—Marco Trask could at last claim, "The R&D organization not only has been 'sorted out,' we are more effective and more efficient than either organization was before the merger. We are producing on all fronts."

Its work complete, the R&D FIT was dissolved—for the second time. Marco told me: "I knew this merger could result in the world's best pharmaceutical R&D organization. I honestly had no idea what it would take to accomplish it. It's so difficult to really understand that the experience of the executives is radically different from what the rest of the organization is going through. I learned the hard way that other people have a different experience and that I need to understand it. I realize now that our decision to disband, which seemed so obvious and right to us at the time, was exactly the wrong move for the organization—we sent the wrong signals and caused disruptions that we never thought of. When I look back on other projects, I realize that I had made the same mistake before. We're always so eager to get on to the next thing that we pull resources away too quickly and take our eyes off the ball, then wonder what went wrong.

"The other important take-away for me is the necessity of being in constant touch with people. I didn't have enough contact with Elena Margolis or, for that matter, with Piet Jansen. I didn't understand Elena's views and her extreme emphasis on values, and I certainly didn't expect her to react as strongly as she did. I still think she was wrong, but the fact remains that I didn't see it coming. With Piet, he has a job to do and it was in my best interest to help him do it. I just got so focused on putting the new company together that I didn't take the time to see the people involved."

One of the R&D FIT leaders reflected on the experience, "We are now where we could and should have been months ago. We have learned an extremely expensive and difficult lesson. We're just lucky we were able to pull this one out of the fire."

Micro Switch has continued to perform beyond expectations, but CoVen enjoyed its success only for a short period. Within three years, market pressures brought about a new wave of mergers and joint ventures in the pharmaceuticals industry. Kloorg, the Swiss-based conglomerate, sought a stronger presence in the United States and purchased CoVen, with its state-of-the-art DevCenter and strong North American sales and marketing operation. Marco Trask found himself facing another integration process. But, thanks to his eventual success with the CoVen integration, Marco was named Executive Vice President of R&D at the new entity, KCV. He made sure that he began the communications process early; the first people he talked with when the merger was announced were the key physicians and scientists. He had no desire to live through another talent drain like the one he had experienced when Dr. Margolis had left CoVen. Another early call Marco made was to Piet Jansen, who was now not only published internationally but the host, on CNN International, of a highly respected weekly report focusing on the pharmaceutical industry. Marco gave Jansen an in-depth exclusive interview and never once got defensive (or mentioned his summer home).

AVOIDING THE SLUMP TOWARD STAGNATION

Life seems so successful and positive during the early days of Fruition that it is easy for people in the organization to want to prolong the good feelings. Often, the best way to do so seems to be: Keep doing things the same way. This impulse can lead, all too quickly, to rigidity and obsolescence. After a period of celebrating the wins and sharing the rewards, the leaders need to ensure that the proclivity for change becomes "institutionalized"—if that is not an oxymoron. Here are six ways to do so:

1. *Don't make today's innovations into tomorrow's sacred cows.* Just because a "new way" was right for the time doesn't mean it continues to be right. No process or structure should be exempt from scrutiny. As one change leader put it, "Question everything—especially the things that are off limits."

2. *Stay abreast of the external environment.* When a company enjoys significant success, and particularly when it reaches a certain size, it often loses sight of its competitive environment. It may then fail to recognize when things are changing, when new competitors emerge, and when new technologies or approaches are introduced. I recall a cartoon in which a man is entering an office and his secretary is saying, "Here are the paradigms that shifted while you were at lunch." To keep up with what's happening, the leaders and their people must keep talking with and listening to customers. They also must keep a sleepless eye on competitors and potential competitors.

3. *Keep listening to and communicating with the organization.* The listening and talking internally must continue, not just in happy-talk recognition events, but in the informal breakfasts, the hallway conversations, and the leaders' off-sites. One CEO makes a point to meet with people he has never met before at every location he visits. He learns all sorts of interesting bits about his organization. Meanwhile, the organization sees him as involved, caring, and clairvoyant. Effective executives constantly have their finger on the pulse of their organization.

4. *Recruit fresh blood.* People who have led teams during major transitions often need a respite. They get change-weary. Besides, if they've worked long and hard to make the most recent set of changes occur, they're not likely to be ready to dismantle it the next morning. Bringing in "fresh eyes" from other parts of the business, or from the outside, helps the organization to question the assumptions and practices rather than screaming, "You don't understand how far we've come!"

5. *Leverage your champions.* A few people become so energized by the change process that they become champions and change advocates. When the initiative reaches Fruition, redeploy them. Allow them to lead other changes in other parts of the organization or to act as consultants and mentors to other internal leaders. Sometimes they may even develop a "shtick"—a training program or a presentation—that they can deliver to other groups. Such people can even become good representatives for the company at outside events, such as seminars and conferences.

6. *Build skills of self-observation and correction; teach the Change Curve.* An understanding of the Change Curve and the fundamentals of managing change should become common knowledge within the organization. As with any new learning, the more it is practiced and developed, the more valuable it becomes. One executive includes, in his quarterly management reviews, a period of reflection on what is being experienced by the organization. What started out as a requirement has now become a valued habit. "By stopping to reflect every quarter, I'm forced to think through not just the numbers but the morale, pace, and spirit of the organization. It helps me to know if I'm demanding too much or too little."

16

When the Old
Becomes New Again

Continuous Change

APROBLEM WITH WRITING about change is that it seems as if everything has been said before—and it probably has. I remember hearing Bart Starr speak at my high school. He was at the height of his popularity as quarterback of the powerful Green Bay Packers. Having a pro-football hero as an alumnus was thrilling for all of us, and we hung on every word he uttered. I rushed home that night to share this new enlightenment with my parents: "You have to give 100 percent!" My father rolled his eyes; my mother quietly agreed with Starr's revelatory pronouncement. When I pressed Daddy as to why he wasn't more impressed, he backed off, agreed, and then added, "Each generation and each individual has to discover the truth for themselves." Daddy was right. The lessons we learn as we experience major changes are lessons we must each learn for ourselves. They are the critical, often unexpected, life lessons that we tend to learn the hard way. But once learned, they stay with us forever.

The phases an individual experiences in a major life event (leaving home, finding a job, marriage, divorce, parenthood, moving) are essentially the same as the phases an organization goes through during any fundamental change initiative. Sometimes, because we fail to make a connection between our personal experience of change and a corporate change, we do not allow our personal experience to inform our business experience. Many of us shy away from introspection or are too busy to examine our own lives very deeply. Besides, we're so close to the change, it's difficult, if not impossible, to see it objectively or clearly. When we think about a change that is now long past, the specifics are usually pretty fuzzy, but we remember with tremendous clarity certain moments and the emotions associated with them.

I remember, for example, the moment I decided to end the Stagnation of my first marriage and to begin preparing myself to be a single mother. It was a hot and sticky August afternoon in St. Louis, and we—my husband, daughter Jennifer, and I—were driving home in our rattly old car that had no air-conditioning. We had been inching along in rush-hour traffic for over forty-five minutes, and no one was in a good mood. My husband had taken the opportunity to subject me to an inquisition and critique of my day's accomplishments, or the lack thereof. Given another few minutes in traffic, I knew he would move on to instructions for the things that I needed to do the next day. Thankfully, I was spared that delight because we pulled into the driveway. My husband lifted Jennifer from her car seat and took her inside. I remember sitting in the car for a long time, thinking, "Life on the outside has got to be better than this." I recognized that my situation absolutely had to change, in a big way.

I had allowed myself to stagnate in a marriage that wasn't working, but I could not do so anymore. I deserved better. More important, my daughter deserved better.

I had understood, intellectually, that our marriage was not working for quite some time. My husband and I had discussed the possibility of divorce many times, and we had been in counseling together for months. Divorce was clearly one of my options, but it was a change that I resisted. I wasn't sure it was the right answer for Jennifer or for me. I was uncertain about what life "on the outside" would be like. I had some very deep beliefs about the importance and value of marriage, and divorce did not really square with my values or my perceptions of myself. Although I had been the primary wage earner while my husband went through medical school, the prospect of being the sole provider and a single mother was scary and intimidating. No one in my immediate family had ever been divorced and, in 1971, there was still a societal stigma about divorced women. I intellectually understood that I could divorce and that it was probably the best course for Jennifer and for me, but I had resisted until that epiphany in the driveway.

After all the divorce papers were signed, Jennifer and I left St. Louis one December morning and headed for my parents' home in Alabama. Everything we owned was packed into a borrowed car. I felt a bit like the Beverly Hillbillies, except that I had a lot less stuff than they did. As I drove, my feelings took turns: relief, hope, fear, sadness, anger, excitement, and worry. I was tired one minute and energized the next. Crying, then laughing; laughing, then crying. It was exhausting! But I knew I possessed two extremely important things: I had my daughter (then age two years) and we both had a new chance for a happy and healthy life. In fairness, I should say that the divorce gave my husband a new chance, as well. I'm not placing all the blame for our breakup on him.

My parents welcomed us with open arms and clean beds, and I thought it was great to be home. My father was the classic curmudgeon with a heart of gold. Although he had a sharp wit and delighted in taking a cynical perspective, he had a deep sense of mission and unflinching compassion. He had begun the practice of adolescent medicine at the University of Alabama in Birmingham, and he volunteered as Head of Pediatrics for the Hope ship. My mother, whom I've mentioned many times, was—and still is—a wise and strong positive force. She has always taken pride in looking at reality straight-on and bringing hope and grace to the encounter.

At about the time I returned home, my sister and her college roommate came to live at home while they attended graduate school. Then my brother's wife and baby stayed with us for a few months while my brother was in Australia doing research. I thought this was great because Jennifer and I were with so many people whom I loved and who loved us. After the isolation and emotional starvation of my marriage, this was a rich balm, and I allowed myself to enjoy it for perhaps a little longer than I should have.

That time in my parents' house was a kind of Preparation phase for me. I was getting my resume together, thinking about what kind of job I wanted, adjusting myself (and Jennifer) to the idea of single motherhood—getting myself operationally and emotionally ready for the next phase of my life. If I had had to plunge directly from the Stagnation of my marriage into a new job and new apartment (Implementation), I think I would have had a much harder time of it. That period of adjusting to the ending of the marriage and the beginning of a new phase, and then planning, visioning, and setting new objectives, was crucial—even though I'm sure I didn't define it that way. Without it, the onset of Implementation would have been a tremendous shock. I'm not sure how well I would have coped.

One day, Implementation began with a bang. I had been running errands and called home to see whether anyone needed anything from town. Mama informed me that I had gotten a call from the First National Bank of Birmingham and they expected me to be at an interview for a new training position in exactly thirty minutes. I didn't have enough time to get home, change clothes, and get back to the bank. My only option was to go as I was—in a housedress, with dirty hair and no makeup. Oh brother! I wasn't ready! Couldn't I reschedule? Why does this always happen to me? But after a moment of ranting, I pulled myself together. My weeks of Preparation had given me enough self-confidence to go into the interview, do the best I could, and accept the outcome.

I met with a vice president, whose first question was, "Do you always dress this way?" "No," I said calmly, and explained the circumstances of the morning. (I didn't mention that I usually looked worse. I was doing a lot of sculpting at that time, and spent my days in jeans, covered with plaster of Paris.) We moved on to my qualifications and I whipped out my recommendation from Pratt Institute, which Mama had suggested that I carry with me at all times. It was so full of praise it practically glowed in the dark.

The interview went well and, after a while, the VP went away for a few minutes. When he came back, he said, "Come back in an hour to meet the Chairman of the Board." I agreed, even though I didn't know what a Chairman of the Board was. The only one I had ever heard of was Frank Sinatra, and I knew he wouldn't be there.

I came back in an hour, still in my housedress and with dirty hair, and the VP took me upstairs to the Chairman's floor. It was very quiet and filled with very big desks. We waited outside an office that I could see was furnished with Oriental rugs and expensive lamps. I watched as the older gentleman in the office pulled out a desk drawer and punched a button inside the drawer. The drapes opened. I said to myself, "Now I get it. Anybody with power drapes has power. This is *the man.*"

I had a great conversation with Mr. Woodrow, the chairman, and he teased me about my recommendation from Pratt. At the end of an hour, he stood up and said, "I'll give you a job for three months. If at the end of that time you've proven useful, I'll give you a job description and a raise."

I thought to myself, "Why not give me the job description now so I can know how to demonstrate my usefulness?" Nonetheless, I was thrilled to get the opportunity, so I stood up to shake his hand and promptly fell on the floor. Poor Mr. Woodrow. He peered over his desk wondering where I'd disappeared to, not knowing whether he should come pick me up, act as if everything was normal, or what.

I, on the other hand, was groveling on the floor wondering what in the world had just happened! I finally realized that my leg had gone to sleep during the interview but it hadn't tingled. It was totally numb, so when I stood up, it gave way.

I managed to pull myself up on the chair and steady myself on Mr. Woodrow's desk. I quipped, "Sir, I was wounded in Viet Nam. So, by hiring me, you get two minority employees—a woman and a wounded vet—for the price of one. I think you ought to give me that raise right now!" And then I limped out of his office before he could rescind his offer. That was how I got my first job in corporate America.

Working at the bank was full of challenges but, much to my surprise, I discovered that I loved them. I had a great time—everything seemed new and exciting. I was learning a lot, making new friends, and discovering a great deal about myself. I created a training program, focusing on customer service and problem solving. The first classes were for the tellers; I had a lot of respect for those women and thoroughly enjoyed our sessions together. First National (now Am-South) was the biggest bank in the state, so it took all of my three months to complete the training for all the tellers. The evaluations of my work were highly positive, and Mr. Woodrow kept his word; I was given a job description, a raise, and even a title: Director of Training. I was put on the fast track for career development. Within a year, I was made an officer of the bank. It was a happy leap from Implementation to Fruition. I didn't have a serious Determination phase at the bank because I was so happy (and relieved) to be engaged in meaningful work and providing for my daughter.

I would never have pursued a business career if I hadn't been forced into it by my divorce. It had never occurred to me that business challenges could be exhilarating, or that I would find such fulfillment in working outside the home. Perhaps I had had very little self-awareness. None of us knows how we will respond to a great change in our lives until we face it.

I talk to many people who want to see change in their work situations—or say they want to. Often, they have a love-hate relationship with their jobs. On the one hand, they love their work, believe strongly in their mission, and genuinely care about the outcomes. On the other hand, getting anything accomplished requires jumping over endless hurdles and competing with colleagues who should be helping. When they do manage to "pull it out of the fire," their managers take their extraordinary performance for granted. Miracles become expected. Last-minute fire drills become standard operating procedure. Even the most capable and caring employees end up feeling abused by the company and their work environment. They desperately want things to change.

Yet, when the company actually decides to make a major change, those same abused employees hesitate and begin to feel doubtful. Who is going to be calling the shots? Will I do well in the new organization? How will my daily routine be changed? Will I be ready to make all those changes? Will the plan work? The very people who have been begging for change are often the ones who experience what I call "retroactive resistance." Now that the reality of change is at hand, the old ways don't seem quite so bad. Perhaps there is a way to make the old ways work after all. This phenomenon always reminds me of the Israelites wandering through the desert longing for the onions and good food they had while living in bondage under the Egyptians.

An individual who faces organizational change is, in effect, undergoing a kind of forced personal change—not unlike the divorce I had to undergo. And although I recognized that divorce made sense, intellectually and operationally, it took me much longer to prepare emotionally for the change. This is true of many people who are asked to participate in organizational change. They will agree with the mission and its objectives, the strategies, and the tactics, but when the moment of truth comes—the moment of actually moving forward into the change—they balk. Generally, they have not been engaging in duplicity. They genuinely didn't know how strong their own emotional resistance would be until it was tested.

I sat next to a real estate lawyer on a plane one day. We got to talking about change, and he told me a story about two clients of his, Alice and Ken Morison, a sister and brother. They had inherited a large piece of property in a vacation area. It had been in the family for three generations, and had been the scene of many Morison family events and holidays. In the past twenty years, the area had become extremely popular, and the land had skyrocketed in value. Both of the Morisons, who were successful but not wealthy, decided that the property had become too valuable and they would be smart to sell. The lawyer worked with his clients for more than a year—developing ideas, reviewing, discussing, and negotiating every possible option. They finally decided to sell the majority of the property to a developer, for a very attractive price. At closing time, the Morisons were an hour late. When they finally arrived, they looked like they were both in pain. Ken paced. Alice sighed. "We just can't do it," she said. "We can't sell. Sorry." And with that, they left. The Morisons reminded me a little of Mrs. Gordon who rebuffed any offers of help when she clearly needed help. There is often a difference between intellectual understanding of one's situation, and emotional readiness to move forward in changing it. (The day we met on the plane, the lawyer was en route to close a new deal for the Morisons. It had been two years since they had walked out of the first closing and now they swore that they were emotionally ready to sell.)

Even people who embrace the idea of change may feel uncertainty when it actually starts to happen. They may agree with the plans but distrust the leaders—or vice versa. Others who seek change may be too exhausted by the old ways to be able to really contribute to the new. They just long for a rest.

Stress is a stimulus, and it can play different roles in our lives. Eustress is "good stress," the kind you might get when something wonderful and exhilarating happens, like winning the lottery. Distress is what you feel when something negative and prolonged happens. Distress can cause damaging wear-and-tear on mind or body, and may seriously interfere with daily life. At work, people feel most distressed by three factors, especially when they are experienced in combination:

1. High demands are placed on them, and they have little control over what those demands are.
2. High visibility. The actions they take are being carefully watched and will have real impact on the success of the venture and their careers.
3. Concern for competence. People worry that they may not have the skills and abilities to accomplish what needs to be done.

In a major corporate change, all three factors are often in play. If your work processes are the center of a redesign effort, for example, the visibility is high. What is being planned may entail a completely new way of working—which you won't control. And you may be, understandably, unsure of how you'll perform. No wonder people get *distressed*-out. Not only do they have a lot of learning to do and operational changes to make, they also have a major emotional adjustment to make, and it's all in public view!

However, when the change initiative works, people can discover that the new work provides them with ample opportunities to shine, to exhibit qualities they didn't know they possessed or had not taken to this level before—resilience, leadership, being a quick study. The pride of accomplishment is powerful and should be enjoyed. When a company comes through a transition successfully, the entire organization benefits in renewed pride, confidence, and a sense of control. People feel better about themselves and the corporation. This kind of experience can lead to the courage needed to step up to a future challenge and assume they can succeed—and possibly even be role models for someone else. No one gets tired of winning. It is especially sweet if the difficulty experienced decreases even as the stakes increase.

The opposite is also true: People do not want to think of themselves as losers, and they don't want to be part of a losing team. When managers allow an initiative to fail, or pretend that no one will notice if it's ignored and no longer discussed, they do themselves and the corporation a real disservice. People will begin to believe that half-measures are all the company is good for, that spectacular results are beyond the realm of possibility, and that mediocrity is all that's expected. Seeing a change through—all the way from Stagnation to Fruition—changes not just the operations or structure, but also the beliefs the organization has about itself, for better or for worse.

That's why I see my divorce—not as a failure—but as a major change experience that was successful. I experienced Stagnation and was able to force myself to face it—intellectually and emotionally—and to provoke change. I took time for a Preparation period, and managed to put myself into an Implementation phase that was professionally fulfilling. I was quite fortunate that my work experiences went so well because my personal life was much harder. Starting over in a new town, with a new job, and newly single seemed like an endless Determination phase. What I remember most about that period was the excruciating loneliness. I have no doubt that the responsibility of Jennifer forced me to establish a new home, to do all the daily chores, and to "buck-up" when I was tempted to quit. Her existence forced me to do what needed to be done. Her presence brought me joy and comfort. I saw the complete arc of change, and understood—if only intuitively at that point—that the change process could lead to growth that was far more rewarding and positive than it was painful or difficult. I credit the lessons I learned from that experience, in many ways, with giving me the courage to pursue other goals. I have succeeded in ways I only dared to hope—a strong, twenty-year second marriage—which I am still enjoying greatly; a happy, well-adjusted daughter; and an always challenging and stimulating career as a consultant. And I expect that those experiences will fuel the pursuit of a long-shelved dream in my "retirement" years—to sculpt again.

We know that organizations must continuously change in order to survive and prosper. But they have to change in ways that bring strength and exhilaration, rather than debilitation and distress. That's where understanding the Change Curve can make a positive impact. The change monster is always lying in wait and ready for battle, but, believe me, we can be victorious.

ACKNOWLEDGMENTS

I LIKE BEING EXPLICIT about feelings so, to me, one of the best parts of writing a book is writing the acknowledgments. It gives me the opportunity to publicly thank people who have been inspiring, encouraging, kind, and helpful, and especially those who have been steadfast in their support. The worst part is the certainty that words are inadequate and that someone who deserves to be thanked will be omitted. For that I apologize in advance. I have much to be thankful for; I have had outstanding clients and colleagues over the years—people I've been crazy about. I learned a great deal from them. They have enriched my life significantly.

Honeywell will always hold a special place in my heart. It was my first major client, and one that welcomed me into its life. The women and men of Honeywell's Micro Switch division have my deep admiration for all that they accomplished, and my appreciation for allowing me to participate with them and to write their story.

The extended family of The Boston Consulting Group, past and present, has contributed intellectual stimulation, energy, challenge, and nurture. Being a part of BCG really is an honor and a privilege—one that I do not take lightly. Without the worldwide network of BCG, these ideas would have never been tested and refined. The tools cited here are the work of the total partnership.

I owe special thanks to many. Carl Stern and John Clarkeson took the "creative challenge" of inviting me to join The Boston Consulting Group when such radical diversity of education, professional background, and perspective was a new idea. I have always appreciated who they are—smart, thoughtful, visionary leaders—and their interest in my career. Anthony Miles not only suggested that I write the book; he also sponsored the project in its early days and has seen it through to Fruition—reading every word and making spot-on suggestions. For my entire career at BCG, Anthony has been a mentor, a challenger, and a source of wisdom. David Fox, one of our senior advisors, was also an early supporter and reader. The early research and limitless enthusiasm of Mark Byford, Aaron Kushner, and Kerty Nilsson really pushed me into action. I could not say *no* when their *yes* was so strong.

The BCG storehouse of ideas, experiences, and knowledge is an intellectual pot of gold—and an enormous asset for anyone writing a book! Over the years, I have benefited greatly from the ideas and methodologies developed by my colleagues, in particular: Felix Barber, Mary Barlow, Barbara Berke, David Brownell, Stephen Bungay, Phil Catchings, Phil Deane, Christina Fernandez-Carol, Grant Freeland, Francine Gordon, Thomas Herp, Kristen Lange, Susan Littlefield, Jan McDougal, Yves Morieux, Dennis Rheault, Joshua Rymer, Tammy Shulstad, Marty Silverstein, Theanne Thompson, Nick Viner, and Krischan von Moeller. Working with them over the years has been a joy.

Technical and/or emotional support was supplied by Jim Andrew, Marge Branecki, Paul Basile, Ted Buswick, Christina Coffey, Derren Connell, Daryl Dean, Pat Degbor, Alastair Flanagan, Peter Goldsbrough, David Hall, Bill Hagedorn, Jennifer Healy, Tom Hout, Bob Howard, Jon Isaacs, Bill Latshaw, Joerg Matthiessen, Sara June McDavid, Ron Nicol, Pamela Parker, Lon Povich, Heiner Rutt, Gail Stahl, George Stalk, Peter Strueven, Terri Siggins, Tony Tiernan, Virginia Trigg, Nancy Vassey, Bolko von Oetinger, Bob Wolf, and Dave Young. The partners in our Atlanta office have been enormously hospitable to me. (And they've let me off the hook on many firm duties so I could focus on writing.) Each of these people has contributed to the realization of this book, for which I am most grateful.

I was lucky to find a truly top-notch team of professionals to work with on the book. My agent, Kristen Wainwright, provided excellent advice and kept the faith during the long proposal-writing stage. Her experience, enthusiasm, and professional perspective were invaluable. John Butman was a dream come true as editor and collaborator. He is a thorough professional who brings intelligence, understanding, candor, and skill to the project and pushes (me) to make it the best it can be. I am also particularly appreciative of John Mahaney of Random House. John expressed keen interest in the ideas and approach of the book and stayed firmly rooted in his commitment to it from Day One. I thank them all for contributing their exceptional talents and for their steadfast commitment.

A very special note of thanks goes to my family. My parents, Jean and Bill Daniel, have alternatively pushed me and reassured me, and I've needed both. My father, in spite of failing eyesight and health, provided expert editing of the early drafts. I am sad that he did not live to see the final work. He was a gift beyond measure. I have benefited from my mother's love and wisdom my whole life, and I'm glad to have the opportunity to share a little of her with others via this book. My husband, Charlie Carroll, has provided me with a base of love and support that I had thought impossible, but which made everything else possible. Our children and their spouses— Sarah Carroll, Tim Carroll and Laurie Gold, Jennifer Duck and Chris McKee—constantly bring pleasure to our lives, keep me abreast of other perspectives, and challenge my thinking. My siblings—Andy, Kim, Ginger, and Twinkle—challenge me every way they can think of. And they provide lots of laughs.

To all, I say a heartfelt thank you.

JEANIE DANIEL DUCK

Coral Gables, Florida

INDEX